Living with
RELIGIOUS DIVERSITY

Looking beyond exclusively state-oriented solutions to the management of religious diversity, this book explores ways of fostering respectful, non-violent and welcoming social relations among religious communities. It examines the question of how to balance religious diversity, individual rights and freedoms with a common national identity and moral consensus. The chapters discuss the interface between state and civil society in 'secular' countries and look at case studies from the West and India. They study themes such as religious education, religious diversity, pluralism, inter-religious relations and exchanges, Dalits and religion and issues arising from the lived experience of religious diversity in various countries. The volume asserts that if religious violence crosses borders, so do ideas about how to live together peacefully, theological reflection on pluralism, and lived practices of friendship across the boundaries of religious identity groupings.

Bringing together interdisciplinary scholarship from across the world, the book will interest scholars and students of philosophy, religious studies, political science, sociology and history.

Sonia Sikka is Professor of Philosophy at the University of Ottawa, Canada.

Bindu Puri is Professor of Philosophy at the University of Delhi, India.

Lori G. Beaman is the Canada Research Chair in the Contextualization of Religion in a Diverse Canada and Professor in the Department of Classics and Religious Studies at the University of Ottawa, Canada.

Living with
RELIGIOUS DIVERSITY

EDITED BY

SONIA SIKKA,
BINDU PURI AND
LORI G. BEAMAN

NEW DELHI LONDON NEW YORK

First published 2016
by Routledge
2 Park Square, Milton Park, Abingdon, Oxon OX14 4RN

and by Routledge
711 Third Avenue, New York, NY 10017

Routledge is an imprint of the Taylor & Francis Group, an informa business

© 2016 India International Centre, New Delhi

The right of India International Centre, New Delhi to be identified as author of this work has been asserted in accordance with sections 77 and 78 of the Copyright, Designs and Patents Act 1988.

All rights reserved. No part of this book may be reprinted or reproduced or utilized in any form or by any electronic, mechanical, or other means, now known or hereafter invented, including photocopying and recording, or in any information storage or retrieval system, without permission in writing from the publishers.

Trademark notice: Product or corporate names may be trademarks or registered trademarks, and are used only for identification and explanation without intent to infringe.

British Library Cataloguing-in-Publication Data
A catalogue record for this book is available from the British Library

Library of Congress Cataloging-in-Publication Data
A catalog record has been requested for this book

ISBN: 978-1-138-94458-9 (hbk)
ISBN: 978-1-315-67172-7 (ebk)

Typeset in Berkeley
by Apex CoVantage, LLC

CONTENTS

vii: List of figures

viii: Foreword
KARAN SINGH

xii: Acknowledgements

xiii: List of contributors

xiv: Introduction

PART I NEGOTIATING DIFFERENCE IN PRACTICE

3: 1 Religious other or religious inferior?
LINDA WOODHEAD

17: 2 Faith, ethnicity and nationalism:
St. Thomas Christians in India
SEBASTIAN VELASSERY

37: 3 Reframing understandings of religion: lessons from India
LORI G. BEAMAN

49: 4 Islam and religious pluralism in India
ARSHAD ALAM

PART II RELIGION AND CASTE

69: 5 Intimate desires: Dalit women and
religious conversions in colonial India
CHARU GUPTA

105: 6 Buddhism in Indian philosophy
A. RAGHURAMARAJU

126: 7 Religious diversity and the politics of an overlapping consensus
GOPAL GURU

PART III   RELIGIOUS EDUCATION

137: 8 Education in secular democratic societies: the challenge of religious diversity
RATNA GHOSH

153: 9 A cultural and dialogic approach to religious education
SOLANGE LEFEBVRE

168: 10 Religious education in a secular state
RAJEEV BHARGAVA

182: 11 Teaching 'religion' and 'philosophy' in India
SONIA SIKKA

PART IV   INTERROGATING LIBERAL SOLUTIONS

203: 12 Diversity, secularism and religious toleration
ASHWANI KUMAR PEETUSH

219: 13 Religious diversity and the devout
BINDU PURI

238: 14 The international politics of religious freedom
ELIZABETH SHAKMAN HURD

FIGURES

5.1	Lion and lamb on the same river bank	75
5.2	Thirst for water	75
5.3	Left is the state of being Hindu (untouchable). Right is the complete change on becoming a Christian	81
5.4	See the difference between two women of the same species: one is an English madam and the other a servant-untouchable. The former walks ahead with an umbrella, while the latter walks behind with her child	82
5.5	The Christian woman is the master of the dog, while the outcaste woman is her servant. But they both were of the same caste, Hindus please see carefully	83
5.6	One has become a madam-lady, and the other a fish seller. Blessed be the religion of Christ, which is all powerful	84
5.7	Cover of a book: Only for Married Women and Men	87
5.8	Tending the feet	90

FOREWORD

Religion deals with something very deep and fundamental in the human psyche. Despite centuries of liberal dismissal, despite Bertrand Russell's statement that human beings are only a 'fortuitous conglomeration of atoms' and Arthur Koestler's theory that the human race is 'programmed for self-destruction', religion is still with us, along with its sense that there is a higher purpose for our existence. The point is that you cannot dismiss religion, and it is dangerous to think otherwise. For half a century, the Indian intelligentsia has adopted a supercilious and dismissive attitude towards religion. That has been a major dereliction of duty, because, then, the interpretation of religion is left to the most vicious, the most backward, the most fundamentalist elements in societies. This is why enlightened people in all societies must speak up about religion, in view of its potential for both good and bad. It is true that religion poses social problems, but we have to face these; we cannot solve them merely by avoiding the topic.

Recently, there has been a revival of religion, as I have just noted, and it has some very good aspects. Unfortunately, at the same time, there has also been a resurgence of fundamentalism and fanaticism in every religion. While these negative currents within Islam have become well-known because of the jehadis, which is a recent development, there has also been a growth of fundamentalism in Christianity, as well as in Hinduism which in the past had never been a proselytizing religion. For whatever reason, certain groups have created unfortunate and unhappy situations, such as in Ayodhya, or Gujarat, or the attacks upon Christian missionaries who were doing excellent work in the service of the people. This is something which cannot be accepted; it has to be opposed not merely by the law, but by the common people.

I know we have been through difficult times. In our own lifetime, India was partitioned on the basis of religion. The Muslim majority provinces opted out, rightly or wrongly. But not only did the Constitution makers not react by setting up a Hindu state, they went out of their way to set up a strongly secular state and incorporate in it special provisions for religious minorities. I do not think that there is such an example anywhere else in the world, and that India has received sufficient credit for the fact that while a nation was divided on the basis of religion, the remainder of the nation struggled to create a Constitution where everybody is equal in the eyes of the law. It is a very great thing – a very remarkable thing – and we must now continue to strengthen the foundation of our constitution, not only legally, but also among the general public.

The academic study of religion can play an important role in this respect, and especially reflections on religious diversity, such as those contained in this volume. What is especially important about the theme these essays address is that it is about *living* with religious diversity, directing attention not only to laws and governmental policies, but also to the place of religious diversity in people's lived experience. This is a subject with which I have been personally occupied for a long time, through my now 30-year-long participation in the Interfaith Movement. As a child, moreover, I was involved with three great religions. I was born a Hindu, and have studied and lectured on Hinduism around the world. But I belong to a Muslim majority state and, therefore, from childhood I would pay my homage to the great Muslim dargahs which are located in Kashmir, whether it is Charar-e-Sharif, the great monument to Alamdar-é Kashmir Shaik Nooruddin Noorania or whether it is Maqdum Sahab in Srinagar, Baba Rishi in Gulmarg, Hazarat Bal itself or the Dargah Sharif in Ajmer. From childhood we have been taught to respect these dargahs with the same *shraddha,* the same devotion, as we do our own temples. As far as Christianity is concerned, I have been very ecumenical. The first school I went to was the Presentation Convent in Srinagar and the second was the Cathedral High School in Bombay. Thus, I covered both the Catholic and the Protestant traditions, and I was raised by European and Christian guardians. I have lived the Interfaith Movement personally, and it has been very much a part of my consciousness and my whole life experience. I have also tried to encourage peace and conflict resolution studies, which involves inter-religious studies as well.

We need further ways of thinking about religion and educating people about it. It is astonishing, for instance, that there is not a single institution of comparative religion in India. India is the land where four of the world's great religions were born – Hinduism, Jainism, Buddhism and Sikhism. Five religions came to us from West Asia and have flourished here for centuries: the religion of Zarathrustha, prophet of Iran; Judaism; Christianity; Islam; and the Bahai faith. And yet in this country, the study of religion is badly lacking. Such study can help to bring about harmony between religions, without which there can be no abiding peace on this planet. Religion, we should recognize, has played an astoundingly significant role in human civilization. Much of the world's art and architecture, its music, dance and literature, its moral codes and spiritual practices can be traced back to one or the other of the great religions of the world. But it must also be said that more people have been killed and tortured, persecuted and terrorized in the name of God than in any other name. This is a very strange dichotomy. History is replete with millions perishing in inter-religious and intra-religious wars. Thus, although on the one hand religion has given us great riches, on the other it has also often been used in a very negative manner.

In my view, we have to be very clear in our minds that the time has now come when we must choose those elements in our religious traditions that are compatible with the requirements of the global society. For example, let me take Hinduism: if somebody today argues that human sacrifice is part of our Hindu tradition and, therefore, we will indulge in it, we will not accept it. It is incompatible with the Constitution. Again, if somebody says that untouchability is built into the *Manusmrti*, therefore, I will practise it, it is not acceptable. Similarly, with Islam, I am afraid there are situations which may, or may not, have religious sanctions, but which are simply not compatible with global society, or even with our own Constitution. Therefore, thinking people have to now boldly speak out. For my part, I believe that when you come to the actual problems people face, you will find much compatibility between religions. These are the problems of poverty, for example, or the status of women or the problems of both children and the environment. It is not important whether you believe in a multiplicity of lives, or in one life, whether you believe in the multiplicity of paths to God, or in one path to God. What is important is: What is your *kartavyam karma*, what are you doing? As long as all of us are doing what we need to do, that is enough.

We can certainly say that our own path is the best, but we cannot say that because you are not following my path, therefore, you have to be killed, tortured or persecuted. Who are we, denizens of a tiny speck of dust in the unending universe around us – there are a billion suns like ours in the Milky Way galaxy and there are billions of galaxies in the unending universe around us – to say that the divine can appear only at this time, and in this place and in this form? You can certainly say that this particular descent of the divine is something which is of great value to the human race and should be venerated. But you cannot claim monopoly of divine wisdom. There are no sole selling agents for divine wealth. I believe that until we recognize the multiplicity of paths to the divine, there will never be peace and harmony on earth.

◆

KARAN SINGH

ACKNOWLEDGEMENTS

The editors gratefully acknowledge the financial support received from the Social Sciences and Humanities Research Council of Canada, the University of Ottawa and the India International Centre for the seminar on which this volume is based. We acknowledge the support of the Canada Research Chair in the Contextualization of Religion in a Diverse Canada as well as the Religion and Diversity Project. We also express our heartfelt appreciation to Marianne Abou-Hamad, Tess Campeau and Heather Shipley for their editorial and organizational assistance.

CONTRIBUTORS

ARSHAD ALAM is assistant professor, Centre for the Study of Social Systems, Jawaharlal Nehru University, New Delhi.

RAJEEV BHARGAVA is currently the director and senior fellow at the Centre for the Study of Developing Societies, Delhi (CSDS).

RATNA GHOSH is James McGill Professor and William C. Macdonald Professor of Education (formerly dean of education) at McGill University.

CHARU GUPTA is associate professor of history at the University of Delhi.

GOPAL GURU is professor at the Centre for Political Studies, Jawaharlal Nehru University, New Delhi.

SOLANGE LEFEBVRE is research chair in Religion, Culture and Society and professor in the faculty of Théologie et de sciences des religions at the Université de Montréal.

ASHWANI KUMAR PEETUSH is associate professor of philosophy at Wilfrid Laurier University.

A. RAGHURAMARAJU is professor in the Department of Philosophy at the University of Hyderabad.

ELIZABETH SHAKMAN HURD is associate professor of political science at Northwestern University with a courtesy appointment in religious studies.

SEBASTIAN VELASSERY is professor of philosophy at Panjab University.

LINDA WOODHEAD is professor of sociology of religion at Lancaster University.

INTRODUCTION

SONIA SIKKA,
LORI G. BEAMAN
AND BINDU PURI

RELIGIOUS DIVERSITY: CONCEPTUAL AND PRACTICAL CHALLENGES

In recent years, the problem of religious diversity has been the subject of increasing academic attention and debate. In India and elsewhere, most of the discussions have focused on managing religious diversity through governmental institutions and legislation. The idea of secularism, with its commitment to maintaining some form of separation between religion and state, has featured prominently in both public policy and academic debate as the primary method of ensuring a constitutional guarantee of religious freedom. More recently, in countries like Canada, commitments to multiculturalism as a state policy have also played a role in debates about religious 'accommodation'. This is perhaps unsurprising, given that culture and religion are significantly overlapping categories. The present volume, however, is motivated by the thought that further research, reflection and dialogue are needed on alternative non-legislative strategies for living with religious diversity.

This concern has arisen from an experience of the limits of constitutions, laws and courts in bringing about social harmony across differences and ensuring the protection of vulnerable minorities. Several problems can be highlighted in this context. One problem is that the actual enactment and implementation of laws and social policies inevitably reflects majoritarian attitudes and fears. That remains true, no matter how many legal and constitutional protections a state may put in place to protect religious minorities. Another problem is that policies of state recognition for religious groups often have perverse effects, incentivizing the formation of rigid identities. This often means that minority communities end up being liminal or excluded in relation to the categories recognized by the state.[1]

INTRODUCTION

In response to such considerations, this volume attempts to look beyond exclusively state-oriented and purely legal solutions to the management of religious diversity. It involves an attempt to consider other dimensions of society involved in fostering (ideally) respectful, non-violent and welcoming social relations between religious communities that have come to identify themselves as distinct from one another. It is important to note that this theme does not exclude consideration of the role of the state but seeks to examine this role in its interactions with civil society, religious organizations and private individuals. In the process, the volume examines the ways various actors participate in the negotiation of religious diversity and the quest for equality. In this context, one question is simply, how do religious and state actors collaborate to create particular models of religious behaviour in various contexts? Additionally, in the face of an emergent discourse of the 'other', both in India and Western democracies, what are the interactions that both ground and subvert that tendency? Another question is whether a close examination of the challenges individuals face in their everyday lives reveals more subtle barriers to equality for members of minority religions? If it does, it becomes urgent to ask how these might be remedied.

We are also interested in understanding the kinds of conditions, beliefs and practices within religious communities that either foster or hinder both inter- and intra-group equality under legal regimes where these communities are granted different forms and degrees of autonomy. What forms of religious discourse and behaviour, we wonder, serve to reinforce or to undermine hierarchies within and between religious communities? How do these interact with legislation, and with national and transnational discourses of equality and religious freedom? What should one do about entrenched intra-group domination supported by religious views? And what is the role of religious education in shaping people's beliefs about the nature of various religious communities and the relations between them? In relation to these issues, we felt it important to explore possible measures, including those that draw on the internal resources of religious traditions, that may help to counter tendencies towards exclusive, rigid and hostile definitions of identity.

These are the broad questions guiding the selection of specific topics in the following pages. That selection is also guided

INTRODUCTION

by a special focus on two nations in particular, India and Canada. Although these nations are vastly different in many ways, there is much to be learned, we feel, about diversity and its negotiation by bringing them into comparative focus. Despite their differences, both countries confront the basic question of how to make room for religious identity and diversity within a national framework, in a manner that is fair and helps to minimize conflict. Canada and India have both struggled to determine the forms of differential legislation and policy that such accommodation legitimately requires, and face the problem of balancing these efforts at accommodation with a respect for individual rights and freedoms, as well as with the search for a common national identity and moral consensus. Both countries also struggle with the majority–minority structure as a way of realizing genuine equality between religious groups. This structure problematically assumes the dominance of a particular community, but also seems to be indispensable in safeguarding the rights of non-dominant religious groups. Furthermore, in both Canada and India, as in many countries, the precise meaning of 'secularism' is a sharply contested issue.

In view of these common problems, cross-cultural comparison can help scholars from both countries to learn from one another in envisioning creative solutions. Contexts and histories vary, of course, and what works in one nation can rarely be simply transferred without modification to another. Yet perhaps Canada can learn positive lessons from India's deep religious pluralism and its model of secularism, while India can learn from Canada's way of balancing individual and community rights as well as its policies regarding religious education. There are also common dangers posed by the fact of religious majorities in both nations, and by the politics of recognition. At the same time, expanding the conversation to include some comparative discussion of how religious diversity is negotiated in other societies facing similar realities and challenges, such as the United States and Europe, is beneficial. Not only does this enrich our imagination of possibilities and alternative frameworks but also processes of migration, exchange and internationalization mean that countries are not best studied as self-contained units.

Indeed, the use of the term *comparative* should not mislead us into thinking that we are dealing in our case studies with nations comprising wholly separate histories and peoples, arriving

INTRODUCTION

independently at distinct ways of doing things. The world has never been quite like that, and is less and less so. Globalization has led to an increase in cross-border traffic, of many interlinked varieties: trade, communications, tourism, migration, education, to name a few of the most significant. Religion is part of this traffic and is affected by other elements within it. There are large diasporic communities whose members keep in close touch with their homelands through new media and frequent travel, in ways that were not possible in the past. Consequently, in comparison with migrants in earlier eras, members of these communities are far better able to preserve the patterns of life and belief they bring with them from their countries of origin. They also exert greater influence on religious communities in their homelands, with which they sometimes maintain close ties. The fact that in India, for example, people of Indian origin living elsewhere have their own legal and social category, complete with the well-known acronym of NRI (Non-Resident Indian) reveals the cultural and economic importance of this group within the country's landscape.

One also cannot overestimate the impact on the lives of religious people, of international discourses regarding justice and human rights, revolving around concepts like religious freedom, secularism and equality. The normative principles that underlie these concepts exert varying degrees of influence in different nations. Hardly any nation remains unaffected, however, by the transnational moral and legal discourses that employ them. Equally influential is the spread of ideas via the internet, which has contributed to a globalization of knowledge, as well as misinformation, about the world's religious traditions and communities.

In this context, transnational knowledge and 'comparison' (for lack of a better term) is more important than ever if the goal is to understand one another across religious differences, especially given that these 'others' are also part of who 'we' are in so many ways. Such knowledge can help in developing adequately sophisticated approaches to particular cases of injustice, and in correcting orientalist and occidentalist caricatures deployed to justify modes of exclusion and subordination. Many educators and policymakers have come to believe, for these reasons and others, that teaching citizens about the world's religions is important, and religious

INTRODUCTION

education is one of our primary themes. Too often, however, learning about religion has taken place primarily through the study of religious scriptures and the words of religious authorities. It is equally essential to examine how people negotiate living together in their day-to-day lives, and to look at the traditions of religious thought and practice they evolve in doing so.

The volume is divided into four broad parts. In Part I, 'Negotiating difference in practice', we explore the ways that religion is woven through day-to-day life and the plural manifestations of what are often imagined to be unitary or monolithic religious 'traditions'. We also situate what is called religion in context, demonstrating that as a category religion is woven through other social and political realities that blur its boundaries. How does lived religion inform the ways in which people work through and negotiate diversity? Attention to the actual religious behaviour and interactions of individuals often reveals a very different picture from the one presented by dominant media, political leaders or the proclamations of official religious authorities. In many cases, while the latter sources project an image of sharply distinct communities with opposed systems of belief and practice, living in confrontation with one another, the former reveals quotidian practices of flexibility, compromise and sometimes even of borrowing and fusion, grounded in attitudes of friendship and respect. Here, one needs to examine views on religious plurality within different communities and traditions, but again in relation to how religious individuals and communities actually live and engage with one another rather than exclusively through the authorized texts of the so-called world religions. At the same time, of course, it is important not to romanticize the popular level over the state one, and we must recognize that sometimes there are excellent laws and compelling speeches by state actors that set a tone of inclusion and equality, while on the ground patterns of aversion, discrimination and violence persist.

A number of themes characterize the strategies that people use in day-to-day life as they interact with others and difference at numerous levels. Some of them, such as love, are themes that social scientists are often reluctant to explore, leaving it to theologians and others to deal with. Yet love, respect, friendship, neighbourliness, forgiveness, flexibility and a desire for peace all characterize and motivate the ways in which people just get along. As we think about this theme one of the major challenges is the recovery of what we might describe as 'non-event'. The small day-to-day interactions that characterize negotiations are difficult to recover: they are often so insignificant that they don't register in people's memories as being anything of significance. And this is partly what makes what we are thinking about so difficult to research. How do we ask people about those moments in day-to-day life that don't really leave their mark but that are in fact the important moments, where people have simply negotiated or worked out a moment of difference? How to capture those fleeting moments of shared understanding, common ground and understanding that make a peaceable everyday life and interaction possible. It is much easier, it seems, to focus on conflict, problems and competition, rather than on the ways in which people find similarity as a point of reference.

Stories about the non-event can soften the hardened lines of the religious boundaries that impede such harmony, offering new models or traces of others' paths. Rather than a purity of difference, they may point to blurred boundaries, as in the case of the St. Thomas Christians. Destabilizing the notion of purity is important, and reflects the ways in which the shape of religion is constantly changing. In his chapter 'Faith, ethnicity and nationalism: St. Thomas Christians in India', Sebastian Velassery documents the ways in which Indian Christians in Kerala, who make up approximately 27 per cent of the population, have navigated their religious and cultural identities, maintaining both distinction and similarity with their Hindu neighbours. Through Velassery's example, the notion of purity is challenged and the ways that blurred boundaries act to create a shared space is illustrated. In common with Hindus, Christians in Kerala have a concept of sacred, and observe similar social customs related to birth, marriage and death, such as giving newborns powdered gold mixed with honey, and not cooking or eating food in the house of the deceased till after the burial. At the same time, they have drawn on Christian themes in their work as agents of social, economic and moral transformation. Their preservation of identity by adaptation to the cultural space of India provides an instructive case that challenges exclusionary categories such as Christian and foreign.

In her chapter, Woodhead points out that discussion of religious diversity is often narrowed down to discussion about inter-religious relations at the level of the (nation) state and state politics, including the governance of religion. She argues for a broadening of the discussion to include (a) intra-religious and religion-secular relations, as well as inter-religious diversity and (b) attention to the ways in which diversity plays out across society, including in key domains such as schools, the workplace, hospitals and prisons. In her examination, Woodhead finds that far from confirming a picture of intensified difference and conflict, which is often rehearsed in national media and politics, much of the research shows that there has been considerable progress in moving towards constructive forms of 'multi-faith' engagement in the United Kingdom since the 1980s. Key to understanding this movement is understanding the dynamics of shifting perceptions.

Arshad Alam examines textual expressions of Indian Islam to point to the tensions that arise from the exclusivist doctrines of the Deobandis (reformists) and the Barelwis, which developed in colonial times and can be characterized as, in part, a strategy of self-preservation. Nonetheless, in contemporary India this raises the broader question of how, exactly, one achieves successful interaction and exchange in the face of such doctrines. From the viewpoints of religious communities making certain kinds of exclusivist claims for their religion, such as the communities Alam's essay examines, the only possible solution to the problem of religious diversity would seem to be that of arriving at an arrangement for living together on purely practical grounds. Given exclusivist salvationist religious doctrines, it is hard to see how there could be a more than practical agreement vis-à-vis diversity. Yet, in keeping with the overall theme of the workshop, it is exactly these practical negotiations and navigations that are in need of deeper scrutiny. Alam's chapter raises a broader issue that is relevant on a much larger scale: what to do with exclusivist religious teachings that would appear to impede the model of living together in a diverse society we might want to create? This is not solely an issue for Indian diversity, but for religious diversity more generally. It is only through an examination of the practical strategies for living together that the exclusivity of doctrine is challenged or rendered more malleable. Practices of living together can create an alternative narrative that acts as an important counterbalance to narrower constructions of religious practices.

Beaman's chapter challenges the notion of purity by suggesting that North American religion has more permeable boundaries than is often thought. While the story of religion is frequently told as one of categories of belonging, examining lived religion reveals that boundaries are much blurrier. The dominance of rather rigid conceptualizations of religion means that an imagined purity has been relatively easy to sustain. By drawing on lessons from the Indian context to reinforce the notion of lived religion, argues Beaman, religion becomes understood as a much more fluid, flexible and messy phenomenon. The erosion of identity purity can open new space for living with difference and diversity by challenging categorical rigidity, generalization and essentialization.

Although we focus on the everyday and the emergence of practical solutions, and the chapters in this section illustrate that practical solutions are sometimes more readily available at informal and local sites than at the level of the state, it is important to return to the question of the role of the state in regulating diversity. Examining the everyday leads one to reflect on when differences matter and when they do not, and why. What role, if any, does the state have in intervening when difference causes tension or conflict? Although the chapters in this section illustrate the ways that everyday actors successfully navigate difference, they also point to places where policy or law may play an important role. Not everyone, for example, is in a position to negotiate: Woodhead's chapter illustrates that status can matter in this process. Arshad Alam's examination of Islamic reform movements, moreover, shows that processes internal to religion may threaten both intra- and inter-religious diversity, creating silenced insiders as well as hostility towards outsiders. Such phenomena may point to the need for the state to play a more aggressive role, or for other measures to be found that could counteract such dangers. Thus, although we highlight successful strategies for living with diversity that are enacted in everyday life, we also recognize that the state may play a useful role in creating conditions of empowerment.

The problem of religious diversity is further complicated by patterns of subordination within and across religious communities. This is especially a problem in India, where caste hierarchies have been maintained for centuries by religious sanction. Part II of this volume deals with caste, a case that cannot be either properly conceptualized or redressed through ideals of peaceful coexistence or negotiation of difference, for it involves a drawing of internal boundaries between 'us' and 'them' whose essential logic rests on deep inequality. Those designated by Brahminical ideologies and institutions as lower caste or outcaste obviously cannot and should not make peace with a religion whose basic beliefs and social structure require their subordination. The question arises here of whether the identity of what has come to be constructed as 'Hinduism' does rest fundamentally on this act of self-distancing from others, who are included only in order to be cast out to the margins as lesser and abject. Solutions in this case cannot involve a respect for the boundaries established by such an act, but must come from attempts to dismantle these boundaries, including rejection of the religious views that serve as a foundation for their creation and policing.

Charu Gupta's chapter on the role of inter-religious and inter-caste intimacies in religious conversions by Dalit women in colonial India looks at one example of boundary transgression across caste hierarchies, drawing attention to intersections between caste and gender. The question of Dalit female desire, she points out in this chapter, has been intrinsic to everyday forms of caste and religious violence, producing deeply politicized discourses, particularly in relation to inter-caste and inter-religious intimacies. These are also tied to elevation or decline in social status, mobility and religious conversions. Gupta's account examines religious conversions by Dalit women in colonial North India as acts which embodied desires and were accounts of resistant or stubborn materialities. It focuses on police reports, court cases and writings of caste and reformist ideologues, to show how the right to conversion produced increasing anxieties, framed around the bodies of Dalit women. These also reflected the insecurities of Hindu publicists to flexible and liminal religious spaces. Through this analysis, Gupta implicitly attempts to recover an aspect of Dalit female agency, choice and aspiration. The localized, quotidian practices of these women and their expressions of new inter-religious intimacies and desires exposed the inherent vulnerabilities in the dominant Hindu logic.

Raghuramaraju's chapter on the differing interpretations of the relations between Hinduism and Buddhism by Radhakrishnan, Ambedkar and T.R.V. Murti illustrates the unfeasibility of always trying to iron out the differences between religions, given the plain facts about their content. It also points to the loss of resources for social critique that may accompany such attempts to dissolve difference into unity. He argues that the colonialism–modernity combination imposed on Indian society an imperative to engage with unity and diversity in a new way, posing fresh challenges to Indian philosophers. The latter employed different strategies; some conformed to the colonial model of modernity, while others relapsed into orthodoxy. Against this background, Raghuramaraju discusses how S. Radhakrishnan, while initially acknowledging differences between Hinduism and Buddhism, eventually renders them as insignificant. By contrast, B. R. Ambedkar, rejecting the politics underlying caste discrimination, highlights the radical difference between these two schools of Indian philosophy. T.R.V. Murti takes into account both differences and commonalities between Hinduism and Buddhism, and exposes the underlying interaction between these schools of thought in shaping their developments. The three provide examples of how philosophy in India engages with surviving traditional philosophies regarding unity and diversity in view of the challenges of coexistence in a modern plural state. Raghuramaraju's presentation of these examples shows how stressing commonalities while downplaying differences – a dominant tendency within modern Indian philosophy, especially among those also involved in political life – does not always serve the cause of bringing about true equality.

In a similar vein, Gopal Guru points out the historical incommensurability of Brahminical Hinduism and Neo-Buddhism, while raising concerns about purely tactical attempts to achieve consensus between the leaders of Hindutva and Dalit political parties.

He argues that in India the religious diversity which exists at the social level is being articulated at the political level, but is in this articulation being converted into what Rawls describes as an overlapping consensus. The result is a 'thin' notion of religious diversity that does not provide an adequate foundation for developing the policy measures required to ensure genuine equality between religious communities, and between individuals within those communities. Guru then works out a thicker notion of diversity, taking account of the realities of life for subordinated groups in particular. He also proposes that profound ethical, and not merely legal and political, change is required to foster true equality and dignity for members of these groups.

Another important theme on which we reflect in this volume concerns the potential role of publicly funded schools and universities in educating citizens about religion, the topic of Part III. It would seem that education about religion could contribute to or enhance the possibility of successful negotiation of difference, but it also poses difficulties and has potential drawbacks. One issue here concerns the possibility of a conflict between religious education and political secularism. It might be thought that public funding for any form of religious education, whether in religious or secular schools, is simply incompatible with the commitment to secularism in countries like India and Canada. However, it is interesting that in Canada, Quebec – a province now very strongly committed to secularism – has instituted a programme for mandatory education about religion in all schools. The argument for this model is that it enhances mutual understanding by providing all citizens with knowledge about the different religions among which they live, while encouraging dialogue and critical reflection. At the same time, though, this kind of education may be thought to conflict with secular values as well as principles of religious freedom, especially if it is mandatory. Furthermore, it is one thing to debate the permissibility and value of non-sectarian religious education at a theoretical level; it is quite another thing to implement it effectively. The design and delivery of non-confessional education about religion in public schools pose numerous pragmatic challenges, given the religious sensitivities of students and teachers, as well as the difficulty of developing an approach that is genuinely neutral or unbiased (or of knowing what even means in relation to religion).

In 'Education in secular democratic societies: the challenge of religious diversity', Ratna Ghosh surveys a number of these issues, asking about the relation between religious education and secularism, and the feasibility in practice of providing non-sectarian education about religion. The global context, she notes, is one where religion is being pushed to the periphery in secular democracies, a process that leads to reactions on the part of those who feel their religious identities to be threatened. Given the dangers of religious fundamentalism, sometimes motivated by such reactions, and the fact that religion remains a deeply important aspect of many people's lives, Ghosh argues that there is a pressing need for critical education about religion. Cultural theory and critical pedagogy, which connect education and the politics of difference with the economy and citizenship, provide a good conceptual framework for its formulation and delivery. Ghosh surveys a number of topics that arise in relation to implementing such education, focusing on the situation in Canada, particularly in Quebec. Ultimately, Ghosh maintains that teaching strategies can be and have been devised that take account of the sensitivities and hazards of teaching the subject of religion in public schools to pupils belonging to different faiths or no faith.

In the next chapter, Solange Lefebvre draws attention to the intertwining of language, religion and Quebecois identity within the process of negotiating diversity in relation to what becomes a rather controversial education programme about religion. She looks at the content of the programme Ethics and Religious Culture implemented in 2008 in both the public and the private school system in the province of Quebec, along with its vision of diversity and intercultural relations. She examines as well the various debates surrounding this programme: fears on the part of proponents of interculturalism as opposed to multiculturalism; contestation in courts by parents and one private catholic school; and contestation by secularists. The final part of her chapter offers a comparison with the French and British visions of diversity in schools. The French model refuses teaching religion as particular discipline in public school, providing instead teaching about the 'religious fact' in disciplines like history and literature. The British model promotes interfaith religious education as a specific discipline. Quebec offers a hybrid approach, between the French secularist and the British interfaith models. Lefebvre demonstrates that behind these various models lie specific comprehensions of state and school neutrality, and of the function of religion in social and individual life.

Rajeev Bhargava discusses the broader issue of whether state-funded schools in a secular society should in principle be providing education about religion, arguing that they can and should, subject to a number of conditions. He contends that state-provided multi-religious education is not incompatible with appropriately formulated secular principles, but is rather necessary and valuable in nations characterized by deep religious diversity. At the same time, though, the curriculum design of such education assumes the existence of mutually distinct 'religions', to which members owe exclusive commitment. Historically, Bhargava points out, Indian traditions have not been 'religions' in this sense, but they have increasingly come to conform to a modern Western idea of religion, which multi-religious education tends to reinforce. He suggests that there is something to be learned from traditional Indian (and other Asian) approaches to religious questions and claims, and a way of adapting these lessons to the teaching of religion in India and elsewhere.

Building on Bhargava's analysis, Sikka also affirms the value of teaching religion in schools, but asks how it may be done in a way that respects the character of Indian traditions, to which the idea of 'faith', along with the distinction between religion and philosophy, is not entirely appropriate. She agrees with Bhargava that the state has a significant interest in providing its citizens with non-sectarian education about the various religious communities it includes, and that interpretations of secularism in India that have sought to exclude the teaching of religion from publicly funded institutions of education are mistaken. Yet it is a fact, she points out, that education about religion tends to be organized around and thereby to reinforce the idea of religions as settled and mutually exclusive systems of belief to which members of separate communities adhere. Such a conception distorts the character of Indian traditions, Sikka maintains, while promoting a generally problematic understanding of religion. She proposes that teaching so-called religion through the discipline of 'philosophy', against the background of an Indian historical context where no such distinction existed, can help to mitigate this danger, while offering a valuable corrective to an understanding of religion that has become increasingly questionable in the West as well.

The final part of the volume interrogates liberal solutions to religious diversity. It is the 'living with' that makes religious diversity a problem demanding urgent conceptual and practical attention. The minimal solution to the problem would seem to be tolerance and the best case for tolerance has perhaps been made by liberals. However, it can be argued that given the primacy of reason in liberalism, liberal reasons for tolerating religiously diverse others can only come from positions of uncertainty or scepticism about religious truths. This becomes apparent if one examines the celebrated liberal arguments for tolerance, as for instance, those made by Mill and by Locke. Mill (in the meta-inductive argument for tolerance in *On Liberty*) recommends tolerance on account of the fact that we know we are not infallible about matters that concern us deeply (Mill, 2006: 24). In the 1667 essay on toleration, Locke grounds tolerance on the fact that religious beliefs are 'purely speculative opinions' (Locke, 1997a: 137). Contemporary liberals like John Rawls and Thomas Nagel recommend epistemic abstinence about truth. In an essay examining the contemporary philosophical responses of Rawls and Nagel to the diversity of ideologies present in plural democratic societies, Raz (1996) examines the difficulties with the epistemic distance recommended by such liberals. On this view, Nagel and Rawls have argued that 'certain truths should not be taken into account because, though true, they are of an epistemic class unsuited for public life' (Raz, 1996: 61). In this context, Raz argues that for a liberal society 'the social role of justice can be purchased only at the price of epistemic distance' (Raz, 1996: 66). The final section in this volume examines the difficulties with the epistemic abstinence implicit in liberal solutions to living with religiously diverse others.

In 'Diversity, secularism and religious toleration', Ashwani Kumar Peetush starts on a liberal note, making the point that Rawls's theory of international justice provides 'the best theoretical architecture' for liberals to recognize non-liberal non-secular peoples as decent societies so long as such societies protect the 'urgent human rights' of their members. However Peetush departs from Rawls's conception of an overlapping consensus by arguing that such a consensus between diverse people need not be a purely political ideal and can be 'essentially comprehensive in nature'. Peetush differs from a liberal position in two ways. First, he argues that Rawls's distinction between the political and the comprehensive obstructs the possibilities of the emergence of any meaningful dialogue on substantial religious arguments for tolerance in the

INTRODUCTION

public domain. Second, Peetush contends that there can be good reasons for tolerance that emerge from within comprehensive religious traditions. He supports this point by referring to arguments for tolerance that can be reconstructed from within the Indian tradition: the Jain doctrine of *anekantavada*, the Buddhist *pratityasamutpada* and the non-dualism of Advaita Vedanta.

Bindu Puri's chapter on 'Religious diversity and the devout' asks if there can be 'a liberal yet religious citizen of faith'. This chapter addresses the religious believers' hesitation in accepting the liberal's uncertainty and scepticism about religious truths as a ground for religious tolerance. Rawls's overlapping consensus certainly provides a believer with a reason for being reasonable, in terms of expectations of reciprocity, from diverse religious others. However, difficulties arise from the fact that giving reasons for being reasonable transforms the reasonable into an intellectual virtue and obliterates the distinction between the reasonable and the rational. It then becomes difficult to argue that Rawls's overlapping consensus is different from (and more stable than) a *modus vivendi*. Puri's chapter suggests that Gandhi's equation of truth with non-violence presents the believer with an internal route from the love of dissenting others to truth/God. On Gandhi's account the only way to arrive at the truth of one's beliefs was to defer to the beliefs and persons of opposing others. One way to philosophically reconstruct Gandhi is simply to think of the impossibility of arriving at true knowledge of self or other without the practice of non-violence as humility, egolessness and love. What makes Gandhi's position different from that of liberals is that Gandhian *ahimsa* as deference does not come from the consciousness of being fallible but from the recognition that non-violence is the ground of arriving at certainties.

Elizabeth Hurd argues against the international liberal practice of promoting religious freedom. Examining such practice, she suggests that it leads to three paradoxes. First, she points out that official religious freedom advocacy has a tendency to unilaterally project conflicts in plural societies as having arisen from the denial of religious freedom to minorities. In this process liberals end up silencing arguments from human dignity that may sometimes be more relevant to reconstructing such conflicts. The second paradox of religious freedom advocacy is that it inevitably singles out religious identity and thereby actually contributes to the violence it sets out to restrain. Studying legal cases of religious discrimination in hiring that have been initiated against the United States Commission on International Religious Freedom, Hurd points to the third paradox of religious freedom. This is that the promotion of religious freedom may undermine democracy because the forms of religion defended by its advocates diminish the potential for non-established, minority and democratic forms of religion to thrive. She concludes that liberal internationalists who set out to enforce the universal norm of religious freedom are engaged in an essentially flawed exercise, for the government that has set up an institution to safeguard religious freedom 'inevitably becomes involved in deciding which religions…' are 'deserving of protection'. The politics of religious freedom advocacy paradoxically transforms the liberal insistence on religious freedom into a non-liberal discourse.

The essays in this volume persuade us that a greater attention to living with diversity is needed in scholarship. We have only just begun the exploration of this theme, with two countries whose traditions are different, yet inextricably bound together in ways that create and sustain similarities. The almost obsessive attention that has been paid to the ways in which states and social institutions understand, monitor and regulate religious diversity during the past decade has obscured an entire realm of everyday success stories about how people do, indeed, live with diversity. Thus, while the disparities between formal constitutional guarantees and legal regulations have been mapped; the normative contents of particular regulatory regimes identified; and the move from the secular into the post-secular proclaimed, there has been a stunning lack of attention paid to the realm of the everyday. In the midst of this flurry of academic pronouncements, people go about their everyday lives encountering diversity and difference and negotiating their way through it, oftentimes in a manner that achieves a de facto justice, sense of fairness and recognition of equality. This realm of everyday activity has remained largely outside the scope of attention of the conversation about diversity. It is important not to lose sight of these everyday negotiations. Religious violence crosses borders, we all recognize, but so do ideas about how to live together peacefully, theological reflections on pluralism and lived practices of friendship across the borders of religious identity-groupings. We need to reflect further on what fosters or hinders such practices in the case of religious diversity, approaching our subject in an objective spirit, without piety but also without contempt.

◆

NOTE

1. Some of these issues emerged as needing further attention from a seminar held at the University of Ottawa in 2010, which also focussed on Canada and India. That seminar formed the basis for the volume, *Multiculturalism and Religious Identity: Canada and India* (edited by Sonia Sikka and Lori Beaman, McGill-Queen's University Press, 2014). It led to a follow-up seminar at the India International Centre in Delhi in 2013, which resulted in the current volume. The website for the Delhi seminar is available at www.livingwithreligiousdiversity.com.

REFERENCES

Mill, John Stuart. 2006. 'On Liberty', in Alan Ryan (ed.), *On Liberty and the Subjection of Women*. New York: Penguin.

Locke, John. 1997. 'An Essay on Toleration', in Mark Goldie (ed.), *Locke: Political Essays*. Cambridge: Cambridge University Press.

Raz, Joseph. 1996. 'Facing Diversity: The Case of Epistemic Abstinence', in *Ethics in Public Domain: Essays in the Morality of Law and Politics*. Oxford: Clarendon Press.

PART I
NEGOTIATING DIFFERENCE IN PRACTICE

1 RELIGIOUS OTHER OR RELIGIOUS INFERIOR?

LINDA
WOODHEAD

The academic debate about religious diversity, and how Western and other societies deal with it, is now extensive – and often rather 'flat'. By 'flat' I don't just mean boring – though it can be – I mean overly abstract, and insufficiently attentive to the contours of inequality. The language of 'difference' and 'diversity', which is privileged in this discussion, can have the unfortunate effect of making it seem that people of different religious and non-religious persuasions meet to discuss their 'cultural differences' on a level playing field. This problem is bound up with the abstract and theoretical way in which discussion of the governance and negotiation of religious diversity is often conducted. Whilst this is appropriate for legal and political approaches looking at the issue from 'top down', it is important also to take account of case studies of how difference is actually negotiated on the ground – including in the vast mass of interactions which are in some sense resolved before they ever come to the attention of a judge or legislator.

Here I want to suggest that taking the micro- as well as the macro-levels of society seriously while looking at religious diversity makes it easier to be watchful for the power differentials which are always operative in such situations. The most obvious differential is that between religious majorities and minorities locally, nationally and sometimes transnationally. Most talk about the 'accommodation' of difference that has as its backdrop this differential, for it is a religious majority which has to do the accommodating when that is posed as a problem; religious minorities are constantly adjusting themselves to fit in with the norms of the majority, but that is not normally discussed as 'accommodation', since it does not constitute a 'problem' for the majority. As well as religious majority–minority differentials, other intersectional inequalities are often at work in religious encounters, including those of class, gender and race. And then there are the less generalizable negotiations of face-to-face 'dignifying' or 'putting down' at play in such situations – often better captured by the novelist or film-maker than the academic scholar, but not wholly outside the latter's purview.

Before offering some concrete examples of the kind of approach I am advocating, let me thank Lori Beaman for inviting me to do so and, more importantly, for exemplifying the kind of approach I am trying to commend. Through the large Canadian research initiative on religious diversity which she leads, Professor Beaman has done more than anyone to encourage this sort of work. In her own writing, her attention to the contours of particular cases – including those in the court room – has encouraged others to think similarly (Beaman, 2008). Her refusal to discuss diversity without also mentioning equality, and her careful dissection of apparently neutral language about 'cultural symbols' and 'accommodation' to reveal the ways in which they mask privilege, is a provocation (Beaman, 2012: 101–38). It is because of her that I will now discuss a small selection of cases of religious diversity from the large British research programme, the Arts and Humanities Research Council Religion and Society Programme, which I directed between 2007 and 2013, as well as from my own research, including that undertaken in connection with an European Union (EU) project looking at how Muslim dress is dealt with in different European countries (Rosenberger and Sauer, 2011).

The importance of taking power relations, including majority–minority relations, seriously in discussions of 'difference' is apparent in the simple fact that religious minorities are likely to face the most serious difficulties in countries with large, settled (for many generations) and fairly sedentary national majorities who have clear ethnic and religious identities. This obviously helps to explain why Europe has more of a 'problem' with minorities than countries formed by relatively recent migrations, like the USA, Canada or Singapore, or by more long-standing diversity, like India. It also helps explain why some countries – like Denmark – which have large and very homogenous ethno-religious majorities have more of a problem in integrating minority religious communities than others even within Europe. The difficulty is exacerbated where the minority, as in the case of Muslims in Europe, is both sizeable and lower in power and status than the majority, both in terms of socio-economic status, and because of having a history as colonial subjects. Here an intersection of inequalities act together and are further exacerbated when the minority has a clear and assertive religious identity, even to the extent of resorting to terrorist violence. In such situations, a cycle of reaction and counter-reaction, of identity-rejection and identity-assertion can begin to operate, drawing in both individuals and whole communities.

Let me start to explore these issues with a research project from the Religion and Society Programme led by Navtej Purewal, which studied sacred shrines and their uses in the Punjab region today, but using the boundaries of pre-independence Punjab before it was divided between Muslim-majority Pakistan and Hindu-majority India (Purewal and Kalra, 2011). One striking finding is how many of these shrines continue to enjoy sacred status and shared usage by Hindus, Muslims and Sikhs of various hues, and how many sacred songs and other practices remain common to them all. Yet on both sides of the border, particularly in Pakistan, there are regular attempts to cleanse the sites of mixed popular practices and to privilege the practices of a purified majority religion. Such attempts are made both by agents of the state, including the police and army, and by agents of religion, including priests and other guardians of orthodoxy. There are regular clear-outs. Yet people keep returning, like a tide rolling back in, colonizing these spaces for popular practices, time after time. The dimension of gender and class is clear too; often it is women and people of the lower classes who recolonize the space, only to be ejected by men of higher standing.

As with this case study, it strikes me that the idea of 'religious traditions' or 'world religions', as highly differentiated from one another, separated by clear boundaries, teachings and practices – and, therefore, prone to problems of encounter – is one which is most often defended by religious and political elites who have interests in preserving religio-political differences. By contrast, the everyday realities of religion lived by ordinary people are often much more diverse, mixed and 'confused' – and hence less subject to 'problems' of encounter. Certainly, there are counter-examples, as in the case of minorities in positions of injustice or insecurity who come under pressure to bind and define and differentiate their religious identities in order to secure them. Nevertheless, research like Purewal's reminds us that the idea that religions are always clear and distinct from one another, and hence inevitably subject to problems of 'difference', may itself be a construct which serves some people's view of religion more than others.

Turning now to the United Kingdom (UK), we come to a context in which religious diversity is much less deep-seated than in India. With the exception of Jewish citizens, Britain had little experience of dealing with religious minorities 'at home' until after the Second World War, and the largest of Britain's religious minority populations, Muslims from former colonies (most of whom have full British citizenship), has only grown to around five per cent of the population in the twenty-first century.

Rather than beginning with an example of Muslim minority encounter, however, let me begin with the case of Lilian Ladele, a black Christian Pentecostal woman, whose controversial desire to manifest her religious belief became the subject of a long-running legal dispute which has only recently concluded. Ladele was employed as a registrar of marriages in a civil registry office in London prior to the UK passing legislation to allow civil partnerships between people of the same sex in 2004. After the legislation was passed, Ladele told colleagues that she could not, in good conscience, conduct civil ceremonies for gay people because it offended her Christian conviction that sexual relations should only take place between married heterosexual couples. At first, an amicable solution was arrived at; other members of staff would stand in for her to conduct such ceremonies, whilst she in return would take on some of their duties.

Thus far, a solution had been arrived at without recourse to law. In 2006, however, the UK introduced a new equality law which afforded protection against discrimination not only on existing grounds of gender and ethnicity but also on the grounds of disability, age, religion and sexual orientation. One result is that cases of alleged discrimination against religious people, which would previously have been settled out of court and in the local context in which they arose (whether satisfactorily or not), can now be taken instead to a tribunal hearing. And so it turned out with Lilian Ladele. Her refusal to treat same-sex couples led to her being harassed by some colleagues who disagreed with her stance, and thence to difficulties with her employer. In the end she resigned, or was forced to resign, and took her case to an employment tribunal, arguing that she had been discriminated against because of her religious commitments.

Ladele's case ended up going right through the courts – first to an employment tribunal which upheld her claim, and then to an appeal court, where she lost. In the meantime, conservative Christian opinion in Britain was mobilizing, partly in a direct response to the introduction of equality law. A number of organizations like 'Christian Concern' came into being at around this time (2008–10), with the intention of highlighting and supporting the cases of individuals whose religious freedom they believed to be threatened. They supported Ladele in taking her case to the highest court of all, the European Court of Human Rights in Strasbourg. Four cases of alleged infringement of religious freedom in Britain were considered together by this court in 2013. On three of them, including Ladele, the court found no reason to overturn the domestic decisions (on one, concerning an employee's right to wear a cross, the court found against the UK). However, there was a dissenting opinion in relation to Ladele, which argued that the case involved a matter of conscience, and that

> instead of practising the tolerance and the 'dignity for all' it preached, the Borough of Islington [Ladele's employer] pursued the doctrinaire line, the road of obsessive political correctness. It effectively sought to force the applicant to act against her conscience or face the extreme penalty of dismissal.[1]

So *Ladele v Islington Council* is interesting for a number of reasons. One is that it is a case in which the arguments for and against are rather evenly balanced, with merit on both sides. In Ladele's favour, she trained as a registrar before civil partnerships were introduced, so they were a new and unexpected part of her duties. She has a right to hold her beliefs, and her conscience – which here was simply a desire to sit on her hands and do nothing – should be respected. Moreover, because there were other people available to conduct the ceremonies, no harm was done to gay or lesbian people, and an apparently amicable solution had been reached with which all parties should have been happy. On the other side of the argument, however, a law had been passed which prohibited discrimination against people on grounds of their sexuality. Ladele is a public servant and, like anyone else, she is required to act in accordance with the law. The fact that a person disagrees with a law is no defence; whilst they can campaign for a change in the law, they cannot break the law. So it was proportionate to dismiss Ladele if she could not carry out duties which are an important part of her role.

The case is also interesting because it illustrates the difference the law can make in the negotiation of religious difference. Had there been no anti-discrimination law, the negotiated local solution would probably not have been challenged. That might have been a better outcome, since Ladele's conscientious objections would have been respected and no gay couples would have been harmed. However, the mere existence of the law probably influenced those who felt they could complain against Ladele (no one disputes she was bullied), and she and the complainants now had a 'higher' forum in which they could negotiate their differences. Is that a better situation? If real harm were being done to anyone in this situation, it surely is. What happened in practice, however, was that a campaigning group 'used' the case of Ladele to highlight their concern that conservative Christian opinion is being ignored in the 'liberal' UK, and that Christians are being 'persecuted'. So the law becomes a stage for wider religious and political campaigning, not merely a means to work out the justice of a particular case.

Finally, the case is interesting because of the many power relations in play. Ladele is a female member of a black Pentecostal Church and holds opinions about homosexuality which are objectionable to majority liberal opinion. In other words, she belongs to a religious minority whose identity-difference is heightened by its opposition to mainstream secular and liberal Christian opinion. Does this mean that there is *more* reason to be careful to protect her rights, including the right to express religious opinions which many people view as homophobic? Or does it mean that someone with views at odds with those of the majority must bear some cost for acting against a settled view which has been enacted in law? And what about the rights of gay and lesbian people, who would also claim to be a minority, have historically been victimized – even if many now have a higher status than someone like Lilian Ladele in terms of class, wealth and ethnicity? There are no simple answers, and the issues are further complicated by the fact that Ladele's case is championed by more wealthy and powerful, often male and white, conservative Christians, who have their own reasons for wishing to uphold norms of heterosexual sexuality and the traditional family.

Let me turn next to a case from my own research into the wearing of *hijab* (head-covering) and *niqab* (face-covering) in the UK. The broader issue (which the EU project, of which this work was a part, was exploring) is why the wearing of such dress, even full face-covering, has been relatively easily accommodated in a few European countries, including the UK, but outlawed in others. In the course of exploring this topic I interviewed a young Muslim barrister, Aisha Alvi, whose personal story is part of the wider narrative of how hijab-wearing was negotiated into mainstream British life in the late 1980s (Hadj-Abdou and Woodhead, 2011: 150–76).

Aisha and her sister had been pupils at Altrincham Grammar School near Manchester – a state school with a high academic reputation. They wore hijab to class despite the fact that it violated the school's dress code. The school objected, and after negotiations with the headteacher broke down, the girls were suspended. 'We went home', Aisha told me, 'and we just thought, "this is wrong!"' You know, 'we love hijab and we want to wear hijab!' They were teenage girls; this was their rebellion, as well as their piety. Far from being coerced by male members of the family, it seems that their father told the girls to be sensible and do what the school required. But Aisha and her sister felt this was a matter of faith and freedom; so they decided to defy the school and go to class wearing hijab.

Because this was the first case of its kind in Britain, it attracted media attention. Soon there were camera crews camped outside the girls' house, waiting for them to go to school and be ejected each day. This was the point, Aisha explained, when the dispute began to turn. 'It was an out-of-court battle won by the media', she later said. The school was in the limelight for the wrong reasons, not for their usual academic reputation, but for being intolerant of Islam. As the case was publicized, the Alvi sisters won support from the Commission for Racial Equality (a government body), the National Union of Teachers, the *Jewish Gazette* and the Manchester Council of Mosques. The pendulum was beginning to swing in their favour. Eventually, the headteacher and governing body backed down, and the sisters were allowed to add hijab to their uniform. From then on, the issue ceased to be controversial in Britain, even though fuller covering of the face and body did provoke a few disputes. Nevertheless, hijab, niqab, *jilbab* and *burqa* are common sights in British cities, and there has never been any serious pressure to ban them.

I include this example because I was struck by Aisha Alvi's self-aware acknowledgement of just how important her family's socio-economic status and educational background was in this controversy. 'We were articulate, middle-class English girls, from a good school', she said, 'and that made it much easier', She and her sister would talk to the cameramen and the journalists every day, and soon the media began to like them and respect them. They compared them to their own daughters. These were well-educated British girls. Having started off asking, 'Why should these Muslims be allowed to wear a headscarf when other pupils have to abide by the dress rules?' they started to say, 'These are really nice girls! Why can't they wear what they want to wear? This is a free country!' So the way in which majority society treats the claims to different treatment by a religious minority can depend, in significant part, on the socio-economic status of the claimants in question. And high-status members of a minority may be able to play a pioneering role which benefits other members of lower status.

It should be noted, however, that there are other structural reasons why the wearing of Muslim dress has been relatively uncontroversial in Britain – again with interesting implications. One is the fact that the government and judiciary have taken the view that the responsibility for dealing with this issue lies primarily with the institutions in which the issue arises – mainly schools and workplaces. Where possible, the law tries to keep out and push things back to the local level. On the whole, making the people who are directly involved in a disputed issue work out a successful solution amongst themselves – often a compromise – seems to have better outcomes than legislating at a national level, where political interests and pressure groups often intervene, and the issue becomes one of principles, rather than real people you have to live and work with on a day-to-day basis. This approach has led to many different local solutions in Britain, and generally served to de-escalate the issue of Muslim dress.

Also important is the fact that the UK already had a tradition of allowing religious and cultural minorities to wear conspicuous and unusual forms of dress. A decade before Muslim dress became an issue, Sikhs in Britain had campaigned successfully to be allowed to wear the turban, even when the law required the wearing of safety helmets. Sikhs were exempted from such law and were also allowed to carry ceremonial daggers. One reason for this was that Sikh men were a rather high-status minority group in Britain, and that, as well as being very well organized, they won the support of the influential Sikh community in India, and of majority bodies in the UK, including trade unions. Another reason is that Scottish men traditionally carry a ceremonial dagger – a *sgian-dubh*. So here, the fact that a majority community had an analogous custom worked to the advantage of the minority group seeking toleration of its own different but related practice – and the analogy helped to normalize the custom in question. This example takes me back to my earlier point about the fact that Britain isn't a mono-nation like Denmark, but is Scotland, Wales, England and Northern Ireland. That diversity makes it easier to assimilate additional diversity, and there is a feeling that it is also easier for religious minorities to be integrated into one of the minority nations (England being the dominant nation), on the principle that the minorities unite against a common enemy!

My next case comes from a project on the Religion and Society Programme directed by Sophie Gilliat-Ray which looked at Muslim chaplains in Britain.[2] The British state supports chaplains in the armed forces, hospitals, schools and prisons. Traditionally, these chaplains have been Christian, drawn particularly from the established churches. This project was looking at how Muslims have been integrated into this 'majority' system since the 1970s. It found that in many cases the majority church and its chaplain acted as a gatekeeper. Change came largely by way of chaplains acting as gatekeepers and 'hosts' who recognized the need to share the ministry with members of other faiths. That's a kind of integration of difference, but the more difficult step comes when Muslim chaplains (and others) are so successfully mainstreamed that a Muslim chaplain becomes the team leader of others, including Christians. Yet, in a meritocratic promotion system this can, and has, happened. Muslims now occupy senior positions in some chaplaincy teams – and even take Christian services when need arises.

What this highlights is the difference between being a religious minority 'given a seat at the table' by the majority, to being an equal at the table, to being the host. The same project also offers examples of how the minority may bring unforeseen benefits to the majority, even by way of resolving what at first seemed like a problem of accommodation. The 'problem' was that the usual procedure of carrying out post-mortems some days after a death was objectionable to Muslim families, because of the religious obligation to bury the body very swiftly after death. Acting as brokers over this issue, Muslim hospital chaplains had the idea of carrying out post-mortems in body scanners. Because these are often idle at night, they came up with the solution of using them at that time for dead rather than live bodies. So successful did this prove that the practice is now becoming much more common for post-mortems of non-Muslims as well. So here we have a 'problem' posed by a minority practice, which turns into a 'solution' which benefits the majority.

My final example concerns multifaith spaces – the subject of a research project led by Ralph Brand which involved specialists from many different fields.[3] In Britain and some other Western countries, these spaces have in the last few decades become the main kind of 'new build' of a religious or spiritual nature. Sometimes called 'prayer rooms', they can be found at airports, in shopping centres, at roadside stops, in conference centres, hospitals, schools. The research team found well over a thousand in Britain, and more in other countries. But what should the architecture look like? The answer turned out to be: no one knows. Multifaith spaces are an idea, catering to a dream, a reality or a necessity, but searching for a form. The architect on the research project says that their only common factor is that they are hideous – they have no architectural merit whatsoever (and on the whole they are not architect-designed). Nevertheless, the research discovered that three main types of design have developed – each of which says something very interesting about how different religions live together.

The first is an empty space. The idea here is that if you want to include everyone on equal terms and eliminate the distinction between minority and majority, then having no special symbols at all is the best solution. The second is a space with lots of cupboards. So there's a Muslim cupboard and a Christian cupboard, a Hindu cupboard and a Jewish cupboard, among others. The theory is that the space is open to everyone, and when any group or individual is using the space, they can take their things out of the cupboard, and when they've finished, put them away again. The third space is a much messier space, with everything in there all the time. All the symbols and paraphernalia are mixed up. So whereas the cupboard solution tends to fix clear boundaries between faiths, the messy solution encourages a mixing up and blurring of boundaries. The researchers found the messy space to be rarer than the former two types of multifaith space, but a chaplain at such a space told me that all sorts of interesting things happen within it. His was at a university, and he told me he had just had a Hindu who had come and asked to be confirmed as a Christian. He hadn't thought that he would have to give up the Hindu part to do that, and had no intention of doing so. He just wanted to be confirmed as well. So this messy space creates new issues about multifaith identity. In practice, it was found that all three kinds of space can lead to disputes and, very frequently, to one or two religions colonizing the space and pushing the others out – even if not intentionally.

I mention this final project, not only because some wider issues of interfaith relations are played out in microcosm in the design and use of these multifaith spaces, but also because they serve as a further reminder of the importance of the contexts in which religious encounters occur. On the whole, these spaces are not state initiatives; they are the initiatives of corporations, airport authorities, hospital committees, school governing bodies, among others. Their rationale is: 'our clientele wants this'; 'it will make our customers happy'; 'it will improve the ethos of the school'; 'it will cater for all religious people in a single stroke'. So it is generally in the private rather than the public sphere that such experimental spaces for contemporary religious practice and encounter come into being. Unlike synagogues, mosques, temples and other traditional religious buildings, they are not owned or controlled by a single religious body nor indeed by any such bodies. They are more often the product of the market, and a response to perceived consumer demand, than of the state or the voluntary sector. Yet they rarely charge a fee and are controlled by widely varying forms of management, sometimes with input from religious groups or other trustees. The varied forms of origin, design and regulation, and the differences these make to religious encounter and its success or otherwise, are subjects which still require further study.

In summary then, I have been drawing attention to a number of different case studies of religious encounters, with the intention of highlighting how they have to do not just with 'difference', but with differential power relations. I have tried to tease out some of the kinds of inequality which are in play, showing that a simple scheme of 'minority religion versus majority', whilst an essential starting point for analysis, is often intersected by various combined inequalities of class, gender, status of a religion, among others. A particular minority's various political and other alliances, transnational linkages and the way in which it is mediated by various modes of communication are also significant – as we saw in the case of Aisha Alvi, for example. And as the Ladele case illustrated, legal and political regimes not only set frameworks that help shape religious encounters but also impact upon by setting standards and expectations which have real effects even when no formal recourse is made.

One obvious conclusion is that approaches which seek to understand religious encounters and differences by looking only at the religious and cultural factors at play are inadequate. They can even be dangerously misleading when they lead to conclusions about the tolerant or intolerant nature of various religious or secular traditions, and to debates about whether Islam is inherently violent, incompatible with liberal democracy and so forth. Religious identities and encounters are never homogenous or deterministic in this way, and do not take place either in a vacuum or upon a level playing field; there are always other factors at play which help to mould these identities and encounters. Religion and religious identities vary greatly depending on who the actors are and what status they have – and this in turn affects religious encounters. For example, women from quite different religious traditions who utilize their respective religions' resources for healing and other kinds of 'misfortune management' may encounter no incompatibility. They may learn various techniques from one another, pray to the same gods and make offerings to the same shrines. By contrast, priests from two different traditions may have reason to emphasize the uniqueness and difference of their respective practices or teachings. I have written elsewhere about the difference between 'tactical' and 'strategic' uses and modes of religion (Woodhead, 2013: 9–22). When used strategically, religion consolidates the power of those, like religious professionals, who have a stake in it. They engage in operations to delimit and guard its sacred spaces. They have a stake in creating sacred spaces, places and objects which are clearly demarcated from profane or mundane ones. When used tactically, people 'carry out' forms of the sacred to resource their lives and networks. They don't necessarily shun the spaces and controlled enchantments of the strategic, but appropriate aspects of them turn them to new uses and gain some control over them – as well as supplementing them eclectically. To relate this to Purewal's study in the Punjab, for example, there is a constant battle between tactical appropriations of sacred space by a whole range of 'unorganized' actors and groups, and strategic attempts to clear and purify these spaces by political and religious authorities. The strategic tries to hedge and concentrate power, whilst the tactical makes raids and stages occupations and takeovers. The consequences for religious encounters are important, and it is always worth asking which mode of religion is in play.

None of this is easy, and an important practical and methodological conclusion of the discussion is simply that there is a great deal to be gained from the wide-ranging expertise that comes together in inter- and multidisciplinary study of religious encounters. So far, the debate has been framed largely by perspectives from legal and political studies. As I have hoped to show, empirical studies by people trained in anthropology, sociology, gender studies, architecture, religious studies, history, among others, also have a great deal to offer. But the richest outcome is likely to be when the different approaches – from top down and bottom up – truly come together. Genuine disciplinary encounters of this kind are propitious for appropriately holistic studies of religious encounters, studies which are able to take account of the manifold dimensions, including power relations, which are always integral to them.

◆

NOTES

1. *Eweida and Ors v United Kingdom* [2013] ECHR 37. Judgement at http://www.bailii.org/eu/cases/ECHR/2013/37.html (accessed 1 December 2013).

2. Details at http://www.religionandsociety.org.uk/uploads/docs/2012_11/1352818739_Gilliat-Ray_Phase_1_Large_Grant_Block.pdf (accessed 1 December 2013).

3. Details at http://www.sed.manchester.ac.uk/architecture/research/mfs/ (accessed 1 December 2013).

REFERENCES

Beaman, Lori G . 2008. *Defining Harm: Religious Freedom and the Limits of Law.* Vancouver: University of British Columbia Press.

————. 2012. 'Battles over Symbols: The "Religion" of the Minority versus the "Culture" of the Majority', *Journal of Law and Religion*, 28(1).

Hadj-Abdou, Leila and Linda Woodhead. 2011. 'Our Choice, Our Freedom, Our Right', in Sieglinde Rosenberger and Birgit Sauer (eds.), *Politics, Religion and Gender: Framing and Regulating the Veil.* London: Routledge.

Purewal, Navtej and Virinder Kalra. 2011. 'Gender, Caste and the Practices of Religious Identities'. http://www.religionandsociety.org.uk/uploads/docs/2011_01/1294134862_Purewal_Phase_1_Large_Grant_Block.pdf (accessed 1 December 2013).

Rosenberger, Sieglinde and Birgit Sauer (eds.). 2011. 'VEIL: Values, Equality and Differences in Liberal Democracies. Debates about Female Headscarves in Europe', in Sieglinde Rosenberger and Birgit Sauer (eds.), *Politics, Religion and Gender: Framing and Regulating the Veil.*
London: Routledge.

Woodhead, Linda. 2013. 'Tactical and Strategic Religion', in Nathal Dessing, Nadia Jeldtoft, Jørgen S. Nielsen, Linda Woodhead (eds.), *Everyday Lived Islam in Europe.* Aldershot: Ashgate.

◆◆

2 FAITH, ETHNICITY AND NATIONALISM
St. Thomas Christians in India

SEBASTIAN
VELASSERY

The major contemporary challenges that can generate certain complex issues with regard to the idea of togetherness in living are centred on (religious) faith, ethnicity and nationalism. These notions have caused a new attentiveness within ourselves in terms of our identities which we so persistently defend. Ethnic, religious and national identities are highly complicated and variable phenomena that resist simple diagnoses of any kind, including not only those related to one's religion and the structural forms and processes in any religious faith but also the ethnic identity and nationalist feelings that one endorses. Moreover, religious faith and practice, as they bear on ethnic and national identity, are characteristically shaped and influenced in a powerful way by particular historical circumstances. To put it differently, religious faith and ethnicities are sources of both human sociality and societal turmoil. The underlying implication is that the influence of these symbolizations and their equal capacity with nationalism as identity factors must be recognized as articulations from which the logic of togetherness of living, social harmony or disharmony, may be understood. Therefore, there is something interesting and worth examining about the recurring correlation of religious faith with ethnicity and nationalism.

The intent of this chapter is to re-examine notions such as faith, ethnicity and nationalism as constituting causes of intolerance in a given society which can act as hurdles for such a model. I intend to develop the thesis that any reduction of conflict can be possible if mankind shares common values, has common interests and is guided by common aspirations which are the criteria for societal living. Although our life-world is constituted by different kinds of identities based on faith, ethnicity or nationalism, the construction of our religious, ethnic and nationalist boundaries is, in itself, not grounds for saying that we are not answerable for the results. The issue can be addressed in another way: Why does the assertion of religious, ethnic and national identity so frequently involve intolerance and discrimination with regard to religious and other forms of violence, including fundamentalist acuity and divisions? Why, for example, are people belonging to certain religions or political parties, who claim to be nationalists, inclined to favour a 'repressive ideology demanding strict adherence to the authority of the official embodiments of religious/national tradition', and thereby try to compel and control not only behaviour but also other religious faiths and people who belong to different ethnic origins? The question, therefore, is: What are the constrictions which act as obstacles to the idea of togetherness in living?

THE NOTION OF IDENTITY
The notion of identity has a long history that manifests itself everywhere as the relation between 'us' and 'them'. Each community has its own identity, and identities tie people together and define their world view to a large extent. Identities could be ethnic, confessional, racial, cultural, psychological, political, class, caste, among others. Identities are never static, but dynamic. The ancient Greek world, although culturally and ethnically united, was, at the same time, a clear manifestation of 'unity in diversity'. The major spiritual and political task of Greek philosophy represented by Socrates, Plato and Aristotle was to enhance, deepen and strengthen the all-Hellenic identity vis-à-vis the rest – the outside world, the others whom they called the Barbarians, i.e., not civilized – and, on the other hand, to contain the divisive role of local identities such as the Athenians and the Spartans. Both the Renaissance and the 'Enlightenment' in Europe have also developed new identities – the ethno-national – among the Europeans by destroying the all-embracing and all-encompassing spiritual unity and identity of the Europeans – the Christian faith, epitomized at that time by the church.

Philosophically understood, the concept of identity is an abstract one that has a metaphysical import. Its referent cannot be pointed at and said to be this or that. In other words, one may be able to describe the term which may be understood as a state of being the same in nature, quality and so on, and in contradistinction to others which are different. To identify, therefore, is to delineate or isolate the features which mark out from others and cause disagreements. Thus, to talk of identity is to talk of a conflictual relation, which forms the basis of the underlying philosophical problem of identity.

Employing the notion of identity with our present concern of togetherness in living undergirds the idea that the query is addressed with one's faith identity, or ethnic identity, or with one's national identity. Identity means a state of being which is the same in nature, quality, etc., and in contradistinction to others which are different. Against this background, we can maintain the following: epistemologically, identity is, prima facie and a priori, a conflictual relation. This is the existential reality which must be recognized as such. Social identities like ethnicity are the result of the nexus of the human subject as an invariable factor, on the one hand, and his/her environment, on the other. Social identities, including ethnic identity, suggest the existence of 'manifold identities', which have a supervening effect in religious faith. The ethnic community is a reference group for the people included in it. People perceive themselves as affiliated with the group and as having their own ethnic identity. But ethnic identity is not just a role. To have ethnic identity means not just to play an ethnic role but to be ethnic, to have ethnicity as the essence of one's 'self'. We play our role; we are our identities. People can live without their roles, but they cannot live without their identities, because these identities are their internal feelings, values and meanings. Their loss would mean the loss of meaning or sense of life, of one's internal essence. Thus, people who lose their identities experience many more behavioural deviations or a desperate search for new identities.

These observations suggest that the most important and frequently appearing characteristics to describe ethnicity are the following: descending order of frequency, common ancestral origin, same culture or customs, religion, race or physical characteristics, and language. Other attributes are based on status or feelings such as the sense of peoplehood, common values or ethics, *Gemeinshaft* relations and belonging to an ethnic group, not by personal choice, but by virtue of taking birth in it. Nationalism, on the other hand, is an ideological movement for self-government and independence as an independent group. Essentially, nationalism fuses three ideals:

collective self-determination of people; the expression of national character and individuality; and the vertical division of the world into unique nations.

RELIGION AND NATIONALISM

Thinkers like Max Weber laid much emphasis on the 'artificial' and 'accidental' character of ethnic and nationalist identity, which is significant; but such an emphasis must not be allowed to obscure some special affinities between religion and nationalism, which have been the basis of other forms of fundamentalist beliefs. The point is obvious: if ethno-national groups are at bottom constituted by a 'subjective certainty in their common descent', a belief that naturally becomes 'the special, even sacred focus of group attention', then we have already begun to describe something very close to 'religious faith' (Little, 1997: 23–24). It is pertinent to note here that there are strong religious rings of ideas associated with ethnicity and nationalism, as in the case of the Jews as a 'chosen people with a providential mission'; and Brahmins in India being noble by virtue of their being born into a particular caste, etc. We may also understand that in many parts of the world, people started forming groups as nation-states, which are based on ethnicity and religious beliefs. In countries like India, which is multicultural and multi-ethnic in its character, conflict lines often correspond with membership to a particular ethnic or religious group. Recent developments in India's cultural, social, political and economic aspects have shown that there is already a structural patterning of Indian societies which are formed in terms of religion, or minority groups, or the marginalized. Consequently, groups such as Dalits, minorities and the economically deprived sections have identified themselves as the 'other' parts of the Indian cultural self, as they were known to be the oppressed and broken.

The notion of identity that misconceives conflicting attitudes in one's religious faith is based on an ideology of exclusion. In other words, identity and conflict are inseparable. This occurs not only at the level of nature or the cosmos but also at the level of human persons and societies. Conflict occurs not only internally but also externally; not only bodily but also spiritually. Despite the fact that the human subject is endowed with free will, social identity is influenced by the vivacity of the nexus of the operating forces. The Hindu nationalist vision – as expressed by such figures as Vinayak Damodar Savarkar and Madhav Sadhasiva Golwalkar, and promoted by organizations such as the Rashtriya Swayamsewak Sangh, the Shiv Sena, the Rama Sena and some of the political parties of India – typically conceives Hindu-ness or *Hindutva* as coextensive with Indianness. To be a Hindu is to be an Indian and to be an Indian is, in some sense, to be Hindu. Such a notion of Hindu identity provokes a plethora of questions and problems. To start with, such a conception necessarily annihilates the idea of India as a nation-state. As this conception questions the Indianness of non-Hindu Indians, like Indian Muslims and Christians, this view also fuels communal tensions in the subcontinent. It has been capable of marginalizing and excluding a group of people who are rendered 'foreign'. The advocates of contemporary cultural nationalists advance the same argument with the same mixture of amusement and horror, implying that religious minorities are aliens and have no right to coexist in a dignified manner in the Indian state. As a result, in many societies, including Indian societies, modernization has accompanied religious revivalism instead of secularization. Today's Islamist movements in several parts of the world, the Hindu revivalist movements in India (by Togadia, Thackeray and Acharya Giriraj Kishore), Buddhist revivalism in Sri Lanka, Jewish fundamentalist movements in Israel and Christian fundamentalist movements in the United States, are all modern phenomena that express the bonding between religion and nationalism.

Indeed, since there are many of us who still have residual, if not substantive, hope in the interfaith processes, why can we not pose and begin to explore the 'how questions' on the implication of living with religious diversity? Let us begin with an inevitable question: How can we avoid the repetition of Bosnia, Rwanda, Godhra (Gujarat, India) and the atrocities that were enacted in the name of religion more recently in Muzaffarnagar (Uttar Pradesh, India). All these acts of violence were performed in the name of religion. These man-made tragedies, which are deeply rooted in man's inhumanity to man and which are daily brought into our living rooms, tell us a great deal about ourselves and about the strange and sometimes bizarre psychology which defines our identity, our self-image and our self-worth. Watching such gory tragedies in our living rooms encourages us to ponder over the meaningfulness of religion and its teachings. The question is:

Is religion and its message to human kind still relevant? As we know, the 'Declaration of Independence' of India and Pakistan as two nation-states and the arbitrary division and subdivision of the subcontinent has spelled some of the ghastliest human tragedies in human history. The Hindu–Muslim bloodletting over the creation of Pakistan cost 800,000 lives and uprooted 14 million people. The question is: How do we hypothesize the meaning of togetherness in living if our human conditions are solely controlled by factors such as faith, ethnicity and nationalism?

MULTIFAITHS AND CONSTITUTIVE JUSTICE

These observations obviate the necessity to argue that religion, when combined with politics, has always played a dominant role in the creation of ethnic conflicts, fundamentalist attitudes, including religious and nationalist dogmas. The specific role of the Hindu religion, as manipulated by certain Hindu organizations of this country, attempts to revive a nationalism as though only Hindus are (eligible to be) nationalists. Such manipulative and skilled appeals have done much to mobilize support for Hindu nationalism – as for example, Hindutva among the sadhus and laity – and provided the movement sacred authority with political connivance. A glance at the newspapers in this country on any given day is likely to reveal a grab bag of stories involving the struggles of various religious groups to redefine the shape of the societies in which they want to live. What is at stake here is the boundaries between societies, which we carve purely in terms of those religious faiths, ethnic and caste identities that have unfortunately become our core identities. Often, we overlook a crucial, logically prior question: Who belongs to society? The problem of fundamentalist perceptions thrusts us back upon the broader question of the justice of the political community, too. Many of the actions of the adherents of fundamentalists, whether they are ethnic or nationalist, point to the fact that political communities formed in the name of religious faiths do not simply grow on trees. They are, rather, products of a sort of a genetic engineering in which collectivities are moulded through the manipulation of religious faith, ethnic considerations and nationalist perceptions which have certain other parameters implied therein. This point may be stated in the following way: That the construction of our religious, ethnic and nationalist boundaries is not always carried out in an explicit or intentional manner and is not in itself grounds for saying that we are not answerable for the results.

EXTERNAL AND INTERNAL ISSUES

Who belongs to which community and in what ways? These are questions pertaining to external and internal issues in a democratic polity like ours and revolve around notions such as faith, ethnicity and nationalism. The external issues (who belongs?) deal with the scope of the outlines of the communities, and the internal questions (in what ways?) bear on the character or constitution of the community. Do all belong equally? Who has a voice? How are power and resources distributed? Is belonging based on religious and ethnic identities? In societies which are not culturally homogeneous – and it is difficult to think of any that truly are – the internal dimension of constitutive justice often takes the form of religious fundamentalism in the minority communities. What is emphasized here is that a body politic that neglects the internal question of multifaiths cannot nurture and foster a cohesive national civil culture and can never incorporate all citizens with the commitment of a civil society to egalitarianism and inclusiveness. Therefore, togetherness in living necessarily implies an interrelated national civil culture that goes beyond ethnicity and faith. These considerations of religious conflicts should enable us to transcend our boundaries, at least for two reasons, in the pursuit of togetherness of living: first, that we should transcend our beliefs from the particular bias towards our individual faiths and cultures. From this vantage point we see readily the human dignity, worth and rights of individual persons, but only secondarily what pertains to the people at large. We follow a contractarian's interpretation of the polis, thinking in terms of one's own religious, cultural and ethnic considerations. And, second, our religious faith ought to appreciate the inspiring value of freedom in the acceptance of the other as the other. Without such recognition of openness to the other, and his/her faith as the unique reality of transcendence, our religious faiths, in the name of preserving one's inalienable rights, become a hollow shell.

THE PRESENT CHALLENGE

If religion and faith are only incidental factors in one's life, why do religious conflict and religious fundamentalism flourish in so many places – Sudan, Sri Lanka, Tibet and China, Israel, India, Nigeria, Lebanon, Northern Ireland, among others? Even if religion is used or manipulated for ulterior and fundamentalist purposes, why exactly does religion repeatedly get used for fundamentalist and nationalist purposes? In short, why does the assertion of religious and ethnic identities involve intolerance and discrimination in our societies? This question may be answered by examing the notion of 'one Indian culture'.

We need to look back at our history, geography, sociology and philosophy in order to understand the reality of 'one Indian culture'. There is not enough historical proof to suggest that India, as it now exists, was one sovereign country in the past: not during the prehistoric period, not even when this piece of land was part of the ancient Lemuria continent. Even at the time when Alexander the Great's invasion was thwarted by King Purushottam, India was not one single country as it is today. The Mauryas, the Guptas or the Mughals could not, and did not, rule over the whole of India. The British Empire, with all its might, could not win over present-day Goa, Diu, Daman and Pondicherry. Until the peak of the freedom movement, the Hindustani was deprived of one flag and one identity. The reasons are manifold. The Indian subcontinent is vast and is made up of different climatic, ethnic and geographical conditions and includes a variety of people from different races, castes, creeds, complexions and languages. It may also be noted that the Indian culture that is depicted in the classical literature of India is merely half the story. That there were peoples whose identities were marginalized and not accorded the minimum of dignity as human beings is also the historical offshoot and conditioned India as a nation-state. The paradox of the Hindu social order is that while the original concept of Varna, with its four categories, as found in the *Purusha Suktam*, embodied an organic view of society where unity is emphasized through the differences, most aspects of the caste system, which were social and philosophical products of the Indian Varna system, were capable of dividing all of society in terms of colour and have provided an oppressive philosophy of prohibition on inter-marriage and inter-dining.

What is astonishing is the fact that not everybody in the country, including Brahmins, is totally conditioned by caste factors and ritualism. The Buddha – himself a Kshatriya – rejected both these conditionings in these institutions; and the fact that a large number of Brahmins, as well as non-Brahmins, became his followers shows that a dent could be made in the system if enlightened men undertook to preach the moral offensiveness of caste, with its pollution rules and unnecessary ritualism. In other words, a Brahmin who became a follower of Buddha did not find any difficulty in overcoming the pollution-purity complex as well as the ritualism because of the Buddha's enlightened vision. A Brahmin, or an upper-caste convert to Christianity, does not have any problem in interacting with lower-class people. These illustrations explain the indomitable supremacy of 'believing in something' and function for such a belief. In fact, the greatest example was Gandhi who had enlightened the Indian psyche by demonstrating that with belief alone certain things could be done, a great deal could be achieved, and the use of Satyagraha for its powerful implementation. Therefore, it is pertinent to underline the fact that togetherness in living gets its realistic significance only when it is (a) capable of generating the need for interdependence; (b) ideal of inclusiveness; and (c) appropriating and participating in other religious faiths, ethnic groups, cultures and contexts, which is based on a firm belief.

◆◆◆

We have attempted to describe the dynamics that are involved in living together with religious and ethnic diversity. These dynamics also can be termed the dynamics of tolerance – the term 'tolerance' is used here in a positive sense. If we accept that 'tolerance' is the watchword in sustaining togetherness in living, we must begin by understanding the idea of 'tolerance' from an honest position. We shall understand by tolerance an acceptance of difference, patience and permissiveness towards those who express these differences in their lives, together with an effort at their rational understanding and emotional forbearance, but without the obligation to incorporate or be limited by them. In addition, it is compulsory to discriminate between the 'different good' and the 'different bad' and not to accept the latter.

The principle of tolerance necessarily implies the admission of the existence of an original aggression: physically or ideally, there is certain interference by one individual with another by the mere fact that the first is different from the second. The degrees of aggression vary, as do the perception and reaction on the part of the one aggrieved who feels a need for self-defence. Aggression does not always imply violence, but it manifests itself in subtle ways such as demands for adhering to values, principles, ideas, institutions and social systems, very often in the name of 'rights'.

Here, I would like to take into consideration the community of Syrian Christians of Kerala, also known as St. Thomas Christians, who have survived as a 'distinct people', yet living in harmony with Hindus. They may be distinguished by three important factors: (a) they consider themselves as a distinct people, epitomized by the sum total of their community's experiences, narratives, superstitious practices, cults and devotions; (b) one important aspect of the selfhood of the St. Thomas Christians has been, and continues to be, their consciousness of apostolic origin – a consciousness that is fully reflected in their age-old tradition that they received the Christian faith from the preaching of St. Thomas, the apostle of Christ in India; and (c) their belief in the transcendent continuity and the uniqueness of their tradition.

It may be argued that the concept of a distinct people called Syrian Christians with a shared cultural identity with the Hindus may actually enhance the Christian understanding of the universal gospel of Christ. St. Thomas Christians, who are the indigenous Christians of India, trace their origin to the apostolic work of St. Thomas, one of the apostles of Jesus, who is said to have preached the Christian message in India during the period between AD 52 and AD 72. Roughly 27 per cent of Kerala's population are St. Thomas Christians and they are further fragmented into groups such as Syro-Malabar Catholics, Syro-Malankara Catholics, Jacobites, Syrian Orthodox, Marthomites, Madhya Kerala diocese of CSI, among others. Until recently, the concentration of this Christian community was mainly in the areas between Palayur in north Kerala and Quilon in the south.

The earliest reference to the activities of St. Thomas in India is obtained from an apocryphal book called *Acts of Judas Thomas* in the Syriac language in the beginning of the third century AD. According to this source, St. Thomas preached the gospel in several parts of India of which only the kingdom of Gudnapur, that of a Parthian ruler who reigned in the north-western part of India during this period, was identified on the basis of numismatic evidence obtained from this region. The sources of St. Thomas Christians link their origin with the three kingdoms of south India: the kingdoms of Chera, Pandya and Chola, where eight Christian settlements, linked with the apostolic work of St. Thomas, were located. These places are Kodungalloor (Muziris), Palayur, Kokkamangalam, Parur, Nilackal, Niranam, Quilon and Mylapore, where he was martyred (Perumalil, 2008).

THE EAST-SYRIAN CONNECTION
Many feel that the relationship that St. Thomas Christians have established with Syrian churches has affected the original selfhood of the Indian Church. Had the church, which took its origin from the preaching of St. Thomas the Apostle, continued to flourish without any overbearing influence from outside, it would have developed a selfhood of its own with a theology, a form of worship, church laws, institutions and structures appropriate to the Indian cultural and religious context. Unfortunately, this natural growth was adversely affected by the connections established with Christian communities outside, first with the East-Syrian and later the Latin and Western communities. Consequently, Christians have had to lead a life not in one world but in two at the same time; the geographical, political, socio-cultural and economic environment of India, and the ecclesiastical world of the East-Syrian Church. This was somewhat an artificial and unnatural kind of life. The core elements of Christian life remained foreign, adopted only peripherally, that too in a country which possessed a rich culture, a rich philosophy and a deep religious spirit comparable to, or even surpassing, Greek culture, philosophy and religious thought.

AN INDIAN CHRISTIANITY
In spite of these handicaps to their development into a fully Christian Church, St. Thomas Christians continued to enjoy a measure of autonomy: civil under the local rulers and ecclesiastical under the East-Syrian Bishops. The titles of the Indian Metropolitan, such as 'the Gate of All India' and 'Head of India' are indicative of the quasi-autonomy of the church. It was also the case of the titles and powers of the 'Archdeacon of all India'. Since the Metropolitan was a foreigner and quite a stranger to local affairs, it was the Archdeacon, the national leader of the community (*Jathikku Karthavyan*) who was

practically in charge of the government of the community, both in its civil and ecclesiastical aspects. The Archdeacon discharged his duties with the help of a characteristically indigenous institution, the *Yogam*, or the assembly of priests and lay people, both at the local level and at the level of the entire community.

The ancient St. Thomas Christians of Kerala developed a lifestyle in their early existence. This lifestyle, in Church matters, reflected to some extent the pattern of the Persian Christians. In the socio-cultural realm, it was not different from that of their Hindu neighbours. In the social set-up of Kerala, they emerged as the peers of the higher classes, especially the Nairs and Menons. The long experience they had acquired of the Hindu way of life and the good neighbourly relations maintained with their Hindu brethren enabled them to build a more positive approach towards Hinduism and Hindu practices. Their integration into the socio-cultural milieu of Kerala was most satisfying (Mundadan, 1984: 22ff.).

SHARING CULTURAL SPACE WITH HINDUS

From the very early times of the Christian era, Kerala was an ethnic museum consisting of a mosaic of natives and foreigners. Commercial interests attracted people of various creeds, races and nations to its coast. As a result, a cultural symbiosis already prevailed in the state before the arrival of the Portuguese. Hindus, Jains, Buddhists, Christians, Jews and later Muslims, both Indian and foreign, lived in harmony. Christians received Hindu names, practiced rituals of worship such as the use of the native *nilavilakku* (lamp), built temple-like churches and accepted social customs like the wearing of the *tali* (bridal medal) by the bride (Menachery, 2006).

It was in this symbiotic socio-cultural context that the bulk of the ancient Indian Christians lived and grew. Even a casual student of the history of St. Thomas Christians wonders at the spontaneity with which the community adjusted itself to its milieu, at least as far as their social life was concerned. This natural impulse led to the acceptance of certain practices and customs, a few of which perhaps tended to be prevarications of genuine Christian life, which the Synod of Udayamperur (or of Diampur, 1599) was justified in correcting. But the Synod went a step further and, in a way, so stifled this spirit of spontaneity that from the end of the sixteenth century the community gradually became less adaptive.

The education of the children of St. Thomas Christians consisted of two stages: one, before the child attained eight years of age, and the other from the 8th to the 25th year. During the first stage, both boys and girls received very elementary education. That was perhaps where it ended for the girls. The boys, however, went further. All boys, either Hindu or Christian, began their training in reading and writing, in the art of fencing in a *kalari* (school) under a *panikar* (master/fencing master), from 8 years of age and continued till they reached 25. This illustrates the fact that Christians in India had developed no exclusive attitude like the then Catholics of Portugal or in other European countries. It indicates that there was a healthy interaction between Hindus and Christians in their day-to-day life.

The different factions of St. Thomas Christians carved out a way of life within the cultural space of the Hindu community in which they were located. They understand the concept of sacred space for the erection of places of worship, or even dwellings, which usually face east or north. Besides, they observe common social customs related to birth, marriage and death, such as giving the newborn baby powdered gold mixed with honey; feeding the child with boiled rice when he/she is 11 months old; and prohibiting mothers from entering the church until 40 days after child birth. The marriage ceremony of St. Thomas Christians too has much in common with that of their Hindu brethren. The man ties an ornament called tali, or *minnu*, around the neck of the woman. The Christian tali differs from the Brahmin tali, as the former has a cross of 21 minute beads on it. St. Thomas Christians make the thread for tying the tali from the bridal veil, which is called *manthrakodi*, just as Brahmins do. Married women will never remove the tali. On their death, it is either be buried with them or deposited in the treasury of the church. No food is cooked or eaten in the house of the deceased until after the burial. All the immediate relatives of the dead person are considered defiled (having *pula*) for a given period of time. The time of defilement for St. Thomas Christians is usually 11 days, but not exceeding 13. In the feasts of pula and *chatham* – derived from the Sanskrit word *sratham* – priests would preside and offer special prayers. During the pre-Diampur period, food was offered at the graveyard of the deceased. There were other customs like serving food to the poor to satiate dead people's souls. In Malabar, which is infested with snakes and reptiles, devotion to St. George, who is often pictured as the killer of snakes, was popularized as a substitute to prevent people from worshipping snakes (Vadakkekara, 1995: 118). Similarly, St. Sebastian is projected as a patron who is capable of containing tropical diseases such as small pox, chicken pox, among others, to which Kerala was a victim in summer. Nevertheless, the major saints of the St. Thomas Christians of the pre-Portuguese days were the Blessed Virgin Mary, St. Prothasius and St. Gervasis, who were the leading personalities linked with the ninth-century Christian migration to Quilon.

THE POLITICAL SPACE

Historically, the political activities of St. Thomas Christians were initially linked to a petty Christian kingdom called Villarvattom, probably formed after the collapse of the Kulasekharas of Mahodayapuram. The sceptre, which St. Thomas Christians submitted to Vasco da Gama in 1502, is said to have been used by this Christian king. When the Villarvattom royal family ceased to exist, St. Thomas Christians were brought under the special protection of the king of Cochin and called the sons of the king. As early as 1547, the king of Vadakkenkur mentions 3,000 soldiers serving under him, whom he was ready to give to the Portuguese for the defence of Diu.

Unlike other churches the world over, the church in Kerala is not deeply involved in party politics. Inevitably, it has been touched by the ideological traits of different political parties. Nonetheless, Christian Churches have always been outside of political pre-occupations in both senses – from church to politics and from politics to church. Its actions and interests were far less influenced by the different political games and upheavals, compared to other sectors of civil society.

St. Thomas Christians were pioneers in both literature and the news media. In Kerala, the beginning was made by the Basel Mission. Gundert's (of Basel Mission) *Rajyasamacharam* (June 1847) was the first such newspaper in Malayalam. *Paschimodayam* followed in October. The Kottayam C.M.S. Press published *Jnana Nikshepam* in 1848. The (*Nazrani*) *Deepika* (1887) and the *Malayala Manorama* (1898) followed. In the world of Indian newspaper publishing, the various records established by the (*Nazrani*) *Deepika* and the *Malayala Manorama* are still unsurpassed – both are the products of Syrian Christians.

THE INDEPENDENCE MOVEMENT

The Christian presence was evident in other movements as well. Among those who followed Gandhi on his Salt March to Dandi was a young disciple, Thevarthundiyi I Titus Titus, a member of a St. Thomas Christian family from Travancore. Attracted by Gandhi's life and work, he lived with the Gandhian community, caring for the Ashram dairy farm.

A discussion on the church's contribution to fine arts is incomplete without reference to the various church-sponsored institutions established for promoting – production as well as training – fine arts. Kalabhavan, which began at Kochi, Kerala, as a cultural centre in the mid-1960s under the guidance of the poet-priest Fr. Abel, CMI, was one of the earliest ventures. Kalabhavan excelled in music, dance, mimicry, comic drama and other popular art forms and contributed many stars to the Malayalam film screen.

CHURCH ARCHITECTURE

Through the 19 centuries of their history in Kerala, St. Thomas Christians evolved a distinct style of church architecture. The Syrians, who migrated to Kerala, brought with them West Asian conventions in church architecture. However, Syrian churches continued to retain some of the indigenous features of Hindu temple styles externally. This gives Malabar churches a unique structure of their own which is fully Indian and, at the same time, also Christian. The three-level gabled roofing of Kerala churches, in descending order, over the sanctum sanctorum, the nave and the portico, have all the beauty, utility and traditional scientific perfection of Kerala architecture. The timber roofing, often covering an area of thousands of square feet without pillars, is a marvel rarely found elsewhere in the country during the period. The three objects in front of the churches – the huge open-air rock obelisk crosses rising from a lotus at the top of an intricately carved multi-stepped pedestal or *balikkallu*, the metal-sheathed flag staff or *dhwaja-sthamba* (*kodimaram*) and the rock lamp-stand or *deepasthamba* – are some of the earliest expressions of Indian art. India's national flower – the lotus – and the national bird – the peacock – first appeared in Kerala art on the rock crosses. The gold and silver crosses, bronze lamps, *muthukkudas* (colourful, decorated processional umbrellas) wooden sculptures and, above all, some of the huge pre-Moghul, pre-Rajput mural paintings of Kerala churches are unique contributions of the Christian community to Indian art.

PROMOTING A SECULAR STATE

One of the fundamental conflicts in the politics of nationalism, during the freedom struggle and later in the nation-building process, had been the definition of the relationship between religions and nationhood. The Hindu right-wing and the Muslim League wanted statehood to be subservient to Hinduism and Islam, respectively. Moderate leaders within the Congress, on the other hand, adopting a secular attitude, sought to separate the two affiliations – religious and national – and define nationalism without reference to religious affiliation.

The All India Conference of Indian Christians decided to opt for the secular option. It refused to identify the Christian community as a socially and politically closed communal entity. So it rejected communal electorates, which the British rulers 'awarded' at first to Muslims and then to Christians and other religious communities. The Christian leadership of that time was aware that its value as a minority community – 6 million strong at that time – depended on the contribution it could make to the whole nation, not in insulating itself from outside society. In 1930, the All India Conference of Indian Christians articulated this self-understanding of the Christian community: the value of a minority community 'depends upon the quality of its life, the standard of its preparation for life's various activities, the strenuousness with which it throws itself into all avenues of useful services and the genuineness with which it seeks the common weal' (Thomas, 2006: 66).

CONCLUSION

The contribution of St. Thomas Christians to the shaping of Indian life in modern times has, indeed, been very impressive. They merit high appreciation as pioneers in the fields of education, medical relief, care for the poor and abandoned sections of society, preservers and disseminators of culture, language and literature, and protectors of the weak. It is an indisputable fact that St. Thomas Christians have a long and cherished history and a story of their own. They can no longer be considered as a monolithic group, but a vibrant community with several layers in its composition. What is noteworthy is that this community, although fragmented into several segments in the course of history, was able to keep its identity by adapting to the cultural space of India and its *Weltanschauung*. Antony Mookenthottam (1978) observes that the social and socio-ecclesiastical life, which St. Thomas Christians had been leading before the arrival of the Portuguese, reflects a unique Christian vision of this community. Their oneness with their Hindu brethren implies an implicit, lived, integral approach; it is their awareness that Christ, in becoming man, assumed everything human and redeemed all social and cultural values. Their long encounter with Hindus helped them to develop a Christian vision of other faiths. They have been living in harmony with the cultural space of Hinduism and thereby have shown that their primordial solidarity with other faiths is an existing reality which can be discovered and unfolded in relationships with their oneness with other communities and faiths.

These observations on St. Thomas Christians and their oneness with the socio-cultural milieu with Hinduism points to the idea that togetherness in living with religious diversity demands an awareness of the reality of our religious practices and even beliefs. The question is: Can we afford to desist from emphasizing this relativity in order to safeguard our uniqueness? If we do not come to a new understanding of each religion's uniqueness, the crisis of conflict will disrupt our society. We must learn to accept that mere adherence to a particular religious faith by birth is no special qualification. Such an outlook does not make us believe that it would be beneficial for all people to join one and the same religion. When prohibition was enforced in Pakistan, tens of thousands of Muslims tried to pass off as members of minority communities, that is, they posed as non-Muslims for the sake of a drink. The same happened when *zakat* was introduced as a kind of Church tax. When Sikhs were brutally killed in this country, many Sikh gentlemen were compelled to shave off their beards and pretend to be Hindus.[1] Similar examples can be adduced from many parts of the world. The issue is this: If many of our religious practices are founded on relative considerations, then why not apply the same logic in our faith, too? These observations obviate the necessity to transcend from our constituted faith to a constituting faith of other religions and peoples. We may be able to find clues for understanding and responding to this perspective in Plato's notion of participation. Let us look for clues on how we might handle three central issues generated by the recent emergence of the awareness of religion, as described.

THE DISTINCTIVENESS OF EACH RELIGION

In this era of globalization, it is the responsibility of each religious head to accept that every other religion is the distinctive manner in which a specific people realizes its life, or *esse*. Therefore, all religions are unique inasmuch as each people realizes its life or being, not as univocal instances of the same specific type, but in its own existentially proper manner, as shaped by their faith in Reality. It is crucial to the exercise of human freedom that the religious uniqueness of each people not be compromised, but rather maximized. The real challenge, then, is to be able to live fully our unique identities in the newly global context.

THE COMMONALITY OF INSIGHT AMONG RELIGIONS

What strikes me about the psychology of religion is not the differences in dogma (over which so much blood has been spilled), but the commonality of insight; all religions claim that all men and women are brothers and sisters and that we should treat others as we treat ourselves. Thus, Christianity: 'All things whatsoever ye would that men should do to you, do ye even so unto them' (*Holy Bible*, Mat.7.12); Judaism: 'What is hurtful to yourself, do not do to your fellow man' (*Talmud*); Hinduism: 'Do nought to others which if done to thee would cause thee pain' (*Mahabharata* 5.5.17); Buddhism: 'Hurt not others with that which pains yourself' (*Udanavarga* 5.18). The unity of insight encoded in these sayings is all the more remarkable because they seem, for the most part, to have evolved independently, in different parts of the world under the influence of different cultural traditions, at different times during history. What these sayings tell us is not merely that we should use a common code of conduct in our dealings with our fellow creatures, but rather that, at the tap-root level, the distinctions which divide us are functions of ego and of differing phases of growth.

COMPLEMENTARITY AMONG RELIGIONS

The principle of complementarity necessarily implies the admission of the existence of an 'other'. The term 'complementarity' received greater depth by the widening of the phenomenological meaning of sexual complementarity and was used by Plato (both man and woman have sexless souls), Descartes (both have sexless reason), Christian philosophers and in Judaism and Islam. In the relation of complementarity, one has to be primarily rooted in one's identity and open to the alterity of the different. The purpose of being rooted in one's own is for the sake of growth by extending oneself beyond the accepted facets of one's identity – one's religion, faith, culture, philosophy, nationalism, among others. In other words, one's identity becomes enriched and complete only when it is opened to alterity.

In the context of our present considerations, a philosophy of complementarity is quite in place. From the Christian standpoint, I may say that both India and Christianity are symbols of unity and variety. Complementarity calls for an attitudinal change – a change from the presumption of 'exclusiveness' and 'self-sufficiency' to 'inclusiveness' and 'dependence'. Such a change will bring about a philosophy of complementarity.

THE CONVERGENCE OF RELIGIONS

The relationship among religions must be one of convergence. Living with religious diversity is a matter not of theory but of teleology because all religions uphold not only the view of the One Creator but also are in pursuit of that One as the goal: each religion, in pursuing its own unique and limited perfection, pursues more ultimately the perfection which is one and infinite. Therefore, all religions are convergent in that each in its own distinctive manner tends towards the one divine or infinite perfection (McLean, 2004: 206). In striving actively for their own perfection as images of the same one perfection, all draw together in a convergent manner. The best method for this mode of convergence is to pray jointly. Without joint prayer, I see little hope for overcoming religious strife and religious fundamentalism. If we pray together more frequently or even regularly, this need not prevent us from praying also separately, community-wise, following the rituals of our respective religious traditions. Let me sum up by recalling a beautiful verse of the thirteenth-century mystic, Muhyuddin Ibn Arabi of Murcia:

> There was a time when I used to discriminate against my neighbour because of his ethnicity or religion. That time is long gone. My heart

has become a meadow for the grazing deer, a monastery for the monk, Torah Scrolls for the rabbi, a Kaaba for the pilgrim. I profess the religion of love, and wherever its caravan will turn to, I shall follow (Duran, 1997: 340).

◆

NOTE

1. I have a special memory of this incident as my daughter was born on this day. Kanpur city was the second worst affected place in India. At the time I was a doctoral student at IIT Kanpur.

REFERENCES

Duran, Khalid. 1997. 'Vocation of Islam in a Conflicting World', in Paul Peachey, G. F. McLean and John Kromkowski (eds.), *Abrahamic Faiths, Ethnicity and Ethnic Conflicts*. Washington: The Council for Research in Values and Philosophy.

Little, David. 1997. 'Belief, Ethnicity, and Nationalism', in Paul Peachey, G. F. McLean and John Kromkowski (eds.), *Abrahamic Faiths, Ethnicity and Ethnic Conflicts*. Washington: The Council for Research in Values and Philosophy.

McLean, George, F. 2004. *Persons, Peoples and Cultures: Living Together in a Global Age*. Washington: Council for Research in Values and Philosophy.

Menachery, George. 2006. 'Cultural Contributions of Indian Church', in *Indian Christian Directory*. Kottayam: Rashtra Deepika, Ltd.

Mookenthottam, Antony. 1978. *Indian Theological Tendencies*. Bern: Peter Lang.

Mundadan, Mathias, A. 1984. *Indian Christians: Search for Identity and Struggle for Autonomy*. Bangalore: Dharmaram Publications.

Perumalil, Augustine. 2008. 'Christian Contributions to the Building of Modern India', in Sebastien Velassery (ed.), *Foundations of Indian Social Life: Cultural, Religious and Aesthetic*. North Carolina: Book Surge.

Thomas, George. 2006. 'Christians and the Freedom Movement', in *Indian Christian Directory*. Kottayam: Rashtra Deepika, Ltd.

Vadakkekara, Benedict. 1995. *Origin of India's St. Thomas Christians: A Historiographical Critique*. Delhi: Media House.

◆◆

3 REFRAMING UNDERSTANDINGS OF RELIGION
Lessons from India[1]

LORI G.
BEAMAN

In her novel, *The Selector of Souls*, Montreal-born and India-raised author Shauna Singh Baldwin bumps up against the complex ways in which religion weaves through day-to-day life in India in myriad forms. A humorous yet illustrative passage describes a conversation between two of the main characters, Damini and Goldina, who exchange information about family history, trying to place each other in the broader layers of Indian society and history as they attend the birth of Damini's grandchild and each remembers her own mother. The two women negotiate their way through multiple identities: both had mothers from Punjab; Goldina's family are 'outcasts' (in Goldina's words), which she qualifies with 'in those days Hindus began to call outcasts like us Hindu, you know, because they needed our votes', and when the family was displaced by Partition, her mother 'went to the nearest church and promised to be a Christian if they would feed her family'. Damini has also made a practical 'conversion' to Sikhism to accommodate her former employer, an elderly woman to whom she was devoted, and confides, 'Yes, I'm a Sikh, and I'm also a Hindu', situating the turn to Sikhism as less a conversion than an addition. When Damini summarizes 'and that's how you became a Christian', Goldina qualifies 'for a while' and reports that when her mother wanted to arrange her sisters' marriages the priest refused, stating that they were too young. So, Damini's sisters became Hindu and her mother remained Christian: 'my mother liked being Christian – pretty music – so only my sisters became Christian'. But, when Goldina's sister was raped and her mother wanted to take her for a 'cleaning', the priest cautioned that the sister would 'fry in hell'. 'Then', recounts Goldina, 'my mother went to a pandit and paid for a penance ceremony. That way he made her a Hindu again. Then she got my third sister cleaned out, and married her off to a Christian to make her a Christian again. After that, my mother returned to the priest and confessed'. When the priest refuses to bury Goldina's nine-month-old unbaptized nephew who died of dengue fever, Goldina's mother goes to her Hindu relatives for a cremation. She is Hindu again 'for a while', but when her mother is beaten by her Hindu employer for touching a cup of water intended for her mistress, she finds a priest to re-baptize her (Baldwin, 2012: 224–28).

Describing religion in India is no small feat, and indeed Western scholars, if I can use such an essentialized category, have engaged in a long-time struggle and debate about how to do so. In her chapter in this volume, Sonia Sikka outlines some of the basic challenges and limits of non-Indian constructions of religion, including a tendency to situate any understanding within the antithesis between faith and reason; the focus on religion as having a specified content related to belief and practice; and singular religious identities. These limitations are exactly what Western scholars bring to the table when they think about Indian religion. Understandably, though mistakenly, they use the modes of categorization and study most familiar to them, and with which they have been socialized. What is both difficult and yet vital in a more globalized world with increasingly diverse religious populations is to step outside of these boundaries, drawing on Sikka's suggestion that we turn from a focus on content and faith 'in' something instead to 'towards the world, reality, life, knowledge, matters about which people held divergent beliefs, on the basis of which they adopted different paths of life and action'. I would reframe Sikka's suggestion in the present tense, suggesting that for the contemporary study of religion there is much to be learned from a reorientation that begins with India. I want to avoid reifying an 'us' and 'them' stance in this chapter, but for heuristic purposes, it is useful to stand as an outsider in relation to India to attempt to begin to appreciate what another approach might allow me to see. As a Western scholar, what can I learn from the complexity of religion in India, particularly about living with religious diversity? How might I re-equip my research toolkit to draw on the insights from the Indian context?

To be clear, and as I am sure is obvious, I am not an expert on India, Indian cultures or Indian religion, however imagined or defined.

The reflections in this chapter emerge from my attempts during the last four years to better understand the debate outlined so well by Sikka regarding the limitations of the category 'religion' in relation to India, but with the goal, rather than of becoming expert on India (which, I think, would be completely naïve), of asking questions about how I might take lessons from Indian scholars and 'living with diversity' in India to respond to what I perceive as the limited imaginary of scholarship on religion in Canada, the United States (US) and Europe. How might lessons from India help me to reorient my approach to religion?

Yet, describing what that reorientation looks like is challenging, especially when considering what exactly it is about Indian religion to which we ought to be attending. The passage from Singh Baldwin's novel, while perhaps exaggerated, illustrates the flexible and pragmatic approach that might begin to help us reshape understandings of religion that have been framed in the ways that Sikka outlines. It also illuminates the risky business of pinning down religious identity as a fixed category. While we (Western scholars) claim to have a flexible approach, I do not think that is for the most part true. Once we identify the religious category into which someone fits, it is almost as though a sigh of relief is expelled. Having pegged the identity issue, we reify that identity and category with no sense of shifting allegiances, practices and yes, beliefs, over the course of life, or even over the course of a day. This point is not made to trivialize religion – quite the contrary. Religion, however defined, is inextricably bound to the everyday in simultaneously complex and simple ways.

In his ethnographic study of a group of villages in the Arampur nexus, Peter Gottschalk brushes past the staid categories typically used by American scholarship on South Asia, noting that 'many defer too quickly to Hinduism and Islam as self-apparent terms for exclusive arenas of religious activity' (2000: 3). His fieldwork reveals the deeply complex ways that residents live with diversity: 'residents live interrelated lives with their neighbours – alive and dead – aware of religious differences only within a much larger context of multiple identities, some shared and some not' (ibid.: 158). The importance of local histories, present and shared memories, but also shared experiences, cannot be overemphasized. As Gottschalk found in his study, the expected pivotal event – Partition and Independence – received little mention in the narratives of the village in which he conducted research. Thus, the expected divisions and narrative about it were replaced by a story of local importance that Gottschalk spent extensive time listening to and analysing. This is not to say that broader national and international/global currents are not important – Gottschalk found that the rise of Hindu nationalism had had some important and unfortunate effects on the community's relations between Hindus and Muslims – but the ways in which people negotiate difference, and indeed displace difference with similarity, is very much a local phenomenon. The unfortunate attention paid to broader narratives that often focus on difference, dissent and violence leaves these practices of daily negotiation unnoticed. And it also leaves unnoticed the flexibility, sharing and friendship that are layered through day-to-day life.

It seems to me that a vital meeting place, and indeed an opening for further exploration, is the intersection of what has come to be called 'lived religion' and lessons from the Indian context. Moving away from the congregation-dominated scholarship in the US, and the organized religion focus of Canada and the UK, lived religion, also described as everyday religion, folk religion and so on, offers an analytical alternative to the narrower approach by embedding religion in the everyday.[2] McGuire says, 'Lived religion is constituted by the practices people use to remember, share, enact, adapt, create, and combine the stories out of which they live' (2008: 98). The challenge of studying these minutiae of day-to-day life is that they are much less easy to study than the belief-based, church-located practice that have made up the bulk of much of the study of religion from a social-scientific perspective. To be sure, there are studies such as Ammerman's classic *Bible Believers* (1987) that configured home, church and school as the locus of religion, but even her path-breaking study emphasizes boundaries between her fundamentalist Christian subjects and their surrounding world; and, as the title of the book lays bare, an emphasis on belief. What if, though, we were to turn our attention to the blurred and messy everyday world, attempting to trace religion with a renewed sense of sociological imagination? What if we were to suspend categorization of religious identity, looking instead for malleability, experience and interaction, rather than 'belief in god', 'prayer' and 'knowledge of the 10 commandments'?

Resistance to such a shift has at least two inter-related bases: first is a tendency to categorize only particular kinds of religious beliefs and practices as 'real' religion worth studying; and second is the influence that Christianity has had in framing the study of religion, despite its claims to objectivity and neutrality. Indeed, religion not deemed 'real' is sometimes constructed as dangerous and, in the context of the US, un-American. In *Habits of the Heart* (2007), Robert Bellah *et al.* characterizes as individualistic the practices of one of their study's interviewees. Sheila, a nurse, talked about not having attended church for a long time. She had, she reported, developed her own rituals, practices and beliefs that focused on caring for others and self. Bellah *et al.* used Sheila to illustrate all that is 'wrong' with American society, which they located in the erosion of an imagined public order that had existed 'once upon a time'. Bellah *et al.*'s critical assessment seemed to be based on little more than the fact that Sheila did not root her spiritual life in a traditional church community. In her sound critique of Bellah *et al.*, McGuire asks whose interests are served by such a dichotomous approach to religion that identifies early American Protestantism (the Puritans) with 'desirable' public and unified qualities of an ideal religion. McGuire gives us a hint about what might be possible in her critique of the questions asked by Bellah and his team of researchers: 'Because Bellah's team focused their interviews on respondents' beliefs and commitments, expressed in response to very narrowly focused interview prompts, they did not learn much more about the nature of Sheila's religious experiences or her actual spiritual practices (if any)' (2008: 152). It is important here to note that Bellah *et al.*'s work is extremely influential in the US, but more than that, it carries on a long tradition of framing religion in a particular way, and one which could not be further from the reality of, say, Indian life, and, in all likelihood, American spiritual life either.

The influence of Christianity – obviously tied to the dichotomy of real religion and the 'other' – on the study of religion, poses a different set of challenges. Although I think there is a tendency of critical scholars of religion to be far too cavalier with their dismissal of religion as a Christian construction, and a further temptation to characterize Christianity in rather narrow ways that do not capture the ways in which it is lived, the challenge presented by a critical approach to religion such as that offered by Masuzawa (2005), Chidester (2003), Boyarin and Boyarin (1993: 693–725) and numerous others pushes scholarship toward a much more nuanced and robust understanding of the phenomenon we have come to call 'religion'. This challenge calls for a self-reflexive approach to the residue of Christianity in scholarly considerations of religion. Moreover, policy and government considerations of religion, especially national surveys that measure religious participation, leave little room for the sorts of religious flexibility that are illuminated by the conversation between Damini and Goldina. In the region in which Gottschalk conducted his fieldwork there was only one self-identified Christian in the 1981 census data. Conducting fieldwork in an area in which Christianity is decidedly not the majority religion creates space for seeing anew. However, the real challenge for the Western scholar is to shed the preconceptions about religious categories he transports with him. Gottschalk is well aware of this challenge as he reflects on his research. He does not turn his analytical gaze back on conceptualizations of religion in the US, and I think the next challenge for scholars is to think about how what one learns might be drawn upon to critically reflect on scholarly constructions of religion in the West. There is much to be learned.

If we bracket the 'pick-one category' approach to religious identity that has been so pervasive in Western scholarship, what then might we see? Though there have been some attempts to categorize fuzzy and lived religion, sometimes as syncretism, or blended religion and so on, they are problematic for a number of reasons, and continue to revert back to the drive to unify multiplicities. Understanding some aboriginals as both Christian and as practicing aboriginal spirituality, and that from their perspective both are equally as legitimate, valid and valuable, has presented a particular challenge.[3] Other research has considered the coexistence of Judaism and Buddhism, and there are many other such examples of religious 'combinations'. But, on the whole, we are not entirely comfortable with multiple categories and allegiances. This is perhaps the strongest legacy of a Christian framing of religion, which insists on one god. To say that this is also a feature of Judaism and Islam misses the point of Christianity's privileged position in defining Western life, and indeed its influence on defining Indian, Chinese and African religious life as well.

To be clear, it is not that 'I am x and y' does not exist outside of India, but that social and scholarly boundaries have made it extremely difficult to identify and think about multiple possibilities, or, perhaps more importantly, to shift the focus from 'I am x' to a much broader sense of the contexts and relationships within which people live. Moreover, the requirement for faith and faith-based practice has narrowed the scope of how we imagine people do religion, or live the sacred in varied dimensions. Conversely, there are pressures in India that would push toward a singular identity of Hindu that would hope to erase the fuzzy, flexible and sometimes pragmatic approach to religion illustrated in the conversation between Damini and Goldina, or as discussed by Gottschalk. So, the challenge is to draw lessons from India without simplifying the complicated contextual conditions under which religion exists there, or to romanticize the history of flexibility while minimizing the history of identity-based conflict.

Three scholarly experiences underscore for me this need for a reconfigured approach to understanding religion: Several years ago I conducted research on labyrinths and those who walk them (Beaman 2006: 83–103). Labyrinths have a variety of forms, but, contrary to some popular perceptions, they are not puzzles or mazes, but have a circular trajectory that guides rather than loses the walker. The way in to the centre is also the way out and there is no possibility of getting lost. Labyrinths are commonly recognized to have two predominant forms: Christian and pagan, with the latter being simpler in design and the former having specific references to the Stations of the Cross and so on. Many churches, particularly more liberal ones, have built their own labyrinths, often in publicly accessible spaces. Others have special labyrinth walks for which carpet, plastic or paper labyrinths are specially brought in and temporarily installed in churches. One church I know brought in both a pagan and a Christian design for such an occasion. Countless individuals have built labyrinths in their own backyards. One of the interesting things about the labyrinth walk is that there are multiple interpretations of its function and meaning. Although there is, as mentioned, a 'Christian labyrinth' based on the model at Chartres, the church is somewhat embarrassed by it, and there is little information about the labyrinth's builders and their intentions. When I conducted interviews with some participants in a labyrinth workshop in Chartres, one conversation struck me as particularly interesting, and as illuminating the limitations of how we think about religion, and indeed the very practices and experiences that lie unexamined, uncounted and in some cases forbidden, from the realm of 'religion'. One woman who identified her religion as Baptist said, 'the people in my congregation would be shocked to know I am here. I would be banished!' Her comment raises many interesting issues: How had the Christian imaginary shaped what people perceived as religious experience? What was allowed and what was forbidden? But, more importantly, I think, how were myriad allegiances and spiritualities shaped into a 'unity' simply by virtue of a dominant definition of 'real' religion? Equally as challenging: how does one ask about these sorts of things in the context of a scholarly imagination that has been so shaped by its cultural context?

The second experience is as director of a large research programme entitled the 'Religion and Diversity Project'. As we seek to understand more about religion in Canada while simultaneously engaging in comparative research with a number of other countries, including India, it has become obvious that our understanding of religion in Canada is woefully limited by our narrow concept of religion and the measurements that have typically been deployed to better understand it. We have engaged in the development of an internet survey with a view to overcoming this narrowness. It is an extremely challenging exercise, mostly because we realize that we are seeking to ask about something that is not actually foregrounded in most people's lives. People do not live primarily or completely through religious identities. Yet, when we foreground religion as a subject for our queries we highlight religion in an 'unnatural' way. This was made obvious to me when I conducted interviews with Muslims in St. John's Newfoundland as part of a project entitled 'Religion in the Everyday: Negotiating Islam in St. John's, Newfoundland and Labrador'.[4] At the end of our questions about experiences of being Muslim in this very small city we asked our participants to think about whether there was anything that the state could do to improve things. When we designed the question we thought that people might take this opportunity to talk about religious holidays, prayer space and so on. Yet, this has not been the response. One woman illustrates the folly of this approach very well when she responded by saying 'I'd like a library in my neighbourhood for my children'. Her concern was about a way of life that she wanted for her children, not about a particular and narrowly focused 'religious' need. This same study has hinted at the ways in which imagining religious categories as containing certain beliefs, practices and so on amongst policy makers, researchers and the media may have the consequence of pushing people into more orthodox or fundamentalist positions than they might otherwise be. By erasing or minimizing similarity, and a more fluid understanding of religion, we may contribute to identity hardening which, in turn, may create a situation in which it is much more difficult to live with religious diversity.

A third experience has been in responding to the release of Pew Research Center's data on the increase in religious 'nones' in the US (Pew Forum, 2012). Picked up by Canadian media, and then echoed again in the UK, when they also had a study that showed the increase in nones, a mini-storm of concern about all manner of dire consequences was created (mostly by the media). Nones are those people who respond to survey questions that ask 'what is your religion' with 'none'. The consequences were imagined to be a world without morals, a collapse of volunteer labour and the demise of charitable groups (which were assumed to be mostly linked to religious groups). In Canada, fully one-quarter of the population includes itself in the 'none' category. Yet, interestingly, we know very little about this group and its parameters. If we add in those who claim membership in a church or religion but do not participate in its rituals (attending church, for example), the 'indifferent' figure (including nones) is well over half of the population. As social scientists, we have no idea what, if anything, these people are doing related to spirituality or non-organized religion. What does this have to do with religion and India? While we do not fully understand the contours of those who put themselves in this category – some are atheists, some agnostics, others humanists, the non-committed and so on – we do know that there are rituals, practices and experiences teeming in this space of 'none-ness'. There is also what might be termed 'creative spirituality' which resides in the space of everyday life. To dismiss it as individualistic, Sheilaism or folk religion misses its rootedness in local communities and relational practices. And it is here that we can turn to rethinking religion by drawing lessons from the Indian context. I believe the nones will force us to do this, but that, even in understanding religions that might seem to have more clearly defined boundaries, such a shift is invaluable in framing religion in the way it is lived, rather than in the way it is imagined. This is not to deny that religion as a hard category is sometimes deployed – often in very harmful and dangerous ways. But, if we reconfigure religion as a more flexible and lived phenomenon, we may also have a hope of decentring those who would use it as a hardened identity category, both in India and elsewhere. ·

CONCLUSION

In her chapter, Sikka says:

> Engagement with Indian traditions in their original spirit fosters an alternative way of relating to what we have come to regard as religious subjects. It can thereby help to counteract the twin dangers of religion's becoming equivalent to the acceptance of doctrines on grounds other than reason on the one hand, or, on the other, purely a matter of identity, the content reduced to the status of a symbolic marker of no greater significance than the colours in a nation's flag.

Although I am admittedly a bit sceptical about any argument that claims to understand an 'original' position (my scepticism likely generated by the endless prattle about 'founders' intentions' in the American debates about their constitutional guarantee of religious freedom), Sikka's point is well taken. This was also the point made by a member of a review panel of the accomplishments thus far of the Religion and Diversity Project. He suggested that in the process of struggling with how to better study religion, we might consider this: what would religion look like if its study had originated in India or China? Obviously, it is not possible to recreate this scenario, but at the very least it is an important thought experiment that may facilitate a re-crafting of scholarly thinking about religion. This is an incredibly valuable exercise that may help us to rethink religion outside of the boundaries and limitations identified by Sikka, but also to see in startlingly new ways the world around us, which is, after all, one of the tasks of good social scientists.

Cordoning off the 'holy' from the pragmatic and the flexible, or the division of the world into the 'sacred' and the 'profane' has had limiting effects on our ability to see and to theorize religion. An experience I had while visiting India for the 'Living with Religious Diversity' workshop resonates here: while visiting the

Mehrangarh Fort in Jodhpur we made a small detour up the side of an adjacent hill. Halfway up, as we paused to look at the stunning view (and to catch our breath) we came across a stone with a face painted on it. Two young men came down the hill and paused to chat with us. They were college students, and after some friendly conversation about where we were from and so on, they said, in reference to the rock, 'this is our god'. I do not pretend to fully appreciate the significance of the local god, or the way that such things work, but I do know that to dismiss this as 'individualistic' or 'magic' (which might happen with a narrower concept of religion), or to not take this god seriously in its importance to the two young men who shared this information with us (and to countless others who also worship this god) would be to miss a part of the religious life of these individuals and of this community. It is this sort of minimization and dismissal that characterizes, for example, Bellah *et al.*'s (2007) diminution of the nurse Sheila's religious practices. A rethinking of the concept of religion, and reconsidering the location of the sacred would have resulted in an entirely different approach to Sheila's religion. This is what I think we might begin to take seriously if we were to begin to think about religion as though it had originated in India. Rather than fetishizing the local god, deeming it to be apart from everyday life, or dismissing it, we would explore its social and cultural links, the relationships that surround it, and the activities and practices that enfold it as both special and simply part of everyday life.

◆

NOTES

1. I would like to acknowledge the support of the Religion and Diversity Project in the preparation of this chapter as well as the ongoing financial support of my research through my Canada Research Chair in the Contextualization of Religion in a Diverse Canada. I am also grateful to Marianne Abou-Hamad for her editorial assistance, and to my friend and colleague Sonia Sikka for reading and commenting on this paper, as well as for her generosity and patience as I struggle to put into words my thoughts about India.

2. See Bender (2003), McGuire (2008), Heelas *et al.* (2005), Lorentzen *et al.* (2009) and Orsi (2005).

3. See James (2012).

4. Principal Investigator for this project is Jennifer Selby (Memorial University of Newfoundland). We have interviewed 50 people.

REFERENCES

Ammerman, Nancy T. 1987. *Bible Believers: Fundamentalists in the Modern World*. New Jersey: Rutgers University Press.

Baldwin, Shauna S. 2012. *The Selector of Souls*. Toronto: Knopf Canada.

Beaman, Lori G. 2006. 'Labyrinth as Heterotopia: The Pilgrim's Creation of Space', in W. Swatos Jr. (ed.), *On the Road to Being There: Studies in Pilgrimage and Tourism in Late Modernity*. Boston: Brill Academic Press.

Bellah, Robert N., Richard Madsen, William M. Sullivan, Ann Swidler, Steven M. Tipton. 2007. *Habits of the Heart: Individualism and Commitment in American Life*. Berkeley: University of California Press.

Bender, Courtney. 2003. *Heaven's Kitchen: Living Religion at God's Love We Deliver*. Chicago: University of Chicago Press.

Boyarin, Daniel and Jonathan Boyarin. 1993. 'Diaspora: Generation and the Ground of Jewish Identity', *Critical Inquiry*, 19(4).

Chidester, David. 2003. *Salvation and Suicide: Jim Jones, the Peoples Temple, and Jonestown*. Revised edition. Bloomington: Indiana University Press.

Gottschalk, Peter. 2000. *Beyond Hindu and Muslim: Multiple Identity in Narratives from Village India*. New York: Oxford University Press.

Heelas, Paul, Linda Woodhead, Benjamin Seel, Bronislaw Szerszynski, Karin Tusting. 2005. *The Spiritual Revolution: Why Religion Is Giving Way to Spirituality*. Cornwall: Wiley-Blackwell.

James, William C. 2012. 'Dimorphs and Cobblers: Ways of Being Religious in Canada', in Lori G. Beaman (ed.), *Religion and Canadian Society: Contexts, Identities, and Strategies*. 2nd edition. Toronto: Canadian Scholars' Press Inc., pp. 55–68.

Lorentzen, Lois, Joaquin Jay, III Gonzalez and Kevin M. Chun (eds.). 2009. *Religion at the Corner of Bliss and Nirvana: Politics, Identity, and Faith in New Migrant Communities*. Durham: Duke University Press.

Masuzawa, Tomoko. 2005. *The Invention of World Religions: Or, How European Universalism Was Preserved in the Language of Pluralism*. Chicago: University of Chicago Press.

McGuire, Meredith B. 2008. *Lived Religion: Faith and Practice in Everyday Life*. New York: Oxford University Press.

Orsi, Robert A. 2005. *Between Heaven and Earth: The Religious Worlds People Make and the Scholars Who Study Them*. Princeton: Princeton University Press.

Pew Research Center's Forum on Religion and Public Life. 2012. '"Nones" on the Rise: One-in-Five Adults Have No Religious Affiliation', *Pew Forum*, 9 October, http://www.pewforum.org/files/2012/10/NonesOnTheRise-full.pdf.

◆◆

4 ISLAM AND RELIGIOUS PLURALISM IN INDIA

ARSHAD ALAM

THE PROBLEM

At the outset, let me establish the difference between diversity and pluralism. While the world has been diverse for centuries altogether, it need not necessarily be plural. Invoking pluralism means a shift in which people have thought about what to do about diversity. Pluralism, therefore, is different from plurality or diversity in the sense of being an active and reflexive perception of the other. It implies more than the coexistence of two or more communities at the same time and in the same space. It presumes that coexistence was made into an issue either by those who were/are politically in charge, or/and by the concerned religious communities themselves. Pluralism, thus, is also a political project in the sense that it implies and involves a polity, a civic context which provides some 'rules of the game', refers to an ethos and evokes a response. Consequently, pluralism is only one of the possible responses to diversity. Diversity can also become threatening and it would not be out of place to suggest that some people are very hostile to the idea. In short, pluralism is something which is not a given: it has to be made consciously, it has to be achieved (Eck, 2006). In this chapter, an attempt is made to interrogate whether Indian Islam has developed a theology of pluralism. Have Indian Muslims developed an understanding about other religious traditions and, if yes, then what kind of an understanding is it? How does Indian Islam interact with them? Does it have a philosophy of living with religious diversity around and within? In raising these questions, one is conscious of the fact that Indian Muslims have been living with different religious communities since centuries and that this coexistence has provided for the development of shared cultural and social traditions (Ahmad, 1984; Assayag, 2004; Mayaram, 1997). However, the question is: Has this popular practice of living and sharing together been able to generate a philosophy and theology of living with the other? Is there space for religious pluralism in Indian Islam? A related question is the attempt to understand how these shared local traditions have been treated within the writings of hegemonic Islamic scholars.

In trying to answer these questions, the chapter will attempt to understand the position of two important *maslaks*[1] within Indian Muslims – the Deobandis and the Barelwis – on the question of religious pluralism. In the process, the chapter will interrogate some key figures and texts within both these maslaks in order to arrive at their understanding of living together with other communities, such as the writings of Husain Ahmad Madani (Deobandi scholar), Abul Hasan Ali Nadwi[2] and Ahmad Riza Khan (Barelwi scholar) in order to understand their position on the issue of religious pluralism. The question of popular shared practices between Hindus and Muslims is examined in an attempt to understand how these practices have been understood by these two maslaks. As a consequence, it inquires into the modalities of Islamic reform and its impact on popular Muslim practice, since each of these maslaks has its own understanding and practice of Islam reform. Finally, the chapter will argue that madrasas are deeply implicated in the project of Islamic reform and will understand how madrasas produce an identity which is antithetical to pluralism, both at the inter- as well as at the intra-community level.

DEOBANDIS AND BARELWIS

A clarification on the usage of the labels Deobandis and Barelwis is important – they are both pejorative words. A Deobandi would mean from, or affiliated to, the Deoband madrasa in Saharanpur, implying that his or her loyalty is more towards that particular madrasa than Islam. Similarly, a Barelwi would denote someone from the city of Bareilly in Uttar Pradesh and more loyal to this place rather than to Islam. Officially, in their written discourses, both Deobandis and Barelwis would identify themselves as Sunnis, or the *Ahle Sunnat* (those who follow the *Sunna,* the path of the Prophet). It would indeed be correct to call them Ahle Sunnat, since this is the category which they apply to themselves (Metcalf, 1992; Sanyal, 1999). However, this chapter refers to them as Deobandi and Barelwi and uses these terms, despite their pejorative connotations, for two reasons: first, simply because it makes it easier to map out their differences; and, second, because these terms have become so popular (Alam, 2011) it is common for the respective adherents to speak of themselves as Deobandis and Barelwis.

The Deobandis are a group within Indian Muslims whose ideological universe revolves around the Deoband madrasa, established in 1867, in the wake of the British repression of Indian Muslims after the revolt of 1857, with a view to preserve and propagate religious knowledge. Deobandis also inaugurated the project of Islamic reform in the Indian subcontinent by which they came down heavily upon popular Muslim traditions such as Muharram, visits to shrines, etc., terming them Hindu influences which needed to be cleansed from the Muslim religious universe. In what may be interpreted as the protestantization of Islam, Deoband evolved a theology of personal religious responsibility, thus ruling out mediation through any shrine or *Pir* (Sufi master). As a result, intercession was frowned upon and termed *bida* (reprehensible innovation). The *Piri Muridi* (Master–Disciple) institution was considered alien to the religious universe of early Islam and therefore to be discarded.

The Barelwis, on the other hand, form a community which revolves round the personality and writings of Ahmad Riza Khan (1870–1920). Ahmad Riza defended a mediated experience of Islam. He argued that Pirs had the power to intercede on behalf of their disciples. In fact, Ahmad Riza would accuse the Deobandis of being Wahhabi and destroying the very soul of Islam. This passionate defence of traditional Islam translated into legitimizing and justifying the religious universe of Muslims, which was predominantly surrounded by Pirs and *mazaars* (shrines). Although it might appear that Ahmad Riza developed and defended a theology suited to popular Islamic practice, the reality is rather more complex. Suffice it to say that the Barelwis had their own ideas and practice of Islamic reform. While the Deobandis are the dominant group within Indian Muslims (in terms of access to state resources, representations in Muslim bodies, etc.), the Barelwis constitute the numerical majority of Indian Muslims in this country.

DEOBANDIS AND PLURALISM

An interrogation of Husain Ahmad Madani's text, *Composite Nationalism and Islam*, is essential in order to understand Deoband's position on religious pluralism. Hussain Ahmad Madani (1879–1957) was the principal of the madrasa at Deoband as well as the president of Jamiat Ulama e Hind, an apex body of Islamic religious scholars primarily belonging to the Deoband school of Indian Islam. Madani is considered to be one of the most influential religious scholars of the subcontinent. Besides being affiliated to the madrasa at Deoband, he was also an advocate of the Ulama becoming the leaders of the Muslim community and played a key role in cementing the Congress–Khilafat pact during the 1920s. The Khilafat movement set the path for what would endure as a pattern for Muslim participation in the nationalist movement (Metcalf, 2005). Through a series of lectures and pamphlets during the 1920s and 1930s, Madani prepared the ground for the cooperation of the Indian Ulama with the Indian National Congress. Finally, in 1938, a collection of his writings was published in Urdu as *Muttahida Qaumiyat Aur Islam* (*Composite Nationalism and Islam*) and was translated in English and republished by the Jamiat Ulama e Hind in 2005. The reviews of the book have sought to glorify the virtues of pluralism embedded in the book, although a closer reading reveals a very different picture.

Madani makes a crucial distinction between *qaum* and *millat*. According to him, qaum connotes a territorial multi-religious entity, while millat refers to the cultural, social and religious unity of Muslims exclusively. It is the affinity on the basis of territory (qaum) which becomes the source of Madani's argument that it is religiously justified for Indian Muslims to fight alongside Hindus to overthrow the common enemy, the British. Since the Muslim presence in India went back a long time, they, together with other communities, constituted one qaum and were consequently under obligation to fight the British. This important distinction between qaum and millat enabled him to not only justify cooperation with the Indian National Congress but also to reply to his critics like Muhammad Iqbal, who were arguing against the concept of territorial nationalism. As befits an Ulama, Madani justified his interpretation by recourse to early Islamic history in which Prophet Muhammad had sought a covenant with the Jews of Medina in order to fight against a common enemy: the unbelievers (*Kuffar*) of Mecca. Drawing a parallel to the times that obtained in that original covenant of Medina, Madani argues that it is perfectly acceptable for Indian Muslims to have a 'pact' with Hindus to fight against the British. Hindus and Muslims, therefore, become one qaum. However, this *qaumiat* (territorial unity) does not translate into a dialectical understanding of sharing between religious and cultural traditions. Madani is well aware of the plurality of religious and cultural traditions in India when he speaks of the non-Muslim communities living side by side in India. But for Madani, this plurality is an end in itself. In fact, he seems to be very clear that this plurality should not develop into pluralism.

In order to make this transition from plurality to pluralism, Madani would have to forgo his own notion of superiority of Islam over other religions. This he is clearly unwilling to do. Islam for him is the only true religion and it is this conviction which leads him to claim that, 'while being aware of the truth of their (other religions') falsehood' (Madani, 2005), Islam is ready to 'cooperate and tolerate' them. Hence, Madani not only disqualifies other religions as being false, but he is also of the view that, ultimately, Hindustan be Islamized: that the Hindu–Muslim entente (composite nationalism) is only required till the time people of this country do not become Muslims (*jab tak Hindustan ke tammam bashinde mussalman nahin ho jate*) (ibid.: 2005). Such a notion hardly augurs well for any kind of pluralism. Far from taking an approach of mutual understanding and dialogue, Madani speaks from a position of power which derives from his own Islamic understanding of truth and falsehood. We see in the text, therefore, a clear unwillingness to allow any kind of cultural sharing, especially between the Hindus and Muslims. When Madani discusses nationalism, he makes it a point to differentiate it from what he calls 'European nationalism', where the 'curse of nationalism makes religion the personal matter of the individual' (ibid.: 101). Madani certainly wants a more proactive role for Islam in the social life of Muslims in India, and at one point even argues that under a non-Islamic dispensation, they (Muslims) should strive to form an Islamic government.

Sure enough, Madani emphasizes that Muslims in India already cooperate with 'non-Muslims' on a number of issues which are civic and hence non-religious. His plea is to extend this cooperation further by coming together on a national platform to fight the British.

However, for Madani, the 'compositeness' of his nationalism is not an end in itself, as advocates of pluralism would like to believe. In his own words, this composite nationalism is 'temporary and special' and is only required till the 'light of true religion (read Islam) dispels its (India's) darkness' (ibid.: 139–40). Shedding further light on his 'special' and 'temporary' concept, Madani elucidates that 'composite nationalism is needed only till such time as different communities (*aqwam*, sng. qaum) and different religions exist in a country. When the entire nation becomes Muslim (which is the prime real aim: *jo ki awwalin maksad hai*), where is the need for it?' (ibid.: 150). It is very clear, therefore, that for Madani, even plurality (forget pluralism) holds no merit of its own; rather, its advocacy is strategically needed only till Islam becomes the sole religion of India.

Even in the interim period when Madani allows Muslims to 'tolerate and cooperate' with the Hindus, he makes it amply clear that the millat is beyond compromise. The millat is pure and should not be alloyed by the touch of lesser religions such as Hinduism and Christianity. Such an understanding of millat, apart from being orthodox, is also anti-history. Indian Islam is full of examples of sharing from other religious traditions, including Hinduism. This creative interaction has given birth to various heterodox traditions as well as numerous cultural practices which were liminal in nature. Madani, being a member of the reformist tradition of Deoband, questioned many of these and collectively termed them as *bida*, and hence un-Islamic. As in any revivalist movement, an 'authentic Islamic tradition' was being formulated by Deoband headed by Madani, against which all indigenous Islamic traditions were to be measured. Although Madani does not specify it, his notion of millat comprises mainly Arabian traditions rather than Indian ones. And since this Arabian tradition can only be appreciated through the language of Arabic, only those Muslims who are well versed with it will be able to do so. His notion of millat, therefore, leaves the majority of Muslims (forget the Hindus and thus the question of inter-community plurality) outside its fold, since Arabic to them was still something to be memorized, not to be studied, understood and analysed.

Madani's Hindu–Muslim entente is devoid of any cultural sharing and mutual reflexivity. His Islam is suffused with an innate superiority complex which hardly augurs well for inter-religious understanding and dialogue. Moreover, his Islam is also antithetical to the Muslim other – Shias, Ahmadis, Barelwis and women who would fail to find a place in his reinvented covenant of Medina. Far from taking a position on Indian pluralism, the text is itself, in its claims of defining Islamic superiority, antithetical to pluralism within Indian Muslims. To treat the text as the position taken by the Indian Muslim on the question of religious pluralism, which is what some reviewers (see Metcalf, 2005: 'Introduction'; Fazal, 2005) have done, is grossly incorrect reading, to say the least.

Perhaps the most forceful articulation of this Islamic superiority comes from Abul Hasan Ali Nadwi (1913–99), the rector of the Nadwa madrasa at Lucknow. Although the Nadwa madrasa was established with the idea of bridging the gap between 'traditionalist' Deoband and 'modernist' Aligarh, theologically Nadwa is hardly different from Deoband and that is the reason why Nadwi's writings are being discussed in this chapter as belonging to the Deobandi school of thought. In his book, *Muslims in India* (1980), Nadwi talks through the language of power, highlighting the exalted status of Muslims vis-à-vis the nation (read Hindus). The coming of Islam and Muslims marked the beginning of a new era in India's history which, according to Nadwi, was an era of enlightenment, progress and prosperity. He concludes by saying that it would be better if the Hindus do not forget the gratitude that they owe to the Muslims. Apart from teaching the Hindus the message of universal brotherhood and equality, Nadwi also mentions that Islam 'taught' the Hindus how to dress and converse in a cultured manner. Moreover, it was the Muslims who gave history to the Hindus as what existed before the advent of Islam was a collection of mythologies and folklore, which the Hindus regarded as history. In short, everything that was good about India today was because of the Muslims. Paradoxically, everything that was 'bad' among Indian Muslims was because of the Hindu influence. Thus the Muslims, because of centuries of coexistence with the Hindus, had adopted customs and practices which were clearly un-Islamic and which must be repudiated in order to bring back the glory of Islam and Muslims. Similarly, in his other work, *The Musalman* (1977), Nadwi terms Muslim ritual and practices during certain festivals like Muharram to be completely un-Islamic, which has no sanction anywhere else in the Muslim world, particularly within the Arabian heartland. This exercise of measuring religious practices of a community through an

Arabian standard, very similar to that adopted by Madani, places the majority of the Indian Muslims in need of express reform. In fact, Nadwi expresses satisfaction when he notes that some of these seemly un-Islamic customs are being given up due to the increasing influence of Islamic education. Thus we see that in Nadwi, Islamic superiority is coupled with the need to curb internal plurality within Muslims.

BARELWIS AND PLURALISM

In order to understand the Barelwi position on religious pluralism, interrogated here are some of the writings of Ahmad Riza Khan, around whose personality the Barelwi identity crystallized. In his writings during the Khilafat movement (around 1920), a movement which brought the Congress and Jamiat Ulama e Hind on a common platform in order to resist the British, Ahmad Riza argued that it was not permissible for a Muslim to cooperate with a *kafir* (Hindus). It was doubly problematic, he reasoned, because the common enemy was the Christians, whom Islam regarded as people of the Book. The argument, in essence, is that Islamic theology does not allow Muslims to cooperate with the idolatrous Hindu against Christian monotheists. At one level, this might indicate a tactical criticism of the Khilafat movement, but Ahmad Riza's use of the word *harbi* (those with whom one is at war) to describe the Hindus of his day, suggests that his objection to any form of Hindu–Muslim cooperation went much deeper (Sanyal, 1999). What is interesting is that Ahmad Riza did not look at the question of the Hindu–Muslim relationship in political terms, but rather as he would in purely religious terms. And within Islamic theology, he could see no justification for such an alliance. In a fatwa he wrote in 1920 (*al muhajjat al mutamana*), he argued that the Jamiat Ulama was transforming what was clearly forbidden (*haraam*) – cooperation with Hindus – into an absolute duty (*farz qati*). Describing the Hindus as killers, oppressors and infidels (*katilin, zalimin, kafirin*), he reminded the Muslims that the Hindus were even trying to tamper with Muslim religious observances. In this fatwa, Ahmad Riza maintained that a vital distinction must be made between two completely different sorts of relationships between Muslims and non-Muslims: those of mere human relations (*mujjarad muamalat*), which were permitted with all non-Muslims under the *Sharia* (Islamic law), and those of friendship and intimacy (*muwalat*) which Muslims may enter into only with other Muslims.

Thus, although at loggerheads with each other, Ahmad Riza would agree with Husain Ahmad Madani that the millat, comprising the pure religious self of the Muslims, should remain static and free from any influence of other religious communities. Ahmad Riza would in fact go a step further and a passage from his own writings gives us a glimpse of his deep-rooted sense of distance from the Hindus amidst whom he lived. They were kafirs and were to be regarded with enmity for that very reason. Moreover, the Hindu (a Brahmin, no less!) was unclean for him and he felt a deep sense of revulsion even with the slightest physical contact with a Hindu. In a long passage from one of his *malfuzat* (discourses or ancedotes of holy persons), he recounts how he once had a severe bout of colic and was reeling in tremendous pain when a Brahmin happened to pass his cot. The Brahmin placed his palm on Ahmad Riza's stomach and asked: Is this where it hurts? In Ahmad Riza's own words:

> feeling his impure hand touching my body, I felt such revulsion that I forgot my pain. And I began to experience a pain even greater than this, knowing that a kafir's hand was on my stomach. This is the kind of enmity that one should cultivate towards the kafirs (Sanyal, 1999).

Thus, lifelong, through his fatwas and other methods, Ahmad Riza would caution Muslims not to form any fraternal alliance with Hindus. But his greatest diatribe was reserved for fellow Muslims, those who did not follow his interpretation of Islam. The Deobandis and the Shias were often the targets of his acerbic polemics. Consequently, he would refuse to be on the Board of the madrasa at Nadwa because there were Shias on the Board. Moreover, his famous polemical war against the Deobandis would make it difficult for a Muslim to offer his prayers led by a Deobandi imam. In fact, in one of his fatwas, he declared that the Deobandis were kafirs and that all contact should be avoided with them. Thus, his intolerant position on other maslaks within Indian Islam makes it very difficult for any dialogicity to emerge within the Muslim community, let alone a pluralist perspective at an inter-community level.

THE DISCONTENTS OF ISLAMIC REFORM

The position of both Deobandis and Barelwis on the question of religious pluralism is problematic. Both maslaks talk from a position of power, thus asserting the innate superiority of Islam over other religious traditions. To make matters worse, they criticize one another in their polemical debates regarding the correct interpretation of Islam. Most of these skills are honed within the precincts of madrasas which hold specific allegiance to the respective schools of thought in Islam (Alam, 2011). Consequently, at both an inter-community and an intra-community level, the Deobandis and the Barelwis have failed to develop a theology of religious pluralism. If the Deobandis and the Barelwis may be considered as the two most important official expressions of Islam in India, then one can perhaps argue that official Indian Islam has failed to develop a context-sensitive theology, that it never occurred to them that, living as minorities, they should be able to develop a theology suited to the altered political landscape. However, does it also logically follow that Indian Muslims, as a whole, have failed to appreciate the contexts in which they have lived? We find that, to the contrary, popular religious practices within Indian Muslims present a wide array of acculturation, some of them so unorthodox that even Muslims criticize them for being too Hindu! For example, the Malkana Rajputs and their religious and customary practices were deemed to be in dire need of Islamic reform. The Meos of Haryana and Rajasthan had no problem in offering *namaz* and paying obeisance simultaneously to the deity kept inside their homes. This is not merely a difference that I am trying to effect between 'official Islam' and 'popular Islam'; on the contrary, my argument is that centuries of living together produced a curious amalgam of religious tradition in this country and, perhaps, we don't possess the vocabulary to comprehend the religious cosmology of these communities. Hindus and Muslims are both modern constructs and, from the vantage point of the present, it is nearly impossible to gauge the world view of a people for whom it was entirely possible to be Hindu and Muslim at the same time.

It is this popular religiosity which has been under attack from various quarters: beginning with the colonial state which wanted discrete rather than fuzzy communities; from orthodox Hindus and Muslims, who wanted these communities to become either fully Hindu or Muslim. One of the most important reasons for the existence of the Deobandis and the Barelwis is their self-assumed mandate of reforming Muslim practices, bringing them in tune with what they consider to be correct Islamic practice. This brings us to the question of Islamic reform, which can be understood as a process of the return to the fundamentals of true religion, to purify and to rid it of what are seen as harmful or non-essential accretions. Islamic reform calls for the obliteration of various customary practices, which are deemed to be un-Islamic, or Hindu, in terms of its origins in the Indian context. In short, Islam becomes the master frame through which all acts are sought to be legitimated and understood.

In India, as elsewhere, Islamic reformism refers to a wide variety of orientations. The very idea of pure/original Islam is a contested one. Accordingly, in India, the Deobandis, the Ahle Hadis, the Jamat e Islami and the Barelwis, all operate with their own ideas of pure Islam. Within these interpretive communities, there are regimes of Islamic reform and all of them call themselves reformists (*islahi*), seeking to purify Islam by purging religious and customary accretions that have crept into it. These maslaks all have their own network of Islamic schools or madrasas through which they seek to reform Muslims by teaching them 'correct' Islamic beliefs and practices. An important, but unfortunate, aspect of scholarship on Indian Islamic reform is that it has mostly concerned itself with what Francis Robinson would have called 'the rationalist' traditions within Islam. Apart from the seminal work of Metcalf (1992) on Deoband, the edited volumes – Hartung and Reifeld (2006), Pearson (2008) and Jamal Malik (2008) – suffer from the same problem. Deoband – not only as a madrasa but also as a movement – the Ahle Hadith and the Jamat e Islami, have all been variously commented upon in the Indian context. However, the project of reformism within the Barelwis who form the majority of Indian Muslims has hardly been commented upon. In what follows I recount the effects of Islamic reform on Mubarakpur, a small weaving town in North India, where I conducted fieldwork.

Mubarakpur is a *qasba* (small town) located in the district of Azamgarh in eastern Uttar Pradesh. Although local estimates put the total population at around 70,000, the 2001 Census puts the figure at 51,000. The literacy rate of the qasba is 49 per cent, with a male and female literacy rate of 56 and 43 per cent, respectively, which compares unfavourably with the overall district literacy rate of 56.15 per cent. The town, dominated by low-caste Muslim weavers who call themselves Ansaris, is primarily known for producing

Banarsi sarees. The qasba is predominantly Muslim and, according to its residents, Muslims comprise around 90 per cent of the total population and are divided into Barelwis, Deobandis, Ahle Hadis and the Shias, with the Barelwis in the majority. These maslaks have their madrasas, with the Deobandi madrasa – Ihya al Ulum – and the Barelwi madrasa – Ashrafiya – being two of the largest in the town.

Interestingly enough, although rivals, both madrasas had a common origin in a *maktab* (elementary religious school) established in 1899, which was called Musbahul Ulum. During the 1920s, the maktab faced a split down the Deobandi–Barelwi line. The Deobandi maktab renamed itself Ihya al Ulum, while the Barelwi maktab continued to call itself Misbahul Ulum and, later, as Ashrafiya Misbahul Ulum. It was only after 1934–35 that both maktabs grew into proper madrasas. Eventually, it was Ashrafiya Misbahul Ulum which grew into one of the biggest madrasas in Mubarakpur and is now the apex madrasa of the Barelwis in North India.

The original maktab was founded with the efforts of Muslims who were Deobandis. Its first teacher, Mahmud Marufi, had spent three years as a student at the Faiz e Aam madrasa in Kanpur, which was closer to the Deobandi school of thought. Ilahi Baksh, patron of the maktab, was an Alim and a Hakeem and had studied in the same madrasa as Mahmud Marufi, thus sharing the same ideological bonding. He was also a *murid* (disciple) of Rashid Ahmad Gangohi, one of the founders of the Deoband madrasa. We also know that during his visit to Mubarakpur, the famous Deobandi Alim, Ashraf Ali Thanwi stayed in the house of Ilahi Baksh. Consequently, as his religious network tells us, Ilahi Baksh was himself a Deobandi. His choice of Mahmud Marufi as a teacher for the maktab also partly explains this, since Marufi had been his student initially and both were students in the same madrasa.

However, this maktab was not looked upon as a Deobandi institution by the people of Mubarakpur. During the early years of the twentieth century, and certainly for some decades after that, the average Mubarakpuri did not know of the finer theological differences between the Deobandis and the Barelwis. For them, the maktab represented something that they did not have so far. It is important here to mention that the appeal of the maktab was only for those Muslims of Mubarakpur who called themselves Sunnis. The Shias and the Ahle Hadis had established their own madrasas. Misbahul Ulum, therefore, was a maktab for the Sunnis of Mubarakpur and represented their collective aspiration to have a maktab/madrasa of their own. This was to change with the coming of Shukrullah Mubarakpuri, a graduate of the Deoband madrasa. True to his reformist Deobandi ideas, he criticized various existing customary practices, such as those associated with circumcision rituals, Eid festivals and marriage ceremonies. As a Sunni reformist, Shukrullah was particularly incensed by the adoption of Shia rituals, strongly opposing participation in *tazia* processions during Muharram. The polemical exchanges between Abdul Aziz and him, the former having taken over as the principal of Ashrafiya Misbahul Ulum, led to the polarization of the Sunnis along Deobandi–Barelwi lines (Alam, 2011). The differences became so pronounced that both maslaks stopped praying together in the same mosque.

It is important to understand that during this time, the Deobandi Ihya al Ulum madrasa was supported by a few relatively educated and prosperous Muslims of the qasba (ibid.). Most of the members of the *shura* (committee) which oversaw the functioning of the Ihya al Ulum madrasa are addressed as *sardar*, which attests that they were important people in Mubarakpur. It is important to understand that the title sardar has various uses. In textile and jute industries, sardars were labour contractors and their status depended on how many labour hands they brought to the industry. Since Mubarakpur was a weaving town, they were important for the local industry. Also, the headmen of a *mohalla* (locality, roughly equivalent to a municipal ward) were referred to as sardars. In both cases, they were socially important and relatively wealthy residents of the qasba. On the other hand, most members on the committee of Misbahul Ulum were petty traders and small shop owners. The emerging Deobandi–Barelwi divide in Mubarakpur thus had some correlation to the social and economic status of its respective followers. Deobandi reformism, led by Shukrullah Mubarakpuri, can be understood as an attempt of one social group (which was relatively wealthy and educated) to redefine the popular practice of Islam in the qasba. Durkheim's argument, as stated by Eickelman, that 'changes in ideas of knowledge in complex societies and the means by which such ideas are transmitted result from continual struggles among competing groups within society, each of which seeks domination or influence' (1978: 486), seems to fit the description of events in Mubarakpur.

What is interesting is the ostensible role reversal between the two madrasas. Today, Ashrafiya has grown into the apex Barelwi madrasa of North India, while Ihya al Ulum has remained a middling madrasa. Over time, Ashrafiya's own outlook has changed. The once-competing Deobandi Ihya al Ulum madrasa is no longer perceived as a threat. Apart from preparing students to become religious scholars, Ashrafiya nowadays also concentrates on advising local Muslims on their everyday problems, offering counsel from its own theological perspective. Its monthly magazine, *Mahanama Ashrafiya*, increasingly cautions Barelwi Muslims against *shirk* (associating partners to Allah) and bida campaigns which were once the prerogative of Deobandis. While in earlier times a famous graduate of Ashrafiya – Arshadul Qadri – took the Deobandis to task for condemning local religious and customary practices, today Ashrafiya encourages Muslims to get rid of 'un-Islamic' practices', such as singing and dancing during marriage feasts, and to keep lifecycle ceremonies as simple as possible. Ashrafiya has also been at the forefront of campaigns to dissuade Mubarakpur's Sunni Muslims from taking out tazia processions during Muharram, reminding them that 'they should not behave like Shi'as'. Thus, Ashrafiya Madrasa today sees itself in a similar reforming role much as the Deobandi Ihya al Ulum saw itself during its heyday.

This role reversal has come about with changes in the economic position of the qasba's Barelwis. Today, as I was informed by the residents, it is the Barelwis who are economically and educationally better off as compared to the Deobandis. While it is true that the reformist project was integral to the Barelwis, as exemplified in the writings of Ahmad Riza Khan (Sanyal, 1999), it is worth mentioning that this project only got going in Mubarakpur with the economic and educational ascendancy of the Barelwis. Islamic reform in Mubarakpur thus appears to be a hegemonic struggle between different social groups within Muslims. At the same time, it is also an expression of social mobility in the local arena. As I have argued earlier, Islamic reform in this context has become the cultural mode of expression of an elite status among a group of newly rich merchants of the 'lowly' community of weavers. Consequently, status and value are asserted by increasing the rigour of Islamic observance and by stressing the importance of simple faith in the fundamentals. The practice of Islamic reform itself becomes a signifier of a different status among Muslims and even within one's own maslak and is, at the same time, a marker of class as well as a sign of a different/better cultural status. But if Islamic reform is an expression of a socially mobile group, then why don't they adopt modern or Western symbols? Bourdieu (1977) reminds us that although the cultural reservoir of symbols is infinitely elastic, in practice groups generally only move in directions in which they feel culturally comfortable. The relatively wealthier and educated weavers of Mubarakpur could not have expressed their new sense of worth and superiority by adopting modern or Western patterns of living, for they do not have pre-existing skills and dispositions of that kind.

The Barelwis' reformism cautions Muslims against practices which they believe are not sanctioned by Islam. Within the qasba, Muslims are advised not to participate in the annual Muharram procession as it is forbidden, that it is a practice followed by Shias, and that Sunnis should not indulge in such religious innovation. It is worth mentioning that the making of taziyas and carrying it in procession has been an age-old tradition, not only in Mubarakpur, but across South Asia. Taziya-making provided one occasion where religious boundaries were blurred as Hindu residents of Mubarakpur participated as well and were equally enthusiastic about carrying it in *julus* (procession). Mohallas vied with each other for the best-produced taziya in the spirit of neighbourhood competition. Moreover, in earlier times, Hindu women performed certain ritual prayers at the taziyas that were placed on different *imambaras* (a raised platform on which taziyas are kept) as their way of showing devotion.

Reformism has sought to end such practices and Hindus complain that they cannot pray to the taziya, as they used to do earlier, because the Muslims object. Reformism, through its diatribe against such common cultural practices, sought to redefine and sharpen boundaries between communities. Muharram processions today are solely composed of the Shias, since Sunnis have almost withdrawn themselves from what was earlier a composite festival of the qasba. Hindus from the qasba are hardly to be found in such a procession now. Clearly then, the institution of Muharram, which was the common tradition of the people of Mubarakpur, gets reduced to a Shia occasion for the Sunnis, but for the Hindus becomes a purely Muslim affair.

Inter-community linkages were also forged through common singing of folk songs (known as *sohar*) by both Hindu and Muslim women. There were many occasions to sing these songs but those during the birth of a son (not a daughter) were most important. It provided space for the women of these two communities to share their problems and recognize the close relationships that they shared with each other. The impact of Islamic reformism has been to term all such practices as outside the pale of 'correct' Islamic practice. Therefore, Ashrafiya's monthly magazine *Mahanama Ashrafiya* would advise Muslim women at length on how to appear Muslim. There are debates within its pages about whether it is permitted in Islam to apply vermilion on the forehead of married Muslim women. And the conclusion is that it is not permitted; that such practices should be termed as *jahilliyya* (the age of ignorance) and that Muslim women must be told not to appear like Hindu women. What is happening is very clear: that reformism, in an attempt to bring back the 'golden age of Islam', is creating markers of difference between communities. The shared practicalities of lived Muslim and Hindu communities are giving way to discrete identity formation where it is possible to mark out a Hindu from a Muslim even in sartorial terms. In this competition to gain Islamic leverage, both Deobandis and Barelwis are equal participants since both have their own understanding of what correct Islamic practice should be. In a sense, the reformist projects of these maslaks are together creating interpretative stress for lived popular traditions in India.

Islamic reform not only diminishes intra-Muslim plurality but also erases inter-community pluralism. A reformist Islam should be differentiated from popular Islam. My intention here is just to understand how popular Islamic practices are coming under increasing interpretative stress, not only from the Deobandis but also from the Barelwis. While I understand that reformism in itself opens up possibilities for both the interpretation of the scriptures and spaces for inter-community civic participation, the point that I am making is different. It seems likely that Islamic reformist projects have nothing to contribute towards the question of religious pluralism. Rather, in their insistence to become scriptural, and their wholesale condemnation of customary practices of Muslims, they affect a divide between communities, a divide which is only deepening. Clearly, then, religious pluralism still remains a problematic question for Indian Islam.

◆

NOTES

1. See Messick (2005). Following Messick, *maslak* (*maslaki*: of *maslak*) may be understood as a named and typically enduring interpretive community which is fundamentally relational in nature; that is, individual maslaks exist in interpretive worlds constituted by other such interpretive communities.
2. The influential rector of Madrasa Nadwat Ulama in Lucknow was close to the Deobandi theological position and hence is considered here as a Deobandi.

REFERENCES

Ahmad, Imtiaz. 1984. *Ritual and Religion among Muslims in India*. New Delhi: Manohar.

Alam, Arshad. 2011. *Inside a Madrasa: Knowledge, Power and Islamic Identity in India*. New Delhi: Routledge.

Assayag, Jackie. 2004. *At the Confluence of Two Rivers: Muslims and Hindus in South India*. Manohar: New Delhi.

Bourdieu, Pierre. 1977. *Outline of a Theory of Practice*. Translated by Richard Nice. UK: Cambridge University Press.

Eck, Diana, L. 2006. *On Common Ground: World Religions in America*. New York: Columbia University Press.

Eickelman, Dale F. 1978. 'The Art of Memory: Islamic Education and Its Social Reproduction', *Comparative Studies in Society and History*, 20(4): 485–516.

Fazal, Tanweer. 2005. 'Muslim and Indian Too', *Biblio: A Review of Books*, X: 7–8.

Hartung, Jan-Peter and Helmut Reifeld (eds.). 2006. *Islamic Education, Diversity and National Education: Dini Madaris in India Post 9/11*. New Delhi: Sage.

Madani, Husain Ahmad. 2005. *Composite Nationalism and Islam*. Translated by M. A. Hussain. New Delhi: Jamiat Ulama e Hind.

Malik, Jamal (ed.). 2008. *Madrasas in South Asia: Teaching Terror*? London: Routledge.

Mayaram, Shail. 1997. 'Rethinking Meo Identity: Cultural Faultline, Syncretism, Hybridity or Liminality?', *Comparative Studies of South Asia, Africa and the Middle East*, 17(2): 35–45.

Messick, Brinkley. 2005. 'Madhabs and Modernities', in Peri Bearman, Rudolph Peters and Frank Vogel (eds.), *The Islamic School of Law: Evolution, Devolution and Progress*. Cambridge, MA: Harvard University Press, pp. 159–74.

Metcalf, Barbara Daly. 1992. *Islamic Revival in British India: Deoband, 1860–1900*. New Delhi: Oxford University Press.

———. 2005. 'Introduction', in Husain Ahmad Madani, *Composite Nationalism and Islam*. Translated by M. A. Hussain. New Delhi: Manohar.

Nadwi, A. H. A. 1977. *Muslims in India*. Lucknow: Academy of Islamic Research and Publications.

———. 1980. *The Musalman*. Lucknow: Academy of Islamic Research and Publications.

Pearson, Harlon O. 2008. *Islamic Reform and Revival in Nineteenth Century India: The Tariqah-i Muhammadiya*. New Delhi: Yoda Press.

Sanyal, Usha. 1999. *Devotional Islam and British Politics in India: Ahmad Riza Khan Barelwi and His Movement, 1870–1920*. New Delhi: Oxford University Press.

◆◆

PART II
RELIGION AND CASTE

5 INTIMATE DESIRES
Dalit women and religious conversions in colonial India

CHARU GUPTA

Religious conversions have been one of the common expedients of those at the bottom of caste hierarchy in India, to improve their position, reject hierarchies, reconfigure social boundaries and as acts of protest and assertion (Clarke, 1998: 4, 125; Fernandes, 1994; Galanter, 1997; Webster, 1994, 1999). The figure of the Dalit[1] convert introduces ruptures in ideas of caste, religion and nation. Dalit conversions to Christianity began largely in colonial India and have provoked various works (Bayly, 1999; Forrester, 1979; Oddie, 1969, 1997; Pati, 2003; Philip, 1925; Phillips, 1912; Pickett, 1933; Vishwanathan, 1998; Webster, 1994; Zelliot, 1992). While insightful in their own right, they have mainly focused on mass movements, and have implicitly been Dalit male-centric, where outcaste women have often remained elusive figures.

However, there is considerable literature on Christian women missionaries themselves, and their position and work within the British Empire (Brouwer, 1990; Burton, 1994; Flemming, 1992; Forbes, 1986; Haggis, 2000; Semple, 2003; Singh, 2000). Again, while deeply perceptive, most of them discuss the opportunities and contradictions faced by missionary women in negotiating the new spaces created by colonial and mission activity, and do not give adequate space to the possible reception and impact of their work on women at the receiving end. In the recent past, some works have emerged, which have attempted to fill this lacuna, the most significant being that of Eliza Kent (2004) and Chad Bauman (2008), which discuss the impact of conversions to Christianity on lower-caste women in colonial South India and Chattisgarh, respectively. In her landmark work, Kent brings out the complex relationship between caste, gender, conversions and colonialism by showing how a 'discourse of respectability' emerged among Dalit Christian communities, which radically transformed the style of femininity to which Indian Christian women were expected to conform. Complimenting her work, Bauman shows that conversions did not lead to a straightforward emancipation of Dalit women. Rather, in many ways they implied an adoption of norms consonant with upper-caste Hinduism and Victorian Christian values, leading to a contraction in Dalit women's range of activities. While agreeing in part to these perspectives, I wish to complicate them by focusing on the relationship of conversions with desire and intimacy. Even while mimicking certain values, Dalits often moulded conversions to their needs and desires, what has been referred to as 'vernacularization' of Christianity (Dube, 2004), and even at times used them to subvert those very norms they were supposed to ape. Simultaneously, such acts produced increasing anxieties among caste Hindus.

Significantly, Dalit conversions in colonial India have been examined largely in the context of Christianity, as mass movements and collective strategies, embedded in community advancement. However, they leave unmarked motivations for individual conversions by Dalit women. It is as if they had no mind or heart of their own; they just followed their families and men. Yet, romance and desire provide us a peep into histories of personal conversions to Islam by some Dalit women, where they attempted to stand as individual subjects, and implicitly questioned both caste hierarchies and Dalit patriarchies.

This chapter concentrates on the representation of the Dalit woman convert by registering a social history of conversions in colonial North India, particularly in the United Provinces (present-day Uttar Pradesh [UP]), through the lens of caste and intimacy. It explores conversions as acts which embodied desires, and were accounts of stubborn materialities. It traces some police reports, cartoons, popular missionary literature in Hindi and writings of caste and reformist ideologues to show how conversions, or the possibility thereof, produced increasing worries, deeply politicized representations and everyday violence, framed around the bodies of Dalit women. These were enmeshed in a particular politics of colonial order, on the one hand, and of incitement, on the other, where there was both a representational heightening and an erasure of Dalit female desire. Through this context of overwriting and silencing of Dalit female subjectivity, it also implicitly attempts to recover in part Dalit female choice and aspiration. It considers how Dalit women found ways of negotiating codified relations, to recast the logic of caste and religious boundaries. To an extent, conversion by Dalit women was an affair of desire, which aided the transformative politics of religious rights. They were possibly employing conversions to also contest their association with sexual availability and degraded female value.

The chapter takes as its cue two entry points. First, it discusses mass conversions to Christianity and how these were also weaved around sartorial desires. Second, it focuses on individual conversions to Islam by some Dalit women, which were embedded in love and marriage. The tensions between such embodied desires reveal attempts to privilege a language of community rights, which were assigned a greater status, over women's individual choices, which were marginalized and silenced.

The chapter also tries to address other concerns. Conversions and their impact on the intimate have bearings on sexualities of Dalit women. In her work, Ann Stoler extends Foucauldian paradigms by combining sexualities with social taxonomies of race, as formative features of modernity. She agrees with Foucault that discourses around sexuality were activated as discursive incitements that facilitated the penetration of self-disciplinary regimes in intimate domains of modern life. But she argues that sexuality in colonial contexts was predicated on exclusionary principles and could not survive without a racially erotic counterpoint, without a reference to the libidinal energies of the primitive, the colonized, which became a marker of critique and desire (Stoler, 1995: 1–54). Extending this insight, I argue that it was not just the colonizers; the indigenous Hindu elite men too underwrote an exclusivist grammar of difference in sexual regimes, be it clothing or inter-religious romance.

Dalit women's rights are also intricately tied to conversions. Gender historians have highlighted the double-edged implications of law and a new language of rights for women in colonial India (Basu, 2001; Chandra, 1998; Chatterjee, 1999; Chowdhry, 2007; Nair, 1996; Singha, 1998). Religious conversions by women particularly produced fraught results in the eyes of law (De, 2010; Mallampalli, 2010). In spite of various limitations, certain laws did help in producing cracks in earlier orthodox mandates and to an extent enabled a new female self-fashioning (Sarkar, 2009). In this chapter too, I mark how disorder crept into the moral order. I do this by extending the language of rights, which have been conventionally and historically defined in terms of codified laws, universal conventions, community needs or institutional sites. But how do we place rights and its possible expressions in everyday life, which take on not just needs but also desires? Dalit women's desires in the realm of clothing or romance, expressed at times through highly ritualized act of conversion, imply a language of intimate rights, creating ripples in codified definitions. Caste then becomes an exploration of not just identity categories or questions of political inequality, on which there is rich scholarship, but also the subtle manner in which it functions as body history, and how everyday life is the site for the social reproduction of a hegemonic caste order *as well as* an enabling ground for the development of practices of dissent.

A SHORT HISTORY OF DALIT RELIGIOUS CONVERSIONS IN COLONIAL UP

At no stage did the Empire challenge caste in the way the Mission did (Copley, 1997: 6). While there had been earlier conversions by the outcastes, for example, to Buddhism in ancient India, the arrival of British and the impetus it gave to Christian missionary activities proved to be one of the biggest influences in altering their position. The Christian community in India was drawn largely from converts of the depressed classes (Webster, 1994: 36). In UP, we witness some Dalit conversions to Christianity (Sharma, 1988; Alter 1986), though not as many as in several other parts of colonial India. However, there was a huge discourse, debate and representation of the issue in popular literature, newspapers, reformist tracts, caste pamphlets, cartoons and missionary propaganda. The Protestant missionaries particularly adopted a variety of techniques for propagation among the Dalits, including bazaar preaching, itinerating through villages, conducting open services in public places, attending religious festivals and fairs, visiting homes and distributing scripture portions and tracts, mostly in local vernacular languages (Webster, 1994: 36; Church Missionary Society [CMS], 1926). The North Indian Christian Tract and Book Society, run by the Church Mission of England, and headquartered at Allahabad, widely disseminated vernacular tracts, including painted story scrolls, books and multitude of songs and hymns amongst the outcastes (Clayton 1911; Lucas, n.d.: 3; Sharma, 1988: 92). Their annual publication and circulation of Christian books reached a staggering height of 908,000 volumes in 1914. A Conference on Urdu and Hindi Christian Literature held at Allahabad resolved that particular efforts will be made through such literature to influence the lower castes and servants (*Conference*, 1875: 4, 15). Every month between 8,000 and 40,000 copies of Hindi tracts were sent out for free distribution. Many of them were thin pamphlets of four to six pages (Lucas n.d.: 41, 53). Tracts like *Hindu Dharm ke Phal* [Fruits of Hinduism] (1905), *Jati ki Chut Chat* [Unreasonableness of Caste] (1905: 1–10), *Hinduon ki Nirdhanta* [Causes of Hindu Poverty] (1909: 7–17) and *Jati Panti ka Varnan* [Explanation of Caste] (1924: 11) launched a stringent attack on Hinduism, particularly on the treatment meted out to the outcastes. Conversion to Christianity was depicted as the biggest boon, which gave the depressed classes dignity, education and clean clothes (*Jati Pariksha* [Test of Caste], 1906: 13; *Devi, Devta aur Murtipuja* [Goddesses, Gods and Idol Worship] 1923: 24). At the same time, their language was guided by a sense of racial and religious superiority, cloaked in a patronizing tone of bringing culture and civilization to the outcastes. For example, a Hindi mission tract stated:

> The untouchables are like lost rupees, on which dust, soil, dirt and mire has gathered. But just as dirty and tattered rupees do not loose their actual value, similarly in the eyes of God the value of these people does not decrease. And we missionaries are here precisely to reform these dirty sinners (*Jati Panti ka Varnan*, 1924: 15).

Besides Christianity, Islam too carried its teachings amongst the Dalits (Mujahid, 1989; Sikand, 2004). Many of the lower castes actively engaged in and creatively reinterpreted Islamic traditions into their lives and cultures during the medieval period (Eaton, 1993: 113–34). It was stated by colonial officials that a considerable proportion of the cobbler caste of UP had become Muhammadan (Nesfield, 1882: 22), and that many Muslim leather workers in the towns were Hindu Chamar converts (Walton, 1903: 12). Muslim organizations continued to actively seek converts in colonial UP from among the outcastes. In Saharanpur, Moradabad, Bijnor, Bulandshahr and Dehradun, they mobilized resources to preach Islam in villages with only untouchables.[2] As an example, in 1925 a Muslim *zamindar* [landlord] of Etah stated that if the outcastes converted to Islam, he would give them 500 *bighas* [3,025 square yards] of land and also have *roti-beti* [food and marriage] ties with them.[3]

Such campaigns and some actual conversions by Dalits created apprehension among the high caste Hindus, the Arya Samaj and the Hindu Mahasabha. While reformist endeavours were guided by other concerns as well, it was conversions which forced many of these organizations to seriously work among the outcastes. Arya Samaj effectively utilized the print public sphere to constantly lament their perceived conversions. This was tied to a number crunching politics, where a picture of terrible calamity was built of rapidly declining Hindu numbers due to Dalit conversions (Chandrikaprasad, 1917: 14; Dwivedi, 1924: 1, 26, 35; Parmanand, 1928: 90).[4] It was stated that every week 2,000 untouchable Hindus converted to Christianity, which meant 104,000 converts in one year. It was also believed that 200,000 untouchables became Muslims every year (Jha, 1925: 4). Massive attempts were made to win them over, by attending their feasts and marriages, allowing them to draw water from wells (Sanyasi, 1919: 65),[5] reconvert them through *shuddhi* [purification ceremony] (*Census*, 1931: 501–2; Freitag, 1989: 230–41; Ghai, 1990; Gooptu, 2001: 144–57; Jordens, 1981: 142–51; Pandey, 1978: 115–17),[6] and showing the relative equality that had been achieved (Figures 5.1 and 5.2).

Many leading Hindi newspapers and magazines gave their unequivocal support to these efforts.[7] Simultaneously, a vast amount of literature, including pamphlets, poems, posters and cartoons, were published to counter conversion attempts by missionaries and Muslims (Banprasthi, 1927; Jha, 1925: 5–15; Sanyasi, 1919; Sharda 1926: 6–9; Shukla, 1934; Upadhyaya, 1925). The supposedly mythical benefits that the outcastes got due to conversions were ridiculed (Banprasthi, 1927: cover):

> *pada akaal bhukh ke mare, taji kutumb, matu, pit, bhaiya.*
> *aat kristan gahiyon lalach bas, jako jagat hansaiya.*
> *gori miss ki rahi vasna, mili ek chamariya.*
> *lalsa rahi phitan charhan ki, mili na ek gadahiya.*
> *main tau gayun din duniya se, bache raho sab bhaiya.*
> *isu masih nahin kahun, prabhu pran bachaiya.*

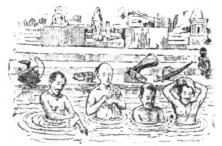

सिंह और बकरी एक घाट
देखिये ! तीर्थराज प्रयागमें श्री त्रिवेणीजीमें छूत और अछूत किस तरह एक साथ स्नान कर रहे हैं ।
Figure 1
Lion and Lamb on the Same River Bank
See at the pilgrimage site of Triveni at Prayag:
The touchable and the untouchable take bath together.]
Source: Kediya (1933: 34).

Figure 5.1 **Lion and lamb on the same river bank:** At the pilgrimage site of Triveni at Prayag, the touchable and the untouchable take bath together.

Source: Kedia (1933: 34).

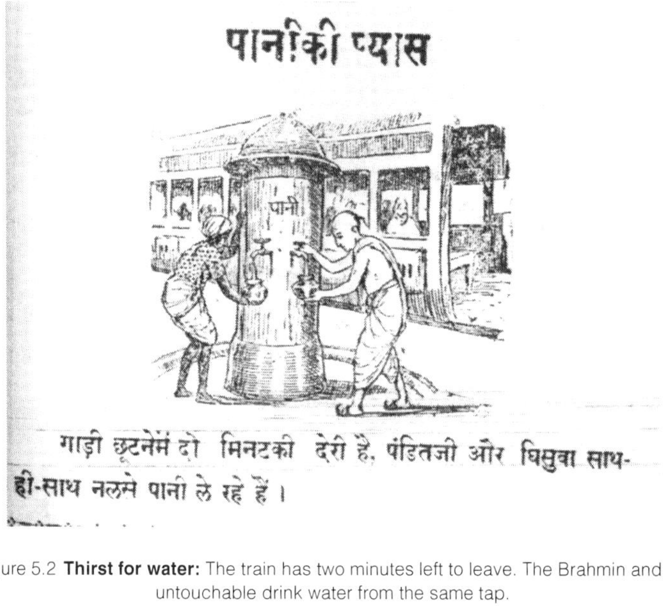
पानीकी प्यास
पानी
गाड़ी छूटनेमें दो मिनटकी देरी है, पंडितजी और घिसुवा साथ-ही-साथ नलसे पानी ले रहे हैं ।

Figure 5.2 **Thirst for water:** The train has two minutes left to leave. The Brahmin and the untouchable drink water from the same tap.

Source: Kedia (1933: 34).

[Comes drought and hunger, you (outcastes) abandon family, mother, father, brother.
The Christian comes with greed and lure, and the world laughs at you.
You crave the fair skinned Miss, but get only a Chamarin.
You desire to ride in a car, but do not even get a female donkey.
I just pray to the world, please all beware.
Christ is nowhere, God save your life.]

Or stated another (Bandhusamaj, 1927: 5–14):

hota nahin anar kabhi amrud badal ke.
tab hindu kis bhanti aaj bhaye muslim dal ke....
brahman, kshatri, vaishya kshetra mein aage awo,
antyaj bandhu samaj vishad saadar apnavo....
teli nai khatik tamoli bhaat bhikhari. dhobi dhanuk lodh bodh se
baarho agari.
kurmi kevat kuril jati ke kori bhangi. aasha tumhin se lagi bano
sache sangi.
[A pomegranate can never change into a guava.
Then how can Hindus today become a part of the Muslim community?...
Brahmin, Kshatriyas, Vaishyas, please come forward,
Accept with respect your junior brothers....
March ahead oil miller, barber, vegetable seller, bard, beggar, washerman, cotton-carder.
Kurmi, boatman, Kuril, sweeper – we have faith in you. Become our true associates.]

Implicit in such literature was upper-caste prejudice, as reflected in these quotes. Moreover, severe tensions on the ground remained. The attempts at keeping the boundaries of Hinduism intact by stopping conversions simultaneously with increasing reconversions could not be easily reconciled with maintaining a difference within Hindu community.[8]

Amidst such campaign by missionaries on the one hand, and Hindu reformers on the other, Dalits often used conversions as a heuristic device, which signalled some dignity, education, clothing, employment, political representation and 'manhood' (Gupta, 2010; Rawat, 2012). Many sweepers, Lal Begis, Chandals, Doms and Chamars of Badaun, Mathura, Meerut, Roorkee, Etah, Cawnpore, Moradabad, Pillibhit, Bijnor and Bareilly converted to Christianity (Allison, 1969: 116–27; *Census*, 1931: 500; CMS, 1926; Phillips, 1912: 34; Sanyasi, 1919: 42; Sharma, 1988: v). Most often, these followed along family and *jati* lines (Singh, 1947: 178). Many converted sweepers and Chamars refused to do *begar* [unpaid labor] in the households and fields of zamindars (Nevill, 1904: 81). Alongside, Dalits often used to their advantage the alarm felt by reformers regarding their conversions, to demand more rights for themselves, and as a way of questioning the stigma of 'untouchability' (Rawat, 2012).

In this background I attempt to read representations of Dalit women's conversions through a gendered lens. First, I underscore conversions to Christianity and its sartorial portrayals, mainly through popular cartoons published in reformist literature. Second, I highlight some police reports to mark individual conversions to Islam, and the fears around them.

CONVERSIONS, CHRISTIANITY, CLOTHES AND CARTOONS

Religious conversions of women were a difficult enterprise for the Christian missionaries. Work among the *zenana* [women's quarters] upper-caste households had resulted in spread of some education, but was a dismal failure in terms of religious conversions (Forbes, 1986; Lloyd, 1882; Pitman, 1906). In comparison, they were more successful amidst outcaste women (Morris, 1917: 2, 9). Some missionary women particularly became active in rural areas of UP in early twentieth century, entrusted with the task of converting, teaching, home visiting and organizing meetings of outcaste women (Survey of Evangelistic Work, 1929: 80). The CMS was very effective in Meerut district, with about 18 to 20 teachers and Bible women working in the mission area (Alter, 1985: 74; Pemberton and Perfumi, 1915: 47–48). Certain missionary publications were specifically aimed at preaching the outcaste women (Lucas, n.d.: 93; *Charitra Sudhar* [Character Improvement], 1910; *Lara Lari* [Story of Quarrelsome Women], 1905; *Ratnmala* [Garland of Pearls], 1969). These included inspiring stories of their conversions, and the dramatic and 'positive' changes it brought about (Campbell, 1918; *Chandra Lila Sadhuni ka Vritant* [Biographical Account of Chandra Lila, a Lower Caste Female Convert], 1910; *Mem Sahiba aur Ayah ki Katha* [The Story of the Lady and the Ayah], 1896). Orphanages, day and boarding mission schools, even though few and far between, were established, which were perceived as removing the outcaste women from a 'useless' and 'dirty' heathen environment. The Jeyi school in Meerut took a pride of place here (CMS, 1926: 2–3, 8–10; Stewart, 1928: 27–30).

As has been emphasized by historians of gender, conversions to Christianity had contradictory implications for women (Bauman, 2008; Haggis, 2000; Kent, 2004). On the one hand, they identify the work done by missionary women amidst their non-Christian 'sisters' in the colonial empires as a 'mission of domesticity', which schooled them into marriage, education, household work, child care, cleanliness and a particular outlook. On the other, they also stress that it was not a straightforward way of making women good, 'clean' Christian wives and mothers. In UP too, these ambiguities were visible. In spite of various limits, at times the condition of Dalit women improved in comparison to the drudgery in which they were living before. Most converted women refused to do unpaid midwife's work or *begar*. Education, even if limited to sewing, hygiene and Bible training, was seen as more appropriate than manual work or unpaid public labor (Philip, 1925: 34–35; Speer, 1939: 81). Mrs. Mohini Das, a Dalit Christian convert, speaking at the All India Depressed Classes Association in Lucknow on 22–24 May 1936, gave a speech titled 'What Womanhood Owes to Christ', where she argued that Christianity opened a new door of opportunity for depressed-class women: 'Wherever His [Jesus] teachings took root the condition of women began to alter. She became not just a glorified courtesan and housekeeper, but a homemaker, a companion to her husband and a fit mother for bringing up his children'.[9] Miss A. M. Stewart, an active missionary in the Jeyi school, stated: 'Girls who have passed out of Jeyi School will make a lasting difference in the village communities amongst whom they live, by their lives and examples' (Stewart, 1928: 277). Some became Bible women. Though there was a severe shortage of funds and their position remained decidedly low in the hierarchy of the missions, Miss P. Emery had this to say on a depressed-class Bible woman in UP (1928: 15–16):

> Their [converted depressed class men] wives had been employed as Bible Readers…. One of the best teachers we have in our district is a woman who has never had but two years schooling in her life, yet she reads the Bible fluently, and last year won the prize for the

> best examination results in the whole district.... She doesn't know
> that there is such a word as methods yet she had taught the boys
> and girls in her village to read with fluency and expression in their
> Readers and Testaments, and they are able to give an intelligent
> answer regarding the fundamentals of the Christian faith.

Another missionary remarked on how a Christian woman sweeper working in the palace of a local Rajah [king] sold 10 gospels to the Rajah's women folk (Heinrich, 1928: 94).

While the missionaries wished to restructure every aspect of converted Dalit women's daily lives, including their physical appearance, sartorial styles, marital relations, customs, language and the people with whom they interacted, many of the religious and social practices of these women reflected highly eclectic borrowing and adaptation (Kent, 2004). Even through processes of mimicry, they often selectively appropriated, reconstituted and at times subverted some of the ideals of upper-caste and missionary life, and imbued it with their own sensibilities and practices. Rev. J. C. Harrison wrote: 'As yet none of our Christians have broken away from their heathen customs.... The household gods are still worshipped by the women. The Hindu festivals are kept, charms are retained, fakirs are consulted – the Sabbath is not kept, marriages are conducted according to heathen rites.'[10]

Conversion to Christianity had particular implications for Dalit women's clothing, as it brought to the fore questions of the body per se vis-à-vis caste. Clothes veil the body. They encode a game of modesty and sexual explicitness, of a denial and celebration of pleasure. They are a form of social control, a mechanism of inclusion and exclusion, mirroring social hierarchies and moral boundaries. They serve as a discursive daily practice of gender, simultaneously communicating and constituting gender, caste, religious and national identities (Barnes and Eicher, 1992; Gaines and Herzog, 1990; Ross, 2008: 83–102). Clothing played an active role in the construction of families, castes, classes, regions and the nation in colonial India (Bayly, 1986: 285–322; Cohn, 1989: 106–62, 312–13; Tarlo, 1996: 23–127). Cloth was inscribed with new meanings by nationalists, particularly Gandhi, and became a key visual symbol of freedom struggle against the British rule (Bean, 1989; Ramagundam, 2008; Trivedi, 2007). However, as Tarlo (1996) argues, there were no singular and stable meanings to clothing choices in colonial India. Feminist historians posit that attempts at re-dressing women had a distinct relationship to idealized upper-caste middle-class wife and mother, to a sartorial morality and to a denigration of sexuality (Bannerji, 2001: 99–134; Gupta, 2001; Sangari, 2001: 344–49).

Clothing hierarchically distinguished women from one another. Dalit women had to endure humiliating dress restrictions, which were also ways to mark their bodies as inferior and sexually promiscuous. Her sexuality was there to be seen and consumed, as her private being was made public through her dress. For example, as elsewhere, among the sweepers of Lucknow, women could not wear the bodice, gold ornaments or a nose ring (Crooke, 1974: 290). Conversion to Christianity was a declaration of an altered relationship with the world through a transformed disposition of caste-marked bodies. We already know how Christian missions in South India encouraged lower-caste Shanar women converts in the late eighteenth and early nineteenth centuries to cover their breasts in public places, which was associated with only upper-caste women (Gladstone, 1984; Hardgrave, 1968; Kent, 2004). Such cross-dressing was not only an appropriation of upper-caste dress signifiers that were forbidden to lower-caste bodies, but was also represented as resignifying the gendered habitus and improve the social standing of lower castes.

Clothing became an indicator to distinguish Dalit Christian women from their unconverted counterparts, and a way to garner dignity. Notions of care and presentation of the body were key components informing the conversion mission. Sewing thus was particularly important, as missionaries were keen to see the 'seminude' outcaste women clad in 'decent' clothes, fit for clean Christian souls. Pictures appeared in popular literature portraying on the one hand a naked, 'dirty' and unkempt outcaste woman and on the other a fully clothed, sari-clad, 'clean' and smiling Christian Dalit woman (Figure 5.3). John Munro, acting as Dewan to Rani Lakshmibai, issued a proclamation way back in 1812, guaranteeing Indian Christian women the right to cover their breasts (Kooiman, 1989: 149). Changes in clothing through conversions became for a section of Dalits a symbolic act and a material marker to transcend systems of inequality, signal upward mobility, write themselves into colonial modernity (Menon, 2006), acquire respect in the public sphere, fabricate their identities and put the ignominy of their past status behind.[11]

Figure 5.3 Left is the state of being Hindu (untouchable). Right is the complete change on becoming a Christian.

Source: *Chand* (May 1929: 51).

Reformist iconography, particularly cartoons, too recognized dress as a terrain for contesting social relations and articulating new religious identities. R. K. Laxman, the celebrated cartoonist of India testifies that a cartoonist attempts to convey the ironies of everyday life through disapproval and complaint (Laxman, 1989: 69–91; 1990: iv; Sahay, 1998). In colonial UP, *Avadh Panch* was the first Indian newspaper to publish cartoons (Hasan, 2007: 9; Oesterheld and Zoller, 1999). Cartoons could make a great impression on a functionally literate population. Soon, many other reformist publications, including those in Hindi, were using them to advocate social reforms, with a central focus on women.

In the early twentieth century, cartoons depicting the crisis of conversions through clothing entered the Hindi print-public sphere in UP, putting on display the perceived insecurities and sexual unease of caste and reformist Hindus. Cartoons published in *Chand* [Moon] (1922–1940s) and Arya Samaj publications, and many of them compiled in *Vyanga Chitravali* [Collection of Cartoons and Caricatures] (1930), usually depicted two outcaste women or men together, of which one had converted to Christianity.[12] Even while lamenting conversions, they could not help but acknowledge the change in demeanour and stature that it brought about in Dalits – in their mode of dressing, walking style, gait and prestige. One cartoon, for example, visualized the converted outcaste woman walking ahead royally, carrying an umbrella, a purse, wearing a hat, skirt and high-heeled shoes, reflecting an elevated status. The unconverted woman walked behind head bent, bare-footed, carrying the child of the converted Dalit woman (Figure 5.4).

Figure 5.4 See the difference between two women of the same species: one is an English madam and the other a servant-untouchable. The former walks ahead with an umbrella, while the latter walks behind with her child.

Source: Vyanga Chitravali.

INTIMATE DESIRES

ईसाइन कुत्ते की मालिक, है अछूत उसकी नौकर !
पर दोनों थे एक जाति के, देखो हिन्दू आँखें भर !!

Figure 5.5 The Christian woman is the master of the dog, while the outcaste woman is her servant. But they both were of the same caste, Hindus please see carefully.

Source: *Vyanga Chitravali.*

Another had the Christian Dalit woman carefully sitting on a chair looking down while the untouchable took care of her dog, looking up (Figure 5.5).

Yet another lamented the loss, showing the converted woman again in shoes, hat and umbrella (Figure 5.6).

Such cartoons can function as our constitutive archives. These banal, ordinary, everyday, popular communications are

Figure 5.6 One has become a madam-lady, and the other a fish seller. Blessed be the religion of Christ, which is all powerful.

Source: Chand (May 1929: 77).

pivotal documents in conceiving the anxieties of Hindu reformers, while also offering a counter-politics of sartorial desire. These representations encompassed the everyday life of Dalits, at home and on the streets. The rhetoric of such repeated caricaturing was meant to manufacture Hindu public opinion against conversions, and warn the caste Hindus not to treat Dalits badly. Such cartoons did not encompass the 'truths' of conversions and its relationship to sartorial styles of Dalit women, as very few dressed in ways illustrated here. In fact, the dress for Dalit Christian women in missionary schools was very modest, with the sari and the blouse. However, their very portrayal in particular ways in these cartoons reflected the traumatized identities of caste Hindus, and their powerful language made explicit the upper-caste perceptions of Dalit women's desires.

For Dalits, clothing representations became a symbol of dignity. It has been proposed that Dalit culture in general does not place any value on an indigenist notion of 'authenticity', including in clothing (Ilaiah, 2003).[13] Discarding the demeaning dress became a code for radical dissent against caste discipline, marking the right to inhabit unmarked bodies (Pandey, 2006: 1785–86). For women from stigmatized communities, sartorial changes, even if sometimes mythical, symbolically associated women's clothing with community dignity. Dalits emphasized the right to ceremonial displays, vigorously policed by upper castes. Good clothing, footwear and bodily comportment – standing erect while speaking, refusing to contort the body in a submissive fashion – were critical to Dalit self-fashioning. Though discourses of sexuality and of female enfranchisement were caste-specific, the focus on the feminized body – how it was experienced and represented – was central to a range of political processes. Clothing representations that conversion to Christianity provided Dalits questioned not only upper-caste religious and symbolic monopolies in intimate spheres, by arguing for the right to wear footwear, wear the breast-cloth or carry umbrellas in the presence of persons of high ritual status, but it also treated them as matters of collective and direct public action, making them politically radical issues (Rao, 2009). At the same time, the converted Dalit figure was an internal embarrassment, an 'inappropriate other', whose sartorial style defied nationalist logic. These women literally wore their difference on their bodies, signifying an uncomfortable anomaly in the reformist–nationalist discourse.

ROMANTIC DESIRES AND CONVERSIONS TO ISLAM

Sartorial representations due to mass conversions to Christianity by Dalits, while giving some room for change, embedded women's desires within community boundaries, sometimes even upholding conservative gender constructs. There were differing perceptions on conversions accorded to collective social groups and to individual Dalit women. This has led some scholars to argue that the political-public Dalit sphere in colonial India was rendered male (Rao, 2009). I do not wish to overemphasize an 'individual versus collective' binary, as these were complex and intertwined issues. At the same time, Dalit men were anxious about individual conversions by Dalit women, particularly to Islam. These were seen as bringing 'shame', since Dalit women were perceived as part of a network of relationships within a community. Dalit men found it difficult to envisage a world of conversions in which Dalit women made personal choices. Such conversions caused disquiet, both among reformers on the one hand and Dalit men on the other. There appeared to be a political and social consensus between them against the desire of Dalit women to convert as individuals, sans familial and community approval.

By focusing on personal Dalit women's conversions, I wish to also historicize love and romance, which are mutable concepts (Collin, 2003; Langhamer, 2007), whose meanings are contingent on gender, caste and religious identities. Scholars have emphasized shifting meanings of romantic love in colonial India (Orsini, 2007: 30–34). Tapan Raychaudhuri (2000) shows how developments in modern print-public culture profoundly altered intimate concerns. Though reformers treated romantic love as an irrelevant joke, a flourishing popular romantic literature in the period brought new intensity in conjugal relationships, with little precedents in pre-modern past. These authoritative archives of intimate histories highlighted the snug connection between marriage, sex and romantic love (Figure 5.7).

However, while the literary turn of both Indian feminist studies and postcolonial theory has provided us with sophisticated insights into love, desire and other forms of subjectivities of middle-class

INTIMATE DESIRES

Figure 5.7 **Cover of a book:** Only for Married Women and Men: *Secret of Love and Sex between the Married Couple* by Yashoda Devi. Allahabad 1933.

women, the same cannot be said about Dalit women. Here I explore how in this climate Dalit women negotiated intimacies beyond its moral and social parameters. The writings from this period provide a window both onto sociological realities and onto their constitution and mobilization for particular political ends, with an inherent politics of exclusion and engagement, reflecting shifting registers of unspoken ambivalences.

I am here also implicitly concerned with everyday violence. The intertwining of gender, religious identities and violence has been richly explored by feminist historians in India. While offering deep insights, their works have been usually embedded in cataclysmic events. Scholars have highlighted the inchoate ways of everyday life (de Certeau, 1984: xi–xxiv). Histories of inter-religious intimacies reflect a mundane texture, where women were ubiquitous, where varied meanings were imparted to sexual affiliations. Even while within hetero-normative paradigms, Dalit female desire produced daily policing and everyday violence, along what Foucault calls the alliance model of sexuality, where – through arrangement of marriages – relations and boundaries of caste and religion were policed.[14]

Ambedkar linked maintenance of endogamy with strengthening of caste, arguing that inter-caste marriage was the most important way of annihilating caste, since it alone acknowledged relationship between maintenance of caste purity and control of women's sexuality (Rao, 2009). In UP, Swami Achhutanand, the leader of the Adi Hindu movement, too exhorted Dalits to abolish sub-casteism by inter sub-caste marriages, and proposed that Muslims and Christians too could help in this enterprise (Jigyasu, 1960; Kshirsagar, 1994: 345). Yet, as Prem Chowdhry (2007) shows, inter-caste marriages took on new contours in the colonial period and became more contentious. Caste endogamy increasingly came to be observed, and often became legally enforceable even for 'untouchable' caste groups who had significantly different norms. Moreover, as Anupama Rao (2009) argues, though caste radicals were preoccupied with challenging caste ideology by rethinking love and marriage, they were by no means immune to extension of novel patriarchal practices into their own households. Caste and gender inequalities reinforced each other, as regulation of women's movement and sexual disciplining emerged as powerful means for consolidation of caste and community exclusivities (Gupta, 2001). Even intermediate and lower castes started imposing restrictions on women in intimate spaces, paradoxically seeing this as a way to claim masculinity, strengthen claims for upward mobility, assert patriarchal control and restore dignity to their women (Bandyopadhyay, 2004; Dube, 1998; Gupta, 2010; Lynch, 1969: 174–81). For example, Chamars of Moradabad, Dehra Dun, Meerut and Saharanpur announced that they would allow their women less liberty of movement and forbade them to visit bazaars.[15] Similar resolutions were adopted by Bhangis, Khatiks and Pasis.[16] Hindu publicists also attempted to 'improve' popular practices of lower-caste women, ostensibly to cleanse them of their perceived lax moral standards. This not only involved a challenging of existing customs associated with low-grade practices but also shaping new ones in keeping with high tradition (Bayly, 1999: 159–60; Chowdhry, 2007). Endeavours to refigure Dalit women subjectivities created fresh norms of conjugal relations, embedded in endogamy and containment of sexuality. Fears were also expressed of illicit collusions and pleasures between upper-caste women and lower-caste men (Figure 5.6).

However, while inter-caste alliances were deeply opposed by caste Hindus, the thought of women, even if from lower castes, eloping or marrying Muslim and Christian men and then converting to Islam or Christianity proved to be more disturbing. Thus even while rejecting inter-caste intimacies, in certain circumstances, lower- and upper-caste Hindu men came together to impose constraints on *their* women. This coincided with the growth of militant Hindu assertion in UP, which reached new heights in the 1920s, with unprecedented communal clashes between Hindus and Muslims (Freitag, 1989: 8–9, 230–41; Pandey, 1978: 115–17), and aggressive participation from a section of the lower castes (Gooptu, 2001).[17] The liberal premise and promise of reformist discourse was considerably overturned, when within it, the woman's body became a marker for enthroning communal boundaries.

Hindu reformers and revivalists started making appeals to upper-caste Hindus to uplift outcaste women. The Hindu Mahasabha emphasized that there was a need to validate by marriage, clandestinely carried amorous relations between a Hindu girl and boy of different castes, even if one of them was an untouchable, to prevent conversions. Cases were cited where the Hindu Mahasabha

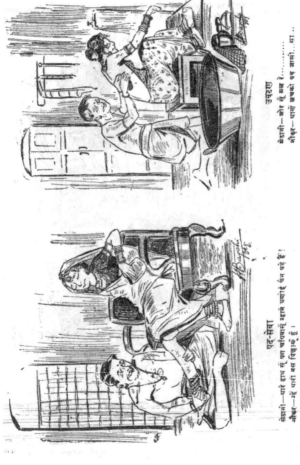

Figure 5.8 Tending the feet
Prosperous Woman: When you rub my feet with your hands, I am deeply contented.
Servant: I know your pulse.
Body paste
Prosperous Woman: Rub a little more....
Servant: I might sprain you.....
Source: *Vyanga Chitravali*

had prevented a Bhangi or a Chamar woman from converting, by marrying her to a higher caste Hindu boy.[18] Conversions of outcaste women were also represented as a loss of numbers and potential childbearing wombs for the Hindu community. A special issue of *Chand* stated that there were millions of outcaste mothers who were full of love, but because of the cruelty of Hindu society, were nurturing wombs and prodigies of Muslim children, and producing cow killers.[19] Stated *Abhyudaya*:

> Many of our Hindu women, whom we consider outcastes, are going into the hands of Muslims and Christians. How can these women, whom we treat so badly, become protectors of cow and worshippers of Ram and Krishna?.... We should make all efforts to prevent our outcaste women from marrying such men. It is imperative so that the number of cow-protectors does not reduce.[20]

Anxieties around conversions to Islam by Dalit women were often expressed in a language of abductions. It was emphasized in magazines and newspapers like *Chand* and *Pratap* [Glory] that women, including outcaste women, were being molested and forcibly converted by Muslim men.[21] 'Samachar Sangrah' [Collection of News Items], regularly published in *Chand*, built a psyche of Muslims as abductors of Dalit women, using it as a plank to woo Dalit men to the side of Hindus.[22] It was reported in 1938 that when a sweeper woman was cleaning the road near a mosque in Kanpur, attempts were made to kidnap her by Muslim *goondas* [evil characters]. Following this, the Mehtar Sabha [Body of Sweepers] resolved to boycott local Muslims.[23] A communal riot occurred in Basti in 1939 due to alleged molestation of a Chamar woman by a Muslim, the trouble assuming serious proportions due to the rivalry between the Hindu and Muslim *lathi akharas* [gymnasium teaching fighting with bamboo sticks] in that vicinity.[24] Dalit men often colluded with such rhetoric, at times overpowering the realities of caste hierarchies. It not only touched an emotive nerve; women were crucial for their material existence. At a meeting of sweepers in Dehradun, it was resolved not to allow their women to work in Muhammadan households. Similar resolutions were adopted by Chamar, Khatik and Pasi caste associations in Agra, Allahabad, Benaras and Kanpur.[25]

More interesting were individual conversions to Islam by some Dalit women due to love, elopement and marriage. Gauri Vishwanathan (1998: 163) states that in many cases of individual conversion, particularly by lower castes, the reason was neither proselytism nor doctrinal conviction, but romance. While difficult to trace such cases in UP, police abstracts of intelligence provide some glimpses, though with a caveat. Only a few cases merited mention, which led to tensions. None of them were described in sufficient details. Yet they provide significant insights. In almost all cases reported, it was individual outcaste women (and not men) who were found to be converting. Their romantic involvements were possibly aided by greater mobility. We get many stray examples. In March 1924, a Chamar woman left her husband in Banaras in favour of a Muslim, whom she married.[26] In March 1926, a Bhangi woman converted to Islam and married a Muslim in Aligarh.[27] In the same year in April, a Muslim of Kanpur had a female sweeper as his mistress, whom he converted.[28] In the next month, a Kori woman, kept by a Muslim contractor at Banda, converted.[29] In December 1928, a sweeper woman of Unao married a Muslim and converted.[30] It was reported from Fyzabad in 1934 that an outcaste woman had married a Muslim.[31] In May 1938, a sweeper woman eloped with a Muslim in Dehradun and subsequently converted to Islam.[32] In 1946, a local Muslim brought with him a sweeper woman whom he claimed had embraced Islam.[33] Such cases point to Dalit women's ambiguous relationship to caste and religious identities, hinting at their desire and experimentation. At times, they chose to defend their conversion as well. In Basti, a Khatik woman who had been converted to Islam was taken to the Arya Samaj office with a view to reconversion but she stuck to her decision.[34]

Outcaste women were possibly 'using' conversion as a mode of coping with and, within limits, transgressing an oppressive social order. It was a strategic manoeuvre with social ramifications, combined with elements of choice, desire and experimentation. It is significant that unlike conversion to Christianity, which required evidence of baptism and other documents, conversion to Islam merely entailed the recitation of *kalma* before witnesses. Also, till at least the 1940s, the courts recognized that conversion to Islam by women of other religions dissolved their former religion and marriage (De, 2010). This moment of transition may have been perceived by Dalit women as providing some leverage in negotiating

INTIMATE DESIRES

personal status and familial, caste and religious power relations, and reconfiguring social boundaries, if only partially and temporarily. More often than not, they were entering relationships similar to the ones they had succeeded in leaving. But is it also possible to see these outcaste women as boundary crossers, where romance offered a momentary amelioration? Can we see these as acts of self-expression, offering possibilities for a liberated Dalit woman's body to emerge through alternative religious belongings?

Causing increasing tensions, such crossings were cited by Arya Samaj and Hindu Mahasabha to raise a fearful scenario and to urge outcaste men to prevent their women from taking such steps (Gupta, 2001). It was emphasized that Muslims continually seduced their outcaste women neighbours, ran away with them and converted them (Sharda, 1925: 33–34). The outcaste woman's self-consciousness as a woman, as a convert, as a person with sexual agency, was consistently erased. Such individual conversions on their own accord, minus 'their men' evoked hostile reactions from Dalit men. The 'rule breaking' by these women was seized as an opportunity to reinforce caste, religious and sexual controls. Thus to repeat the cases mentioned before, when the Chamar woman converted in Banaras, it caused alarm in Arya Samaj circles. A breach of peace was threatened between them and Muslims.[35] When the Bhangi woman of Aligarh married a Muslim, communal feelings were largely embittered. Large crowds gathered, a case was filed against it, many shops in the city shut down and the city Bhangis struck work.[36] Trouble arose in Kanpur between sweepers and Muslims when knowledge of conversion of the female sweeper spread. The Arya Samajists seized upon it as a pretext for anti-Muslim propaganda. They succeeded in bringing about a strike of sweepers, who refused to work for Muslims.[37] In Fyzabad, the Muslim male was arrested on charges of seducing the outcaste woman. Though he was acquitted when she stated that she was his wife, relationship between Muslims and outcastes became strained.[38] The sweeper community threatened to boycott all Muslim houses, following the elopement and conversion of the sweeper woman in Dehradun.[39] The sweepers of Moradabad ceased working for Muslim inhabitants after a case of 'kidnapping' of a sweeper woman by a Julaha.[40] In a village in Meerut, tense situation existed when the sweepers of the locality removed a sweeper woman from the custody of a Muslim.[41] Here the outcaste men colluded in the production of a sense of reality that stigmatized them. While they questioned the dominant order, they at times identified with it, especially when it came to the question of 'their' women.

CONCLUSION

Intertwining Dalit women's conversions with clothing and love provides such conversions with a language of intimate rights, while also expressing Dalit women's desire for dignity, pleasure and autonomy. They also reflect aspirations for things, which were relatively outside the realm of those strictly necessary for the survival of the individual or the community. Such conversions were a site of contestation, whose meanings shifted in specific historical moments. They inspired a great deal of anxiety and ideological diatribes among the Hindu reformers, particularly the Arya Samaj, as they symbolized possible autonomy and recalcitrance of Dalit women's heart and mind in intimate arenas of their lives. Social signifiers of caste and religion tied together with perceived illegitimacy of desire to produce interlocking set of power relations.

Hindu reformers' sartorial cartoons of converted Christian Dalit women exposed contradictory impulses at the heart of their project, as even while lamenting conversions, they paradoxically reflected self-respect through fashion. Here, Foucault's notion of how bodies, and the ways they are dressed and managed through both self-discipline and surveillance and a general panoptic lens, can be relevant (1979). However, its disciplinary strength was often diluted as clothing also became a performative tool for Dalits to adorn dignity and wear themselves into colonial modernity.

Dalit women's individual conversions to Islam evoked a somewhat different response. While promoting caste endogamy, upper-caste Hindu publicists were deeply troubled with fantasies about possible relations between lower-caste women and Muslim men. They simultaneously opposed inter-caste relationships, while urging men of their community to accept lower-caste women to prevent their conversion. There was a complex relationship between caste endogamy and community homogeneity. The contingency of community made the marking of 'difference' slippery. Dalit women's conversion for love was an explosive issue. In such a situation, abduction campaigns constructed sedimented discourses on sexual immorality, in which the Muslim male was carved through repetitive motifs. Simultaneously, the figure of the converted Dalit woman often motivated a kind of collusion among low-caste and high-caste men, helping in claims for a wider pan-caste Hindu community (Dube, 1933). Concerns around such intimacies could appeal, though from different perspectives, to orthodox and reformist Hindus and to Dalit men, who were simultaneously pursuing declarations of separate identities from upper-caste Hindus.

For Dalit men, conversions came to be constituted by values derived from specific moral visions, and came to have shifting meanings. They had different norms when it came to mass conversions by community, and individual conversions by Dalit women. It was applauded as a rational choice representing 'larger' good in one case and condemned as irrational in the other. This helped in marginalizing possibilities of autonomy within or outside the community, and in the reinstatement of oppressive patriarchies. These politicized entanglements generated what a scholar has called 'intimate politics' (Friedman, 2006: 3), a form of embodied struggle in which community agendas were formulated, contested and, in some cases, transformed through the bodies and practices of these women. Through a politics of representational heightening (as in clothing) and an erasure (as in romance), of telling and not telling, there was a complex playing out of Dalit women's desire.

However, the collective identities and patriarchies thus constructed were unstable. Agency was both constituted and subverted by existing structures of power. Through limited, but still subversive ways, the localized, quotidian and embodied practices of Dalit women resituated conversions in a realm of ambiguity, offering a new gendered self. The recalcitrance of desire threw up emancipatory possibilities of intimate rights, where highly ritualized acts of conversion, clothing and marriage could at times become a metaphor for a new vocabulary of body, of interiority, of subjectivity.

◆

This work has drawn upon material from Charu Gupta, 'Intimate Desires: Dalit Women and Religious Conversions in Colonial India', *The Journal of Asian Studies*, 73(3): 661–87, 2014 ©Association of Asian Studies, Inc., Cambridge University Press, reproduced with permission.

ACKNOWLEDGEMENTS

I presented earlier versions of this article at the Macquarie University, Australia, in August 2011, at a Workshop on A Social History of Caste and Intimacy at the Nehru Memorial Museum and Library, Delhi in December 2011, at a Conference on Engendering Rights in India at Chicago University in May 2012 and at an International Seminar on Living with Religious Diversity in Delhi in February 2013. I wish to thank the commentators and chairs, particularly Kaplan Ram, Anupama Rao, Mary John, Tanika Sarkar and Rajeswari Sunder Rajan, for their perceptive comments on these presentations. I am also grateful to the two anonymous reviewers for the *Journal of Asian Studies* for their critical reading.

NOTES

1. The term 'Dalit', literally meaning 'crushed' or 'broken to pieces', signifies a radical identity of 'untouchables' in India. Various terms like 'depressed classes', 'Harijan', 'scheduled castes', 'outcastes' have been used for them in colonial and present-day India, and all are ideologically loaded words. Further, terms like 'Chamar' and 'Bhangi', considered derogatory today, were often used in the writings of the colonial period. I use these terms, keeping in mind the historical contexts in this article. They are not meant to hurt any sensibilities.

2. *(Secret) Police Abstracts of Intelligence of UP Government (PAI)*. 14 April 1923: 241; *PAI*. 19 May 1928: 189.

3. 'Etah Zilla ke 400 Chamar' [400 Chamars of Etah District]. *Abhyudaya*. 22 August 1925: 5.

4. Also see 'Achchut aur Musalman' [Untouchables and Muslims]. *Abhyudaya*. 18 July 1925: 2; Editorial. 'Hinduon ka Haas' [Decline of Hindus]. *Sudha*. June 1929: 541; Editorial. 'Hinduon ka Bhayankar Haas' [Cataclysmic Decline of Hindus]. *Chand*, January 1929: 450–60.

5. Also see *PAI*. 1 July 1922: 1087; *PAI*. 7 April 1923: 226; *PAI*. 21 April 1923: 265, 266; *PAI*. 26 May 1923: 309; *PAI*. 9 June 1923: 332; *PAI*. 30 June 1923: 367; *PAI*. 23 February 1924: 75; *PAI*. 29 March 1924: 118; *PAI*. 31 March 1928: 124; *PAI*. 26 May 1928: 193; *PAI*. 13 February 1926: 84; *PAI*. 5 June 1926: 308; *PAI*. 19 June 1926: 327; *PAI*. 12 March 1927: 92; Editorial. 'Paap ki Granthiyan' [Books of Sin]. *Chand*. May 1929: 2–6 [special issue on 'Untouchables'].

6. Also see 140/1925. Home Poll. National Archives of India (NAI).

7. See, for example, *Abhydaya*. 13 March 1926: 1–2; *Chand*. May 1929: 41–51; *Chand*. May 1930: 268–74, 351–53.

8. *PAI*. 18 March 1922: 350; *PAI*. 25 March 1922: 597; *PAI*. 10 March 1923: 155; *PAI*. 5 April 1924: 126.

9. Mrs. Mohini Das. 1936. 'What Womanhood Owes to Christ'. *Indian Witness*. 11 June: 373, quoted in Webster (1994, 222).

10. *CMS Report, 1904–05*: 214, quoted in Alter (1986).

11. In the present context, a similar point has been made regarding Mayawati's sartorial style. See Nigam (2010, 254–55). He states that Mayawati's 'ostentatiousness' and her sartorial preferences can be read as her symbolic countermove, which mocks at Gandhi's attempt at 'representing poverty' and mourning through the semiotic transformation of his own body.

12. *Chand* was the leading women's periodical of early twentieth century, with a wide circulation. It was first published in 1922 from Chand Press in Allahabad by Ramrakh Singh Sehgal and his wife Vidyavati Devi. It often had voluminous issues of more than 100 pages, covering a diverse range of topics (Nijhawan, 2012; Orsini, 2002). Cartoons were regularly published in *Chand* and many of them were compiled and published by the Chand Press under the title *Vyanga Chitravali*. Conversions by outcastes became a regular subject of these caricatures in many newspapers and magazines of the time, highlighting a broad consensus and opposition to them. See, for example, various issues of *Chand; Vyanga Chitravali; Abhyudaya*. 13 March 1926: 9.

13. Ilaiah goes on to argue that unlike Gandhi and Nehru, Ambedkar always wore a suit, without facing any problems for his community, whereas Gandhi had to really struggle to de-Westernize himself.

14. I am grateful to Kalpana Ram for making this point.

15. *PAI*. 1 April 1922: 642; *PAI*. 13 May 1922: 845; *PAI*. 30 September 1922: 1466. *PAI*. 4 November 1922: 1577; Raghuvanshi (1916); Briggs (1920: 47).

16. *PAI*. 24 March 1923: 186; *PAI*. 29 September 1923: 503; *Abhyudaya*. 25 December 1926: 8; Blunt (1931, 241).

17. Also see 4/1927. Home Poll. NAI.

18. B. S. Moonje Papers. File No. 42/1935. Nehru Memorial Museum and Library.

19. Editorial. 'Paap ki Granthiyan' [Deeds of Sins]. *Chand*. May 1927: 4.

20. Shyambihari Lal. 'Samay ki Maang' [Call of the Times]. *Abhyudaya*. 31 October 1925: 3.

21. Editorial. 'Deviyon Savdhan' [Women Beware]. *Chand*. May 1924: 8–10; 'Achhut Nari ki Durdasha' [Pathetic Condition of Untouchable Woman]. *Chand*. May 1929: 177.

22. 'Stri Haran' [Women's Abduction], 'Samachar Sangrah'. *Chand*. June 1926: 215; 'Samachar Sangrah'. *Chand*. August 1926: 431; 'Samachar Sangrah'. *Chand*. December 1927: 312; 'Goondon ki Zyadti' [Misdeeds of *Goonda*s]; 'Samachar Sangrah'. *Chand*. February 1927: 472.

23. *Pratap*. 27 March 1938: 8.

24. *PAI*. 25 February 1939: 40.

25. *PAI*. 12 March 1927: 92.

26. *PAI*. 29 March 1924: 118.

27. *PAI*. 27 March 1926: 176.

28. *PAI*. 3 April 1926: 195.

29. *PAI*. 1 May 1926: 235.

30. *PAI*. 1 December 1928: 522.

31. *PAI*. 24 November 1934: 625.

32. *PAI*. 21 May 1938: 124.

33. *PAI*. 2 August 1946: 127.

34. *PAI*. 6 March 1926: 127.

35. *PAI*. 29 March 1924: 118.

36. *PAI.* 27 March 1926: 176.

37. *PAI.* 3 April 1926: 195.

38. *PAI.* 24 November 1934: 625.

39. *PAI.* 21 May 1938: 124.

40. *PAI.* 18 February 1939: 35.

41. *PAI.* 2 August 1946: 127.

REFERENCES

Abhyudaya. 1925–1926.

Allison, W. L. (ed.). 1969. *One Hundred Years of Christian Work of the North India Mission of the Presbyterian Church, USA.* Mysore: Wesley Press and Publishing House.

Alter, James P. 1986. *In the Doab and Rohilkhand: North Indian Christianity, 1815-1915.* Revised and completed by John Alter. Delhi: ISPCK.

Bandhusamaj. 1927. *Hinduon ki Tez Talwar.* Kanpur.

Bandyopadhyay, Sekhar. 2004. *Caste, Culture and Hegemony: Social Domination in Colonial Bengal.* Delhi: Sage.

Bannerji, Himani. 2001. *Inventing Subjects.* Delhi: Tulika.

Banprasthi, Premanand. 1927. *Musalmani Gorakh Dhandha* [Frauds of Muslims]. Awadh.

Barnes, R. and J. B. Eicher (eds.). 1992. *Dress and Gender: Making and Meaning.* Oxford: Berg.

Basu, Monmayee. 2001. *Marriage and Hindu Law: Sacrament to Contract.* Delhi: Oxford University Press.

Bauman, Chad M. 2008. *Christian Identity and Dalit Religion in Hindu India, 1868-1947.* Michigan: Wm. B. Eerdmans Publishing.

Bayly, Christopher. 1986. 'The Origins of Swadeshi (Home Industry): Cloth and Indian Society, 1700-1930', in Arjun Appadurai (ed.), *The Social Life of Things: Commodities in Cultural Perspective.* Cambridge: Cambridge University Press, pp. 285–322

Bayly, Susan. 1999. *Caste, Society and Politics in India from the Eighteenth Century to the Modern Age.* Cambridge: Cambridge University Press.

Bean, Susan. 1989. 'Gandhi and Khadi, the Fabric of Indian Independence', in Annette B. Weiner and Jane Schneider (eds.), *Cloth and Human Experience.* Washington: Smithsonian Institution Press.

Blunt, E.A.H. 1931. *The Caste System of Northern India: With Special Reference to UP.* London.

Briggs, G. W. 1920. *The Chamars.* Calcutta.

Brouwer, Ruth Compton. 1990. *New Women for God: Canadian Presbyterian Women and India Missions, 1876-1914.* Toronto: University of Toronto Press.

Burton, Antoinette. 1994. *Burdens of History: British Feminists, Indian Women and Imperial Culture, 1865-1915.* Chapel Hill: University of North Carolina Press.

Campbell, Mary J. 1918. *The Power House at Pathankot: What Some Girls of India Wrought by Prayer*. Lucknow: Women's Christian Temperance Union of India.

Census of India, 1931, UP, Vol. XVIII, Part I, Report. 1933. Allahabad.

Chand. 1924–1930.

Chandra Lila Sadhuni ka Vritant. 1910. 2nd edition. Allahabad: Christian Literature Society for India.

Chandra, Sudhir. 1998. *Enslaved Daughters: Colonialism, Law and Women's Rights*. Delhi: Oxford University Press.

Chandrikaprasad. 1917. *Hinduon ke Sath Vishwasghat*. Awadh.

Charitra Sudhar. 1910. Allahabad: Christian Literature Society for India.

Chatterjee, Indrani. 1999. *Gender, Slavery and Law in Colonial India*. Delhi: Oxford University Press.

Chowdhry, Prem. 2007. *Contentious Marriages, Eloping Couples: Gender, Caste and Patriarchy in Northern India*. Delhi: Oxford University Press.

Church Missionary Society (CMS). 1926. *The Mass Movement in the United Provinces: A Survey and Statement of Needs*. Kottayam: CMS Press.

Clarke, Sathianathan. 1998. *Dalits and Christianity: Subaltern Religion and Liberation Theology in India*. Delhi: Oxford University Press.

Clayton, A. C. 1911. *Preachers in Print: An Outline of the Work of the Christian Literary Society for India*. London.

Cohn, Bernard. 1989. 'Cloth, Clothes and Colonialism: Indian in the Nineteenth Century', in *Cloth and Human Experience*.

Collin, Marcus. 2003. *Modern Love: An Intimate History of Men and Women in Twentieth-Century Britain*. London: Atlantic Books.

Conference on Urdu and Hindi Christian Literature Held at Allahabad, 24–25 February 1875. 1875. Madras: The Christian Vernacular Education Society.

Copley, Antony. 1997. *Religions in Conflict: Ideology, Cultural Contact and Conversion in Late Colonial India*. Delhi: Oxford University Press.

Crooke, W. 1974 [1896]. *The Tribes and Castes of the North Western India: Vol. I*. Delhi: Cosmo Publications.

de Certeau, Michel. 1984. *The Practice of Everyday Life*. Translated by Steven F. Rendall. Berkeley.

De, Rohit. 2010. 'The Two Husbands of Vera Tiscenko: Apostasy, Conversion, and Divorce in Late Colonial India', *Law and History Review* 28(4): 1011–41.

Devi Devta aur Murtipuja. 1923. Allahabad: North India Christian Tract and Book Society, 2nd edition.

Dube, Saurabh. 1998. *Untouchable Pasts: Religion, Identity and Power among a Central Indian Community, 1780-1950*. Albany: State University of New York Press.

———. 2004. 'Colonial Registers of a Vernacular Christianity: Conversion to Translation', *Economic and Political Weekly*, 10 January: 161–71.

Dube, Sukhnandan Prasad. 1933. *Chuachut ka Bhut*. Lucknow.

Dwivedi, Manan. 1924. *Humara Bhishan Haas*. 3rd edition. Kanpur.

Eaton, Richard. 1993. *The Rise of Islam and the Bengal Frontier, 1204-1760*. Berkeley: University of California Press.

Emery, P. 1928. 'The Village Day School', in *Report of the Conference of the Depressed Classes Committee*, 9–11 October, Cawnpore: 13–19. Lucknow: Methodist Publishing House.

Fernandes, Walter. 1994. *Caste and Conversion Movements: Religion and Human Rights*. Delhi: Indian Social Institute.

Flemming, Leslie A. 1992. 'A New Humanity: American Missionaries' Ideals for Indian Women in North India, 1870-1930', in N. Chauduri and M. Strobel (eds.), *Western Women and Imperialism*. Bloomington: Indiana University Press, pp. 191–206.

Forbes, Geraldine H. 1986. 'In Search of the "Pure Heathen": Missionary Women in Nineteenth Century India', *Economic and Political Weekly*, XXI(17), 26 April: WS-2–WS-8.

Forrester, Duncan B. 1979. *Caste and Christianity: Attitudes and Policies on Caste on Anglo-Saxon Protestant Missions in India*. London: Curzon.

Foucault, Michel. 1979. *Discipline and Punish: The Birth of the Prison*. New York.

Freitag, S. B. 1989. *Collective Action and Community: Public Arenas and the Emergence of Communalism in North India*. Berkeley: University of California Press.

Friedman, Sara L. 2006. *Intimate Politics: Marriage, the Market, and State Power in Southeastern China*. Cambridge: Harvard University Press.

Gaines, Jane and Charlotte Herzog (eds.). 1990. *Fabrications: Costume and the Female Body*. New York: Routledge.

Galanter, Marc. 1997. *Law and Society in Modern India*. Delhi: Oxford University Press.

Ghai, R. K. 1990. *Shuddhi Movement in India: A Study of Its Socio-political Dimensions*, Delhi.

Gladstone, John Wilson. 1984. *Protestant Christianity and People's Movement in Kerala: A Study of Christian Mass Movements in Relation to Neo-Hindu Socio-Religious Movements in Kerala, 1850-1936*. Trivandrum: Seminary Publications.

Gooptu, Nandini. 2001. *The Politics of the Urban Poor in Early Twentieth Century India*. Cambridge: Cambridge University Press.

Gupta, Charu. 2001. *Sexuality, Obscenity, Community: Women, Muslims and the Hindu Public in Colonial India*. Delhi: Permanent Black.

———. 2010. 'Feminine, Criminal or Manly? Imaging Dalit Masculinities in Colonial North India', *Indian Economic and Social History Review* XLVII(3): 309–42.

Haggis, Jane. 2000. 'Ironies of Emancipation: Changing Configurations of "Women's Work" in the "Mission of Sisterhood" to Indian Women'. *Feminist Review*, 65, Summer: 108–26.

Hardgrave, Robert L. 1968. 'The Breast-Cloth Controversy: Caste Consciousness and Social Change in Southern Travancore', *Indian Economic and Social History Review*, 5(2): 171–87.

Hasan, Mushirul. 2007. *Wit and Humour in Colonial North India*. Delhi: Niyogi Books.

Heinrich, C. 1928. 'The Church's Responsibility for Evangelism', in *Report of the Conference of the Depressed Classes Committee*, 9–11 October, Cawnpore: 91–96. Lucknow: Methodist Publishing House.

Hindu Dharm ke Phal. 1905. 2nd edition. Allahabad: North Indian Christian Tract and Book Society.

Hinduon ki Nirdhanta. 1909. 2nd edition. Allahabad: North Indian Christian Tract and Book Society.

Home Political Branch. 1910–1938. National Archives of India, Delhi.

Ilaiah, Kancha. 2003. 'Cultural Globalization'. *The Hindu*. 22 February.

Jati ki Chut Chat. 1905. Allahabad: North Indian Christian Tract and Book Society.

Jati Panti ka Varnan. 1924. 4th edition. Allahabad: North Indian Christian Tract and Book Society.

Jati Pariksha. 1906. Allahabad: North Indian Christian Tract and Book Society.

Jha, Brijmohan. 1925. *Hinduon Jago*. 2nd edition. Agra.

Jigyasu, Chandrika Prasad. 1960. *Sri 108 Swami Achhutanandji Harihar*. Lucknow.

Jordens, J.T.F. 1981. *Swami Shraddhananda: His Life and Causes*. Delhi: Oxford University Press.

Kedia, Baijnath. 1933. *Vyanga Chitravali, Part I* [Selected Collection of Cartoons Depicting Social Evils of Indian Society]. Kashi.

Kent, Eliza F. 2004. *Converting Women: Gender and Protestant Christianity in Colonial South India*. New York: Oxford University Press.

Kooiman, Dick. 1989. *Conversion and Social Equality in India: The London Missionary Society in South Travancore in the 19th Century*. Delhi: Manohar.

Kshirsagar, R. K. 1994. *Dalit Movement in India and Its Leaders (1857–1956)*. Delhi: MD Publications.

Langhamer, Claire. 2007. 'Love and Courtship in Mid-Twentieth Century England', *The Historical Journal* 50(1): 173–96.

Lara Lari. 1905. 5th edition. Translated by Rev. W. F. Johnson. NITS.

Laxman, R. K. 1989. 'Freedom to Cartoon, Freedom to Speak', *Daedalus*, 118(4): 68–91.

Laxman, R. K. 1990. *The Best of Laxman*. Delhi: Penguin Books.

Lloyd, H. 1882. *Hindu Women: With Glimpses into Their Life and Zenanas*. London.

Lucas, J. J. n.d. *History of the North Indian Christian Tract and Book Society (1848-1934)*. Allahabad: Mission Press.

Lynch, Owen M. 1969. *The Politics of Untouchability: Social Mobility and Social Change in a City of India*. New York: Columbia University Press.

Mallampalli, Chandra. 2010. 'Escaping the Grip of Personal Law in Colonial India: Proving Custom, Negotiating Hindu-ness', *Law and History Review* 28(4): 1043–65.

Mem Sahiba aur Ayah ki Katha. 1896. Translated by Rev. W. F. Johnson, from a story by Mrs. Sherwood. CLS.

Menon, Dilip M. 2006. *The Blindness of Insight: Essays on Caste in Modern India*. Pondicherry: Navayana Publishing.

Moonje, B. S. Private Papers. Nehru Memorial Museum and Library.

Morris, Miss E. 1917. *Village Education: Its Goal and How to Attain It*. Ludhiana: Ludhiana Mission Steam Press.

Mujahid, Abdul Malik. 1989. *Conversion to Islam: Untouchables' Strategy for Protest in India*. Chambersburg: Anima Publications.

Nair, Janaki. 1996. *Women and Law in Colonial India: A Social History*. Delhi: Kali for Women.

Nesfield, J. S. 1882. *Brief View of the Caste System in North Western Provinces and Oudh*. Allahabad.

Nevill, H. R. 1904. *Meerut District Gazetteer*. Allahabad.

Nigam, Aditya. 2010. 'The Heterotopias of Dalit Politics: Becoming-Subject and the Consumption Utopia', in Michael D. Gordin, Helen Tilley and Gyan Prakash (eds.), *Utopia/Dystopia: Conditions of Historical Possibility*. Princeton: Princeton University Press, pp. 250–76.

Nijhawan, Shobna. 2012. *Women and Girls in the Hindi Public Sphere: Periodical Literature in Colonial North India*. Delhi: Oxford University Press.

Oddie, Geoffrey A. 1969. 'Protestant Missions, Caste and Social Change in India, 1850-1914', *Indian Economic and Social History Review*, VI, September: 259–91.

———. 1997. *Religious Conversion Movements in South Asia: Continuities and Change 1800-1900*. Surrey: Curzon Press.

Oesterheld, Christina and Claus Peter Zoller (eds.). 1999. *Of Clowns and Gods, Brahmans and Babus: Humour in South Asian Literature*. Delhi: Manohar.

Orsini, Francesca. 2002. *The Hindi Public Sphere, 1920-1940: Language and Literature in the Age of Nationalism*. Delhi: Oxford University Press.

———. 2007. 'Introduction', in Francesca Orsini (ed.), *Love in South Asia: A Cultural History*. Delhi: Cambridge University Press India, pp. 1–39.

Pandey, Gyanendra. 1978. *The Ascendancy of the Congress in UP, 1926-34: A Study in Imperfect Mobilisation*. Delhi: Oxford University Press.

———. 2006. 'The Time of the Dalit Conversion'. *Economic and Political Weekly*, 6 May: 1779–88.

Parmanand, Bhai. 1928. *Hindu Jati ka Rahasya*. Lucknow.

Pati, Biswamoy. 2003. *Identity, Hegemony and Resistance: Towards the Social History of Conversions in Orissa, 1800-2000*. Delhi: Three Essays Collective.

Pemberton, J. F. and L. C. Perfumi. 1915. *A Century of Work in Meerut, 1815-1915*. Sikandra.

Philip, Puthenveettil O. 1925. *The Depressed Classes and Christianity*. Calcutta: The National Christian Council and Madras, Allahabad, Rangoon Colombo: The Christian Literature Society for India.

Phillips, Godfrey E. 1912. *The Outcastes Hope or Work among the Depressed Classes in India*. London: Young People's Missionary Movement.

Pickett, J. Waskom. 1933. *Christian Mass Movements in India: A Study with Recommendations*. Lucknow: Lucknow Publishing House.

Pitman, Emma Raymond. 1906. *Indian Zenana Missions: Their Need, Origin, Objects, Agents, Modes of Working and Results*. London: John Snow & Co.

Police Abstracts of Intelligence of UP Government, 1922-40 (PAI). Lucknow: Criminal Investigation Department Office.

Pratap. 1938.

Raghuvanshi, U.B.S. 1916 *Chanvar Puran* [A Caste Tract on the Chamars]. Aligarh.

Ramagundam, Rahul. 2008. *Gandhi's Khadi: A History of Contention and Conciliation*. Delhi: Orient Longman.

Rao, Anupama. 2009. *The Caste Question: Dalits and the Politics of Modern India*. Delhi: Permanent Black.

Ratnmala. 1869. Allahabad: Christian Vernacular Education Society, Mission Press.

Rawat, Ramnarayan S. 2012. *Reconsidering Untouchability: Chamars and Dalit History in North India*. Delhi: Permanent Black.

Raychaudhuri, Tapan. 2000. 'Love in a Colonial Climate: Marriage, Sex and Romance in Nineteenth-Century Bengal', *Modern Asian Studies*, 34(2): 349–78.

Ross, Robert. 2008. *Clothing: A Global History*. Cambridge: Polity.

Sahay, K. N. 1998. *An Anthropological Study of Cartoon in India*. Delhi: Commonwealth Publishers.

Sangari, Kumkum. 2001. *Politics of the Possible: Essays on Gender, History, Narratives, Colonial English*. Delhi: Tulika.

Sanyasi, Shradhanand. 1919. *Jati ke Dinon ko Mat Tyago Arthat 7 Karor Dinon Ki Raksha*. Delhi: Sadharma Pracharak Press.

Sarkar, Tanika. 2009. *Rebels, Wives, Saints: Designing Selves and Nations in Colonial Times*. Ranikhet: Permanent Black.

Semple, Rhonda Anne. 2003. *Missionary Women: Gender, Professionalism and the Victorian Idea of Christian Mission*. UK: Boydell Press.

Sharda, Chand Karan. 1925. *Dalitodhar*. Ajmer.

Sharma, Raj Bahadur. 1988. *Christian Missions in North India 1813-1913 (A Case Study of Meerut Division and Dehra Dun District)*. Delhi: Mittal Publications.

Shukla, Ramgopal. 1934. *Achchutodhar Arthat Kattar Panthiyon ki Chillapon*. 2nd edition. Kanpur.

Sikand, Yoginder Singh. 2004. *Islam, Caste and Dalit-Muslim Relations in India*. Delhi: Global Media Publications.

Singh, Maina Chawala. 2000. *Gender, Religion and 'Heathen Lands': American Missionary Women in South Asia (1860s-1940s)*. New York: Garland Publishing.

Singh, Mohinder. 1947. *The Depressed Classes: Their Economic and Social Condition*. Bombay: Hind Kitab Ltd.

Singha, Radhika. 1998. *A Despotism of Law: Crime and Justice in Early Colonial India*. Delhi: Oxford University Press.

Speer, Robert E. and Constance M. Hallock (eds.). 1939. *Christian Home Making*. New York: Round Table Press.

Stewart, A. M. 1928. 'Education of Village Girls', in *Report of the Conference of the Depressed Classes Committee*, 9–11 October, Cawnpore: 27–30. Lucknow: Methodist Publishing House.

Stoler, Ann Laura. 1995. *Race and the Education of Desire: Foucault's History of Sexuality and the Colonial Order of Things*. Durham and London: Duke University Press.

Sudha. 1929.

Survey of Evangelistic Work, Punjab Mission of the Presbyterian Church USA. 1929. Lucknow.

Tarlo, Emma. 1996. *Clothing Matters: Dress and Identity in India.* Chicago: University of Chicago Press.

Trivedi, Lisa N. 2007. *Clothing Gandhi's Nation: Homespun and Modern India.* Bloomington: Indiana University Press.

Upadhyaya, Gangaprasad. 1925. *Padri Sahib se Bacho* [Beware of Priest]. Prayag: Arya Samaj Chowk.

Vishwanathan, Gauri. 1998. *Outside the Fold: Conversion, Modernity, and Belief.* Princeton: Princeton University Press.

Vyanga Chitravali. 1930. Allahabad: 'Chand' Karyalaya.

Walton, H. G. 1903. *A Monograph on Tanning and Working in Leather in the United Provinces of Agra and Oudh.* Allahabad.

Webster, John C. B. 1994. *The Dalit Christians: A History.* 2nd edition. Delhi: ISPCK.

———. 1999. *Religion and Dalit Liberation.* Delhi: Manohar.

Zelliot, Eleanor. 1992. *From Untouchable to Dalit: Essays of Ambedkarite Movement*, Delhi: Manohar.

◆◆

6 BUDDHISM IN INDIAN PHILOSOPHY*

RAGHURAMARAJU

I

The radical and the ritual are two significant aspects surrounding the phenomenon of religion. The radical consists of elements that differ, disagree, dissent, oppose or even exclude the then existing religion, or religions. This could be with respect to either their ideas or practice. The ritual or regulative is concerned with formulating, systematizing, building, laying the rules, maintaining, emulating and eventually consolidating new ideas. Giving importance to the latter and not factoring in the former can seriously compromise one's understanding of the nature of religion. Further, let me reinforce my argument by introducing a distinction between a leader and a follower. A leader is one who knows how to handle not only what is politically correct but also that which is politically incorrect. The competence about these two realms significantly distinguishes a leader from the followers. The follower mostly deals with what is politically correct. If we take into consideration the second aspect, we then cover only the confirmative aspect of religion, while leaving out its radical aspect. Very often, a new religion begins with a difference; hence, difference forms the foundation of religion. Even the novelty of a new religion comes later in the chronological order. There is an imperative need to take note of these foundations and their chronological order, not only to arrive at a comprehensive idea of a religion but also to understand its later functions. The immediate reason for bringing this to the table of discussion is to make a case for the indispensable significance of difference between two, or amongst more than two religions, or even philosophies. This chapter, therefore, presents a critique of an attempt – an arduous attempt – to deny the difference between two important philosophical or religious schools, between Hinduism and Buddhism.

S. Radhakrishnan tries to absorb Buddhism into Hinduism. He undertook this task in *Volume I* of his magnum opus, *Indian Philosophy*. Radhakrishnan expends a great deal of time upon accomplishing this task; he offers a variety of resources, and advances various philosophical arguments. To begin with, he does acknowledge the originality and uniqueness of the Buddha and Buddhism. With reference to early Buddhism, he writes:

> There is no question that the system of early Buddhism is one of the most original which the history of philosophy presents. In its fundamental ideas and essential spirit it approximates remarkably to the advanced scientific thought of the nineteenth century. The modern pessimistic philosophy of Germany, that of Schopenhauer and Hartmann, is only a revised version of ancient Buddhism. It is sometimes said to be 'little more than Buddhism vulgarized.' As far as the dynamic conception of reality is concerned, Buddhism is a splendid prophecy of the creative evolution of Bergson. Early Buddhism suggests the outline of a philosophy suited to the practical wants to the present day and helpful in reconciling the conflict between faith and science (2008: 287).

Therefore, in Radhakrishnan's assessment, Buddhism is original; it is a precursor, inspiring the pessimistic philosophy of Germany; it is practical and, more importantly, it is up to date. Having thus eulogized Buddhism, Radhakrishnan proceeds to identify certain important shifts in philosophy brought about by the Buddha, the most important being that while the Upanisads were 'a work of many minds', Buddhism, on the other hand, was the 'considered creed of a single individual' (ibid.: 291). Indicating another difference between the Upanisads and Buddhism, Radhakrishnan states that in the 'Upanisads we have an amazing study of an atmosphere, in Buddhism the concrete embodiment of thought in the life of a man' (ibid.: 291). This shift away from many minds to a single individual and the ensuing unity of thought and life was, according to Radhakrishnan, what 'worked wonderfully on the world of the time' and was in fact responsible for the 'success of early Buddhism' (ibid.: 291).

Radhakrishnan proceeds to acknowledge Buddha's contribution. Buddha, he avers, 'wished to steer clear of profitless metaphysical discussions' (ibid.: 297). He first emphasized the special and novel aspects of Buddhism, noting the shift it brought about and acknowledging its contribution. This enhances the image of Buddhism. He, however, goes on to make his move to undermine the position of Buddhism, which we shall see how, through a long chain of argumentation.

Radhakrishnan now reports that the Upanisads and Brahmanism's 'creed' was 'collapsing' and their system 'disintegrating'. The unsaid subtext of this statement is that Buddhism did not take on a strong philosophical system, but one that was already in decline. In that sense, the statement erodes the importance of Buddhism. Radhakrishnan goes on to explain, however, that it was against the background of this disintegrated system that Buddha sought to 'provide a firm foundation for morality' on the 'rock of facts' (ibid.: 300). This firm foundation, provided by ancient Buddhism, claims Radhakrishnan, 'resembled positivism in its attempt to shift the centre from the worship of God to the service of man' (ibid.: 300–301).

Radhakrishnan then asserts that early Buddhism was 'not an absolutely original doctrine' (ibid.: 303). He reads the word 'original' to mean breaking away completely from the age and country. Radhakrishnan thus surprises the readers by claiming that Buddhism 'is no freak in the evolution of Indian thought' and 'Buddha did not break away completely from the spiritual ideas of his age and country' (ibid.: 303). As the statement shows, the definition of originality that Radhakrishnan uses is problematic; at the very least it is an interpolation within Buddhism and is external to it. To substantiate his move, Radhakrishnan offers an argument by introducing a distinction; he writes: 'open revolt against the conventional and legalistic religion of the time is one thing; to abandon the living spirit lying behind it is another' (ibid.: 303). There is something unconvincing about this change in Radhakrishnan's attitude towards Buddhism; but let us move on to analyse his next move. Claiming the Buddha as part of a continuous ancient way of being, he declares that 'Buddha himself admits that the dharma which he has discovered by an effort of self-culture is the ancient way, the Aryan path, the eternal dharma' (ibid.: 303). Radhakrishnan writes:

> Buddha is not so much creating a new dharma as rediscovering an old norm. It is the venerable tradition that is being adapted to meet the special needs of the age.... Early Buddhism, we venture to hazard a conjecture, is only a restatement of the thought of the Upanisads from a new standpoint (ibid.: 303).

In this view, Buddhism is not a break from tradition but a reformed, hermeneutic version of the same tradition from a fresh standpoint. Thus, in his interpretation, Buddhism is parasitic on a Brahmanism in need of reform and possesses no autonomy of its own outside this ambit. Radhakrishnan proposes to substantiate the claim that the 'spirit of the Upanisads is the life-spring of' early Buddhism by pointing out the aspects that these two philosophies have in common:

(i) Both the Upanisads and early Buddhism accept the 'doctrine of impermanence' (ibid.: 313).

(ii) Buddha, 'following the Brahmanical theory, presents hell for the wicked and rebirth for the imperfect' (ibid.: 374).

(iii) Only 'metaphysics that can justify Buddha's ethical discourse is the metaphysics underlying the Upanisads'. And Buddha did not look upon himself as an innovator, but only a restorer of the ancient way, i.e., the way of the Upanisads (ibid.: 397).

(iv) Finally, the incomprehensibility of the absolute by the intellect is accepted by both the schools.

Thus, for Radhakrishnan, Buddhism '... is a return of Brahmanism to its own fundamental principles' (ibid.: 398–99). Having drawn out the commonalities between Buddhism and Brahmanism, Radhakrishnan states, however, that Buddhism brought about the democratic practice of including the masses by breaking open the exclusivism of the Upanisads (ibid.: 398). Nonetheless, even this concession to Buddhism that Radhakrishnan makes, in acknowledging its contribution towards democratizing Hinduism, is immediately weakened when he goes on to say that such 'democratic upheavals are common features of Hindu history' (ibid.: 398). Revealing his desperation and the vulnerability of his position by resorting to examples from the post-Buddha period, Radhakrishnan writes that when 'the treasures of the great sages were the private property of a few, Rāmānuja, the great Vaisnava teacher, proclaimed the mystic texts to even the pariahs' (ibid.: 398).

Having underscored the attributes common to the two systems, Radhakrishnan makes the bold move of ironing out two major differences between Buddhism and Brahmanism, namely, the denial of *atman*, and the rejection of caste, by the Buddha. With reference to the first, Radhakrishnan claims that the Buddha advocated both *atma-vada* and *anatma-vada*. To quote:

> The two doctrines were preached by Buddha for two very different objects. He taught the existence of Ātman when he wanted to impart to his hearers the conventional doctrine; he taught the doctrine of an-Ātman when he wanted to impart to them the transcendental doctrine (ibid.: 328).

The Buddha's adherence to this dual position, according to Radhakrishnan, is played down by later interpreters like Nagasena, who 'drew the negative inference that there was no soul' (ibid.: 331). Nagasena, alleges Radhakrishnan, ignored the Buddha's silence. Hence, according to Radhakrishnan, this difference between atman and an-atman is not a substantial one.

Making a further point, Radhakrishnan claims that the Buddha did not 'oppose the institution [of caste], but adopts the Upanisad standpoint [which is that] [t]he Brāhmin or the leader of society is not so much a Brāhmin by birth as by character' (ibid.: 369). In his view, the Buddha undermines that spirit of caste which later gave rise to inhuman practices. Yet, even this reformist move, for him, is not new to Brahmanical theory, as the latter too 'looked upon the highest status of the Sannyāsin as above caste' (ibid.: 370). Summing up his views on this topic he writes:

> ... in the world of thought both Upanisads and Buddhism protested against the rigours of caste. Both allowed the highest spiritual dignity to the poor and the humble, but neither rooted out the

Vedic institutions and practices, though on this point Buddhism is a little more successful than Brāhmanism (ibid.: 371).

Thus, for Radhakrishnan, the Buddha does not reject caste outright, as has been attributed to him, but only rejects its subsequent corrupt versions. More importantly, the Upanisads, in Radhakrishnan's interpretation, do not clearly advocate caste. Having identified all these common features between Buddhism and Brahmanism, Radhakrishnan makes yet another move in the same direction and claims that the Buddha is dependent on Hinduism. He writes: 'The rules of Buddhist Sangha were borrowed from the Brāhmanical codes, though they were adapted to missionary purposes' (ibid.: 369).

At the end of the discussion Radhakrishnan turns the matter on its head when he points out a central defect in Buddhism. He writes that the 'central defect of Buddha's teaching is that in his ethical earnestness he took up and magnified one half of the truth and made it look as if it were the whole' (ibid.: 399). Radhakrishnan attributes this error to the Buddha's 'distaste for metaphysics' that consequently 'prevented him from seeing that the partial truth had a necessary complement and rested on principles which carried it beyond its self-imposed limits' (ibid.: 399). Explaining Hinduism's hostility towards Buddhism, Radhakrishnan writes:

> The Hindu quarrels not so much with the metaphysical conceptions of Buddha as with his practical programme. Freedom of thought and rigidity in practice have marked the Hindu from the beginning of his history. The Hindu will accept as orthodox the Sāmkhya and the Pūrva Mimāmsā systems of thought, regardless of their indifference to theism, but will reject Buddhism in spite of its strong ethical and spiritual note, for the simple reason that the former do not interfere with the social life and organisation, while the latter insists on bringing its doctrine near to the life of the people (ibid.: 596).

Radhakrishnan goes on to add that:

> While the Upanisads tolerated, even if they did not encourage the caste rules, Buddha's scheme definitely undermined the institution of caste (ibid.: 597).

This is not only important but also interesting, as it discloses the substantial threat the Buddha poses to Brahmanism. While other schools of Indian philosophy offered differences in the realm of ideas, Buddhism threatened to intervene in both its social life and organization. In this context, it sought to diminish the distance between theory and practice. It is this move by the Buddha, according to Radhakrishnan, which threatened to change the organization of social life that incurred the wrath of the Hindus.

Thus, Radhakrishnan begins by acknowledging that Buddhism is original, modern and scientific, a trendsetter and a practical and updated school of thought. He then identifies Buddhism as a system that revolves around a single individual, and which sought to remove abstract metaphysics. Subsequently, as if reversing this view, Radhakrishnan claims that early Buddhism is not an original doctrine but merely presents the Upanisads from a new standpoint. In support of his assertion, Radhakrishnan points out common themes in Buddhism and Hinduism, and explains the differences between the two, such as anatma-vada and the rejection of caste in Buddhism. While conceding that Buddhism broke open the exclusivist tendencies in the Upanisads and facilitated the participation of the masses, Radhakrishnan nonetheless underplays this ostensibly unique characteristic too by claiming that these democratic overtures are also found in Hinduism, thus erasing this difference between Buddhism and Hinduism. In conclusion, Radhakrishnan points out the defects in the Buddha's teachings and states the reasons for Hindus being intolerant of Buddhism. As I have already pointed out, there is something unconvincing about the long and arduous route of philosophical argumentation that Radhakrishnan has undertaken. We must, however, note three points in his discussion: first, the politics of denying differences between Hinduism and Buddhism underlying his attempt; second, his solid and persistent attempt at offering a philosophical argument in support of his view; and third, his acknowledgment of the sociological fact that Buddhism posed a real threat to Hindu society.

While disagreeing with Radhakrishnan's attempt to deny the differences between Buddhism and the Upanisads, we must, however, pay close attention to two other aspects. A close scrutiny of his argument shows that he is making two important points here: (a) he endorses Buddhism's attempt to reduce the gap between theory and practice present in corrupted versions of the Upanisads and Brahmanism; (b) he admits that this attempt by the Buddha angered the Hindus.

Even though Radhakrishnan makes his point on behalf of Hindus, it must be noted that he concedes the fact that Buddhism did perform this act of attempting to reduce the gap. This fact was also highlighted by B. R. Ambedkar, although, unlike Radhakrishnan, he bolstered the radical difference between Buddhism and Hinduism. Before I discuss Ambedkar let me report yet another view, that of Ganganatha Jha, that concurs broadly with Radhakrishnan. Jha, in the introduction to his English translation of *The Tattvasangraha of Shântaraksita with a Commentary of Kamalashila*, traces the attempt to establish common features between Hinduism and Buddhism to Vijñânabhiksu. Agreeing with him, Jha says,

> I have often felt, – as Vijñânabhiksu also felt – that there was deep kinship between 'Vedânta' and 'Buddhist Idealism', – the only difference of importance being that while the Buddhist Idealist regarded *Jñâna*, like everything else, to be momentary, though *real* – more real, at any rate, than the External world, – the Vedanta regarded *Jñâna*, at least, the Highest Jñâna, 'Consciousness', which is the same as 'Soul', the highest Self, to be the only Reality – and *permanent* (1986: viii) .

Tracing this move to reconcile the difference between these rival schools to pre-Samkara and stating his differences with the prevalent view he says,

> We have been inclined to regard this as an achievement of the Great Shankarâchârya who succeeded thus in reconciling Hinduism and Buddhism and thus helping the fusion of the two. – It seems however that this feature of the 'Vedânta', this stressing of the eternality of '*Jñâna*', at any rate, was older than Shankarâchârya, – if we admit the date usually assigned to this great writer (ibid.: viii).

He thus concludes that Shankarâchârya who came after the seventh century can be 'credited only with having *emphasized* this idea and thereby led to the fusion of the two Philosophies or Religions' (ibid.: viii, emphasis in the original). So there is a long history to this attempt and Radhakrishnan is merely a recent participant on this already trodden path.

II

In sharp contrast to Radhakrishnan, Ambedkar emphasizes the radical stand of the Buddha and Buddhism. Ambedkar rejects the Vedas and the Upanisads and accepts Sankhya in addition to Buddhism in Indian philosophy. Interestingly, although he accepts Sankhya, he rejects the Bhagavad Gita. He claims that the aim of the Gita was to 'defend certain dogmas of religion on philosophical grounds' (Rodrigues, 2010: 193). This is intriguing since the Gita is based on the metaphysics of Sankhya.

For Ambedkar, the Vedas are a collection of *mantras*, i.e., hymns, or chants, and are 'mere invocations to deities such as *Indra, Varuna, Agni, Soma, Isana, Prajapati, Bramha, Mahiddhi, Yama* and others'. There is not 'much philosophy in the Vedas' except 'speculations of a philosophical nature' about the 'origin' of the world, the creation of 'individual things' and their maintenance (ibid.: 205). The Buddha, according to Ambedkar, 'did not regard all the Vedic sages as worthy of reverence', but only 'ten Vedic Rishis'. He did not see anything 'morally elevating' in the Vedic mantras. Ambedkar argues that for the Buddha, the '*Vedas* were as worthless as a desert', and so he 'discarded' them as 'useless' (ibid.: 207).

The Brahmanas are a part of the Vedas, and both are called *Sruti*. The Brahmanic philosophy, says Ambedkar, held the Vedas as not only 'sacred' but also 'infallible'. Further, for Brahmanic philosophy, 'performance of Vedic sacrifices and observances of religious rites and ceremonies and the offering of gifts to Brahmins' can save souls from transmigration and give them salvation. In addition to this, Ambedkar points out, Brahmins have a theory for an ideal society, that is the *Chaturvarna*, which entailed the division of society into four classes: Brahmins, Kshatriyas, Vaishyas and Shudras. These classes are not equal but are ruled by 'graded inequality'. The first one is placed at the top, while the last one is relegated to the bottom. There is also a division of occupations, which is 'exclusive' and does not permit trespass. Another rule of this theory of an ideal society is that education must be denied to Shudras and women of all classes. A further rule is that a man's life is divided into four stages. This, Ambedkar explains, is the 'divine pattern of an ideal society called Chaturvarna' (ibid.: 212). Finally, the Brahmanas also endorsed the doctrine of karma (ibid.: 212).

The Buddha, insists Ambedkar, 'strongly opposed' the thesis that the Vedas are 'infallible' and that their authority 'should never be questioned' (ibid.: 212). On the contrary, he declares that 'nothing was infallible and nothing could be final' (ibid.: 213). The Buddha also denies any 'virtue in sacrifice'. While accepting sacrifice in the 'sense of self-denial for the good of others' as true sacrifice, the Buddha regards as false sacrifice the 'killing of animals as an offering to God for personal benefit' (ibid.: 213). He also rejects the theory of Chaturvarna as unnatural, arbitrary, rigid and bereft of freedom. While conceding that inequality 'exists in every society', the Buddha, writes Ambedkar, rejects Brahmanism that endorses graded inequality. Ambedkar explains:

> Far from producing harmony, graded inequality, the Buddha thought, might produce in society an ascending scale of hatred and a descending scale of contempt, and might be a source of perpetual conflict (ibid.: 214).

The Buddha found this ordering of society to be not only selfish but also wrong, designed to serve the interests of a few at the cost of all, particularly, the Shudras and women. Being denied access to learning and education, these segments of society did not know who was responsible for their degraded condition. Their ignorance, instead of causing them to rebel against Brahmanism, made them 'become the devotees and upholders of Brahmanism' (ibid.: 215). So, for these reasons, concludes Ambedkar, 'the Buddha rejected Brahmanism as being opposed to the true way of life' (ibid.: 215).

In Ambedkar's critique of the Upanisads, the '... main thesis of the *Upanishads* was that Brahman was a reality and that Atman was the same as Brahman. The Atman did not realize that it was Brahman because of the *Upadhis* in which it was entangled'. So, the question [as asked by the Upanisads] was: 'Is Brahmana a reality?' In Ambedkar's reckoning, the 'acceptance of the Upanishadic thesis depended upon the answer to this question' (ibid.: 216). In contrast, says Ambedkar, the 'Buddha could find no proof in support of the thesis that Brahman was a reality. He, therefore, rejected the thesis of the *Upanishads*' (ibid.: 216). The question above was put to no less a person than Yajnavalkya, 'a great seer who plays so important a part in the *Brihadarnyaka Upanishad*'. He was asked: 'What is Brahman? What is Atman?' All that Yajnavalkya could say was: '*Neti! Neti!* I know not! I know not!' How can anything be a 'reality about which no one knows anything', asked the Buddha (ibid.: 216). The Buddha had, therefore, no difficulty in rejecting the Upanisadic thesis as being based on pure imagination (ibid.: 216). In contrast to Radhakrishnan, Ambedkar sees no commonalities between the Upanisads and Buddhism. Rather, in Ambedkar's view, the Buddha clearly and wholly rejected not only the Vedas but also the Upanisads.

Although Ambedkar rejects outright the Vedas, Brahmanas and the Upanisads, he accepts, together with Buddhism, the importance of one old system of Indian philosophy – Sankhya. Ambedkar considers Kapila, the founder of Sankhya, to be the most pre-eminent 'among the ancient philosophers of India' (ibid.: 207). An important dimension of Ambedkar's philosophy is that although he endorses the philosophy of Sankhya, he does not accept the Bhagvad Gita, which is based on the metaphysics of Sankhya. Also, Ambedkar made another interesting move, in this context, by revealing the close relationship between the Gita and Buddhism.

According to Ambedkar, the Gita is not a 'gospel', and hence it has 'no message'. It only defends 'certain dogmas of religion on philosophical grounds' (ibid.: 193). The first dogma the Gita defends is the justification of war on the basis of the mortality of human existence (ibid.: 194). Second, it defends the dogma of the Chaturvarna by 'linking it to the theory of innate, inborn qualities in men' (ibid.: 194). The third such defence is of *Karma Marga*: that is, the selfish motive behind performance of the karma is removed by 'introducing the principle of Anasakti, i.e., performance of Karma without any attachment for the fruits of the Karma' (ibid.: 195).

Ambedkar dismisses the Gita's Chaturvarna theory. Referring to Krishna's defence of the Chaturvarna, which is based on Sankhya's Guna theory, Ambedkar writes:

> In the Chaturvarnya there are four Varnas. But the gunas according to Sankhya are only three. How can a system of four varnas be defended on the basis of a philosophy which does not recognize more than three varnas? (ibid.: 197).

Underscoring the carefully timed efforts of the Gita to rescue the doctrines of counter-revolution, Ambedkar writes:

> Nonetheless there is not the slightest doubt that without the help of the *Bhagvad Gita* the counter-revolution would have died out ... if the counter-revolution lives even today, it is entirely due to the plausibility of the philosophic defence which it receives from the *Bhagvad Gita* ... (ibid.: 197–98).

Ambedkar goes on to claim that there is no difference between Jaimini's *Purva Mimamsa* and the Bhagvad Gita. If there were any difference, it would lie, according to Ambedkar, in the Gita being a 'more formidable supporter of counter-revolution' and therefore providing a 'permanent basis which they never had before and without which they [that is, the counter-revolutionaries] would never have survived' (ibid.: 198). In this context, Ambedkar asserts – contrary to those like Telang and Tilak – that the Gita 'has been composed after Jaimini's *Purva Mimamsa* and after Buddhism' (ibid.: 199). Ambedkar rejects those 'typical' Hindu scholars who are 'reluctant to admit that the *Bhagvad Gita* is anyway influenced by Buddhism and is ever ready to deny that the *Gita* has borrowed anything from Buddhism' (ibid.: 202). With reference to these 'typical' Hindu scholars, Ambedkar writes:

> It is the attitude of Professor Radhakrishnan and so also of Tilak. Where there is any similarity in thought between the *Bhagvad Gita* and Buddhism too strong and too close to be denied, the argument is that it is borrowed from the *Upanishads*. ...[to thus avoid] allow[ing] any credit to Buddhism on any account (ibid.: 202).

Pointing out the similarities between the Gita and Buddhism, not only in 'ideas but also in language' he says:

> The *Bhagvad Gita* discusses *Brahma-Nirvana*. The steps by which one reaches *Brahma-Nirvana* are stated by the *Bhagvad Gita* to be (1) *Shraddha* (faith in oneself); (2) *Vyavasaya* (firm determination); (3) *Smriti* (remembrance of the goal); (4) *Samadhi* (earnest contemplation) and (5) *Prajna* (insight or true knowledge) (ibid.: 203).

In identifying the source whence the Gita borrowed the Nirvana theory Ambedkar points out that as 'no *Upanishad* even mentions the word Nirvana' the 'whole idea is peculiarly Buddhist and is borrowed from Buddhism' (ibid.: 203). There are other ideas in the Gita that are borrowed from Buddhism, Ambedkar asserts. They are: the definition of a true devotee: '(1) *maitri* (loving kindness); (2) *karuna* (compassion); (3) *mudita* (sympathising joy); and (4) *upeksa* (unconcernedness)'. These are found in *Mahpadana Sutta* and *Tevijja Sutta*. The other idea that the Gita takes from Buddhism is on the question of what knowledge is and what ignorance is. The explication, in chapter XIII, 'reproduced word for word the main doctrines of Buddhism...' from the Gospel of Buddha (ibid.: 204). Further, even the 'new metaphorical interpretation of karmas' in chapter VIII is a 'verbatim reproduction of the words of Buddha' from *Majjhina Nikaya I, 286 Sutta XVI* (ibid.: 204). Thus, Ambedkar concludes that the:

> ... *Bhagvad Gita* seems to be deliberately modelled on Buddhist *Suttas*. The Buddhist *Suttas* are dialogues. So is the *Bhagvad Gita*. Buddha's religion offered salvation to women and *Shudras*, Krishna also comes forward to offer salvation to women and *Shudras*. Buddhists say, 'I surrender to Buddha, to Dhamma and to Sangha.' So Krishna says, 'Give up all religions and surrender unto Me.' No parallel can be closer than what exists between Buddhism and the *Bhagvad Gita* (ibid.: 204).

Therefore, we have in Ambedkar an acceptance of Buddhism and those aspects of the Sankhya that were accepted by the Buddha, and a complete rejection of the Vedas, Brahmanas, Upanisads and the Gita. The last, Ambedkar argues, is a response to Buddhism, and is a philosophical defence of Purva Mimamsa. While Radhakrishnan denies any significant difference between Hinduism and Buddhism, Ambedkar in contrast, reinforces the differences. While Ambedkar uses the differences between Hinduism and Buddhism to claim the rejection of the former by the latter, Radhakrishnan, on the other hand, explains the differences away to establish continuity between the former and the latter. Although Radhakrishnan attempts to erase the differences between Hinduism and Buddhism – and this may not be a politically correct thing to do – he seriously engages with the issue and persistently pursues his line of argument, philosophically. It is one thing to disagree with Radhakrishnan and another to dispense with him. Thus, there is a need to distinguish between political correctness and theoretical engagement. Not pursuing ideas with theoretical rigour can, at times, cost politics heavily. This is particularly so, not while making political claims, but when it comes to making sure political claims endure. In the case of Ambedkar, he is politically correct. He clearly, but only briefly, states his differences with his contemporaries such as Telang, Tilak and Radhakrishnan. However, what Ambedkar has stated has not been progressively followed up and explored further by the philosophical community.

There is a need to extend Ambedkar's engagement with different traditions and make these philosophically more rigorous, and to bring in rich resources from Buddhism, particularly in relation to Hinduism. In an interesting paper, Gopal Guru makes a claim for Dalits to take to theory (2002). I would want to extend this to include a philosophical engagement with Buddhism and reopen the critical philosophical engagement with Hinduism. Along with the political claims clearly stated by Ambedkar, the philosophical insights and ideas available in his writings can be extensively elaborated. These can be further related to the core, the fundamental philosophical themes in Buddhism as well as Hinduism: this opening between political ideas that are extended to philosophical discussions, and insights that are formulated as philosophical theories, relating Ambedkar to Buddhism and highlighting his critique of Hinduism, and reopening the critical relation between Buddhism and Hinduism – all these can reinvigorate the discussion on Indian philosophy. This manner of the clearing of a space, or making an opening, has successful precedents, since this is what was undertaken by Buddhist philosophers in relation to the Buddha. They extended and philosophically formulated his ideas in a metaphysical discourse, even though the Buddha rejected metaphysics. The rich and extensive philosophical resources from Buddhism can be used to consolidate the critique of Hinduism initiated by Ambedkar. This, in my reading, would not only consolidate the political views that Ambedkar proposed but also make the debate between Hinduism and Buddhism more current. Hence, we may say that Ambedkar brings political correctness to the discussion, making it more contemporary. However, one of the limitations in Ambedkar is that, in his preoccupation with exposing the injustice done by Hindu society to Dalits, he considers only the impact of Buddhism on the Gita, without considering the impact of Hinduism on Buddhism. In other words, both Radhakrishnan and Ambedkar tend to take extreme positions, albeit in opposite directions. It is in this context that I shall discuss the work of T.R.V. Murti.

III

Murti states his philosophical differences with Radhakrishnan's denial of differences between Hinduism and Buddhism. Like Ambedkar and Radhakrishnan, Murti credits Buddhism with offering a modern perspective. In his estimation, the 'egalitarian stand taken by Buddhism, as contrasted with the hierarchical pattern of Brāhmanism, in regard to the cultivation of spiritual life is in closer conformity with the ideals of today' (Coward, 1983: 163). Directly taking on Radhakrishnan, he asks:

> Does all Indian philosophy stem from one original source – the Upanisads? And are all Indian religions variations of the Vedic? Following the lead of Professor Radhakrishnan, the foremost Indian thinker of today, there is a large and impressive body of opinion favouring the unilinear tradition and development of Indian thought (ibid.: 163).

Contesting this dominant view of unilinear development, Murti asserts that in the 'estimation of the Buddhist and non-Buddhist' that includes Jaina and Brahmanical orthodox tradition, 'the differences between the two are radical'. Aside from these extreme positions, however, he claims that 'both these estimates seem to suffer from the fallacy of over-simplification. Probably the truth lies somewhere in the middle' (ibid.: 163). Specifying the nature of this middle path, Murti states that a 'careful analysis would reveal that Hinduism (Brāhmanism) and Buddhism belong to the same genus; they differ as species' (ibid.: 163–64). Using this formula, he goes on to emphasize a third dimension of the relation between Buddhism and Hinduism – their complementary nature. This dimension eluded the attention of both Radhakrishnan and Ambedkar. Focusing on this complementary dimension, Murti clarifies, 'In a sense, they are complementary to each other; one emphasises what the other lacks or slurs over. Without basic affinity they would have been completely sundered from each other ...' (ibid.: 164). And without differences they 'could not have vitalised and enriched each other. In view of the differences in their basic standpoints and the mode of their historical development, we should be alive to their differences as much as we affirm their affinities' (ibid.: 164). Recounting the commonalities between them, Murti writes:

> Both Brāhmanism and Buddhism are types of spiritual religion. They try to realise a state of utter negation of the ego, the abolition of selfishness .... Again in both, the highest state is attained by a non-discursive intellectual intuition, a kind of mystic absorption .... Both religions have always believed in the Law of Karma as the Law of the Universe and as the arbiter of human destiny (ibid.: 164).

Then, turning to the differences in their philosophies, he asserts:

> All systems of Hindu thought subscribe to the *ātma-vāda* – the conception of reality as Being, substance and permanent. In its most radical form, as in the Vedānta of Sankara, it denied the reality of change, and characterised it as appearance (ibid.: 164).

In contrast, writes Murti,

> the Buddhist schools rejected the reality of the soul or substance (*anātma-vāda*) and conceived the real as Becoming (ibid.: 164).

Besides those described previously, there are other vital differences between the two systems with regard to their religious views. Underscoring these, Murti avers:

> The source of religious inspiration in Brāhmanism is the revelation as given to us in the Vedas; in Buddhism it is reason (ibid.: 165).

The other irreconcilable difference between Buddhism and Hinduism, according to Murti is that:

For Buddhism the fundament is the moral consciousness and the spiritual urge is for purifying the mind of its passions (*visuddhi-mārga*). The fundament of Brahmanism is God-consciousness; and the goal is exaltation or deification (ibid.: 166).

Thus, for Murti, the '*en rapport* relationship with God is what distinguishes Hinduism from Buddhism' (ibid.: 167). He states that 'the Mādhyamika, Vijñānavāda and Vedānta exhibit some common features as to their form' but that 'they differ in the mode of their approach, and possibly with regard to that entity with which they identify the absolute' (ibid.: 171). Further, while the 'Vedānta analyses illusion from the knowledge-standpoint ...' the Vijñānavāda, on the other hand, 'analyses illusion from an opposite angle' (ibid.: 173).

Rejecting those who, like Radhakrishnan, do not sufficiently emphasize these 'differences' Murti declares:

> It has been the fashion to consider that the differences between the Mādhyamika *sunyata* and *Brahman* are rather superficial and even verbal, and that the two systems of philosophy are almost identical. At least Professor Radhakrishnan thinks so, and Stcherbatsky's and Dasgupta's views are not very different (ibid.: 177).

Reiterating his own position on this matter of the relationship between Hinduism and Buddhism, Murti says that 'although their generic identity is undeniable, the specific differences are equally undeniable' (ibid.: 219). Disagreeing further with Radhakrishnan, Murti claims that Buddhism's opposition to the Upanisads is not to be seen in Buddha's rejection of ritualism when the Upanisads themselves are wary of this practice, but rather in his rejection of atman. To quote:

> In the dialogues of Buddha we breathe a different atmosphere. There is a distinct spirit of opposition, if not one of hostility as well, to the ātmavada of the Upanisads. Buddha or Buddhism can be understood only as a revolt not merely against the cant and hollowness of ritualism – the Upanisads themselves voice this unmistakably – but against the ātma-ideology, the metaphysics of Substance-view (Murti, 2010: 16–17).

Trenchantly questioning Radhakrishnan's interpretation of the Buddha's silence with regard to atman, Murti writes:

> If the ātman had been a cardinal doctrine with Buddhism, why was it so securely hidden under a bushel that even the immediate followers of the Master had no inkling of it (ibid.: 17).

To support his analysis, Murti elucidates the implications of accepting atman for its spiritualism and moral dimension. He says:

> An unchanging eternal soul, as impervious to change, would render spiritual life lose all meaning; we would, in that case, be neither the better nor the worse for our efforts. This might lead to inaction (akriyāvāda). Nay more; the ātman is the root-cause of all attachment, desire, aversion, and pain (ibid.: 17).

Having identified the genus-like similarities and species-like differences, Murti then highlights the active and negotiated relations between the two schools of thought. Murti's contribution lies in elucidating this transformative relation between Hinduism and Buddhism, rather than merely stating either differences or absence of differences. This is what distinguishes Murti from both Ambedkar and Radhakrishnan. Ambedkar recognizes only the impact of Buddhism on the Gita and does not see any significant influence of Hinduism on the shaping of Buddhism. While Radhakrishnan strategically and infrequently acknowledges the interrelations between the two systems, in the end, he underplays them by subsuming Buddhism within Brahmanism, thus making the process of transformation restricted and less significant. For Radhakrishnan, it becomes a marginal activity overshadowed by his overall concern, which is to correct Brahmanism through the critical application of Buddhism. In contrast, Murti claims that Buddhism and Brahmanism have mutually impacted each other.

Stating the nature of influence in clearer terms, Murti writes that influence can be 'expressed as much through opposition as by acceptance' (Coward, 1983: 168). Accounting for the transformation within Buddhism, Murti asserts that in its earlier phase it 'was a radical pluralism [subsequently has become] in the Mahāyāna a radical absolutism with a different conception of Buddha and the Bodhisatva ideal' (ibid.: 168).

> He attributes this transmutation to both internal and external factors. These are: ... one, that of borrowing from or being influenced by the Upanisadic thought where absolutism and theism are such dominant features; the other hypothesis would deny external influence and see the account for the revolution as the result of an inner dynamism in Buddhist thought itself. These two views are not exclusive, and perhaps the truth lies somewhere between the two (ibid.: 169).

The first view, according to which the

> Upanisadic Brahman is obviously the model from which the *Tathatā* or *sūnyatā* has been drawn. Competent scholars, like Kern, Keith, Stcherbatsky and Radhakrishnan among others, have drawn pointed attention to the probable influence of the Upanisadic thought on the emergence of the Mahāyanā (ibid.: 169).

Murti, on the other hand, gives more importance to the second view. He writes, 'I attach somewhat greater importance to the dynamism inherent in Buddhism itself which engendered the revolutionary change' (ibid.: 169). While holding internal reasons responsible for the changes in Buddhism, Murti does not wholly discount the influence of external reasons. Pointing out another example of influence of the Upanisads on Buddhism he says:

> The dialogues of Buddha, as preserved in the Pāli Canons, are suggestive; they are as little systematic as the Upanisadic texts. Buddhist systems grew out of them much in the way the Brāhmanical systems grew out of the Upanisads (Murti, 2010: 14).

Later in the same work he claims that:

> There were lively interchanges between the Buddhist and the Brāhmanical logicians for centuries. The Mādhyamika and Aupanisada schools were not enclosed in water-tight compartments (ibid.: 113).

After elucidating the influence of the Upanisads in systematizing Buddhism, Murti turns his attention to highlighting the influence of Buddhism on subsequent philosophical activity in India. Thus, Buddhism has drawn from the Upanisads for its methodology of systematizing the dialogues of the Buddha, and Advaita has incorporated the Buddhist dialectical technique. The important point in Murti's argument is the dialectical relation between Hinduism and Buddhism. However, while there are many political dimensions to Murti's critique of Radhakrishnan, which are close to Ambedkar's analysis, Murti either does not perceive these or stops short of relating his work to them.

Thus, we have in Radhakrishnan a philosophical engagement wherein his attempt to claim Buddhism as part of Hinduism he denies or explains away, although less than convincingly, the differences between Buddhism and Hinduism. However, Radhakrishnan does concede, though only in passing, the fact that Buddhism threatened to change the social system of Hindus, and he leaves it at that. Subsequently, we have in Ambedkar a different effort, in sharp contrast to Radhakrishnan, wherein he highlights the differences between Hinduism and Buddhism, and claims the Buddha as being outside the Hindu fold. Murti takes a moderate position, keeps the discussion at a philosophical level and challenges Radhakrishnan on many counts. But Murti's engagement is confined to Radhakrishnan's claims and conclusions and does not refer to his arduous arguments and strategies. This, in a way, bypasses the academic protocols and academic bureaucracy essential in philosophical engagement.

While denying the difference in order to project unity and cultural continuity as a defence against colonialism may be understandable, the manner in which the denial is executed may not be justified. What independent India requires is not mere unity or mere difference nor even unity in diversity. We need to go much beyond these. There is a need to identify and nurture the differences that are available. There is a further need to debate these differences on reasonably objective and common grounds. Arguments are one aspect of a debate. In a debate, the participants only claim what is truth. What is truth is adjudicated not by the participants but an outsider. An outsider could be an expert or, as in a democracy, it could be the common person. So what is suggested here is not mere identification of difference, as was the preoccupation of the

Orientalists nor is expressing ideas in isolation; not even dialogue between two cultures or schools of thought which largely remains less rigorous; not mere arguments, but rigorous and relentless debates. Modern India provides several complex debates for philosophy to rejuvenate itself. The scholarship that focuses on the conformity aspect fails to recognize those foundational structural features crucial to the formation of religions.

More importantly, the instance of this happening in the visible sites of textbooks – that too authored by a well-known philosopher who was also a statesmen, a president of India – eluded the attention of philosophers. Most, if not all, universities in India have a paper, or papers, on Indian Philosophy. *Indian Philosophy* by Radhakrishnan is a prominent prescribed textbook in these courses. Surprisingly, it eluded the attention of scholars working on Ambedkar. If philosophers have not worked on Ambedkar, then that needs to be addressed.

◆

*Reproduced with the permission of Oxford University Press
©Oxford University Press
Unauthorized copying is strictly prohibited.

REFERENCES

Coward, Harold G. (ed.). 1983. *Studies in Indian Thought: Collected Papers of T. R. V. Murti*. Delhi: Motilal Banarsidass Publisher.

Guru, Gopal. 2002. 'How Egalitarian Are the Social Sciences in India', *Economic and Political Weekly*, XXVII(51), 14 December: 5003–9.

Jha, Ganganath. 1986. *The Tattvasangraha of Shāntaraksita with the Commentary of Kamalashila, Vol. 1*. English translation by author. Delhi: Motilal Banarsidass Publisher.

Murti, T.R.V. 2010. *The Central Philosophy of Buddhism: A Study of Madhyamika System*. New Delhi: Munshiram Manoharlal Publishers Pvt. Ltd.

Radhakrishnan, S. 2008. *Indian Philosophy, Vol. 1*. First published in 1923. New Delhi: Oxford University Press.

Rodrigues, Valerian (ed.). 2010. *The Essential Writings of B. R. Ambedkar*. New Delhi: Oxford University Press.

❖❖

7 RELIGIOUS DIVERSITY AND THE POLITICS OF AN OVERLAPPING CONSENSUS

GOPAL GURU

Coalition politics has become entrenched in the life of electoral democracy in India. This political development should encourage us to examine the Rawlsian conception of an overlapping consensus in terms of its implications for religious diversity. It would be interesting to find out whether an overlapping consensus as a comprehensive political doctrine can serve to overcome the mutually incommensurable religious positions that otherwise fragment secular politics and torment minority communities. Taking a clue from Rawls again, one can further argue that the comprehensive doctrine (justice, in the case of Rawls) which could serve as the motivating basis for adopting an overlapping consensus, at the same time also contains within itself a paradoxical element. Viewed from this angle, even the Rawlsian comprehensive doctrine of justice would have within itself the paradoxical element of injustice. In the same way, a comprehensive doctrine of religious pluralism or of diversity would inherently have the paradoxical element of the dominance of a particular religion. In the Indian context a significant question is, to what extent does the politics of overlapping consensus or reasonable pluralism prevent a dominant religion from undermining religious diversity? Or, does it end up enabling a dominant religion to carry out its hegemonic agenda under the garb of the overlapping consensus? In this chapter I will argue that political parties use the idea of an overlapping consensus as a discursive device in order to carry forward their respective political agendas. Before we can move to detect what is the paradoxical element in a comprehensive doctrine such as religious diversity, let us define in brief the meaning of an overlapping consensus.

An overlapping consensus is a kind of compromise among different and conflicting 'reasonably comprehensive doctrines'. I am specifically interested in the overlapping consensus that seems to be emerging between Brahmanical Hinduism and neo-Buddhism in contemporary Indian politics. Overlapping consensus is an outcome of some sort of bargain where each position sacrifices something for the sake of larger agreement. In such a consensus, no one is entirely satisfied or completely happy, and yet they need to take negotiable positions that are just adequate to this consensus. On the brighter side, it could be argued that on such a simple understanding of an overlapping consensus, reasonable people are in search of a permanent solution and hence, logically, they are permanently unhappy. The principle of their life is that they are never happy. An important question is, of course, why an overlapping consensus has got some purchase in contemporary Indian politics. Before I address this question, it is necessary to make a couple of clarifications.

First, in my understanding a significant category, in this context, is not the usual suspect, secularism, but caste. Caste becomes a significant reference point for me because I am focusing my attention on neo-Buddhism vis-à-vis Brahmanical Hinduism. Buddhism is the result of the rejection of caste-based Hinduism. Hence, I have chosen caste as the significant category that induces mediation between these two comprehensive doctrines. Obviously, I am avoiding reference to the established category of secularism which (in the Indian context) has been treated by scholars as a threshold reference point for understanding the importance of an overlapping consensus. Second, I argue that it is dominant parties in the National Democratic Alliance (NDA) that form the relevant reference point for assigning relevance to the present discussion. In the context of the conflicting relationship between Brahmanical Hinduism and neo-Buddhism, importing secularism into the discussion would not yield any significant or exciting arguments. Hence, I would like to articulate my position on an overlapping consensus, taking the NDA coalition as the relevant reference point. I do this to argue that the question of caste, rather than communalism, is intimately linked with the NDA. For certain social and political reasons the constituent members of the NDA do carry the historical burden of the caste question. Here, I am not suggesting that the United Progressive Alliance (UPA) coalition is devoid of elements of Brahmanical Hinduism. In fact, political parties do have either a mild or strong element of Brahmanical Hinduism, although they maintain subtle or not-so-subtle associations with different religions.

The UPA has from time to time been deploying secularism as the threshold reference point for developing an overlapping consensus. In a certain sense, secularism as a comprehensive doctrine which gives peace and harmony a chance does constitute one of the important components of social imagery. But this is not adequate to understand a new dimension that can add to our fresh understanding of the idea of an overlapping consensus in Indian politics.

It is interesting to note that reasonable pluralism that did not succeed at the level of the Dalit movements in the earlier period seems to be working rather successfully in contemporary times. The question that needs to be raised at this point in time is: Why has reasonable pluralism achieved this success? This has to be understood with particular reference to the changes that have suggested flexibility in Buddhist political practices, particularly in the context of Maharashtra. In the early decades of Buddhist conversion there was an ideologically coherent political mobilization of neo-Buddhist masses against both the Hindutva parties like the Jan Sangha on the one hand, and the bourgeois party like the Congress on the other. A comprehensive understanding of Buddhism helped the neo-Buddhists to not only maintain their autonomous political identity but also articulate it as an independent political mobilization. It also helped neo-Buddhists from Uttar Pradesh to achieve this autonomy from the parties using religion for political mobilization. This confidence to fight a political battle for restoring dignity was possible as long as the Dalits kept out of the logic of electoral power. However, Dalit leaders seem to have lost the moral stamina to sustain this autonomy. Buddhism, as a comprehensive principle, seems to have lost its normative hold over at least the neo-Buddhist leaders. In common perception today, this view is almost entirely abstract. In the three decades after independence, it was arguably concrete in the political perception of the people. In reasonable pluralism, reasonable people agree to shave off the rough edges of their political personality. Thus, in the interest of responding to the political compulsion to remain relevant and thereby purely in the interest of personal gains (not in defence of comprehensive principles like perpetual peace), political leaders are prepared to moderate their radical position on religious issues. My argument is directed at the irresolvable contradiction between Brahmanical Hinduism and the neo-Buddhism of B. R. Ambedkar. In my view, this forms a vantage point for understanding the contemporary Indian politics of an overlapping consensus.

Ambedkar's neo-Buddhism and Brahmanical Hinduism are considered as comprehensive doctrines which are historically incommensurate. Why is this so? According to Ambedkar, Brahmanical Hinduism is based on the ascending sense of reverence for the top of the twice-born and an ascending sense of repulsion for the lower castes. For the untouchable it has a withering sense of respect. Neo-Buddhism, on the other hand, seeks to radically even out this hierarchical sense of reverence. Put differently, it advocates a mutual sense of reverence. It actually suggests withering down of (in this context one can take note of the 22 oaths that Ambedkar gave Dalits in 1956 at Nagpur) the ego embodied in *Bhudeo*.

Second, Ambedkar enacted this opposition of neo-Buddhism to Brahmanical Hinduism by emphasizing the meaning of human dignity. Neo-Buddhism is an ethical investment in elevating human stature over the hierarchical social status that singularly defines Brahmanical Hinduism. It is interesting to note in this regard that Ambedkar carefully chose the places to enact neo-Buddhism to Brahmanical Hinduism: for instance, Nagpur, Pune, Nasik and Yeola, arguably places that continue to follow the *prakaha*r (intense) version of Brahmanical Hinduism. In Yeola in 1935, now a *taluka* in Nasik district of Maharashtra, Ambedkar announced that he would leave Hinduism. At Pune, he inaugurated Buddhist Vihar in 1946. At Nagpur, he along with his followers embraced Buddhism in 1956.

The political articulation of the opposition between Brahmanical Hinduism and neo-Buddhism was played out in Dalit cultural practices in Maharashtra, Tamil Nadu and Uttar Pradesh. This opposition was also reflected in the electoral politics where the Dalits did not vote for Jan Sangha candidates, but also socially boycotted those who either voted or shared a political platform with the political leaders representing different Hindutva outfits. The political symbol like the elephant (that was chosen by Ambedkar) was considered to be more powerful in its message than the symbols used by rival parties, which were considered to be grotesque. Thus, during the first three decades, Buddhism as defined by Ambedkar worked for the Dalit political leaders as a robust bulwark which the former used both against the Congress and the Hindutva political parties. However, this opposition has begun to disappear. The political leaders who form the Dalit political formation are now eager to forge an alliance with the very Hindutva parties which do not have a good record on the questions of social justice and Dalit dignity. The question is, what kind of justification do these leaders provide for their alliance with Hindutva parties? Have the Hindutva parties changed their rigid character and become politically flexible? What are the justifications that are provided in favour of a new consensus than the one found in the politics of Uttar Pradesh between the Bhartiya Janata Party (BJP) and Bahujan Samaj Party (BSP), and more recently, between the Republican Party of India (RPI) (Ramdas Athwale) and the BJP and Shiv Sena?

During the last two decades, political leaders from the Dalit community have been trying hard to become part of coalition politics, both at the national as well as the local level. This has implications for religious reconfigurations. Hence, politics of alliance get primarily defined in terms of those political parties that show their open and formal allegiance to religion. Interestingly, Dalit political leaders showed their inclination towards those parties that expressed their association with political Hinduism. In this regard, one will have to think about at least two Dalit political parties – the BSP in Uttar Pradesh and RPI in Maharashtra. In the recent past, the BSP did form an alliance with the BJP in forming the government in Uttar Pradesh. In order to give political effect to this alliance in the electoral battle, the BSP did try to moderate its religious position on Buddhism.

However, it is possible to advance a counterargument against such efforts. One can argue that such consensus in the sphere of electoral politics is purely symbolic. Yet, it has been projected by Dalit leaders as universal, as if representing a larger consensus of the wider community. Second, in my understanding, those taking the lead in reaching a consensus that could be seen as overlapping in political parties are understood to be reasonable persons. In this way, I am already assuming that those (particularly Dalit leaders) who are taking the lead in producing this consensus seem to be using the space that they have acquired through power-sharing for occupying the public place with religious symbols. (Pariwartan Park at Lucknow or Gautam Buddha University at Noida). Common Dalits then have a chance to become reasonable persons only through an indirect participation in the production of an overlapping consensus. Dalits also seemingly agree with their leaders when the latter are involved in making political use of the religious symbols of Brahmanical Hinduism. To put it more dramatically, Dalit leaders seek to genetically modify Buddhist symbols into the symbols that otherwise belong to Brahmanical Hinduism. In this regard, one needs to remember the BSP's political slogan, 'Yeh Hathi Nahi Ganesh hai, Brahma Vishnu Mahesh Hai'. Ganpati is the religious symbol of Brahmanical Hinduism. Similarly, the BJP, through its *samarasta manch,* carries the image of Ambedkar on its head or in the Rashtriya Swayam Sewa (RSS) *shakha.* In both cases, the response of the common people from both sides to participate in the production of the overlapping consensus is abstract or indirect because it is the political leaders of respective parties who produce this consensus on behalf of their supporters. Common Dalits, for example, become reasonable persons only through their participation in terms designated by their political leaders. This overlapping consensus, as we will discuss later on, is vacuous because it does not effect any ameliorative changes in the existential condition of the Dalits and the non-Dalit poor on whose behalf the consensus is reached. For, the translation or moderation of positions is done only by the leaders and not the social groups.

Some of the self-styled neo-Buddhist leaders in Maharashtra are a case in point. Differences get moderated only at the level of leaders, while they remain active at the level of followers of the particular faith. For example, a few minority politicians have joined parties with strong Hindutva leanings, but this has not translated into wider support of the Muslims. The common people are not ready to resolve their disagreements and this is because the contending parties avoid addressing the much larger issues of injustice and humiliation that continue to remain an ontological wound that torments these common people who were affected, either directly or historically, through the victimization of their dear and near ones. Those who have only a symbolic association with the victims and those who are ontologically dissociated from the victimized and humiliated common Dalits and minorities take the lead in producing this overlapping consensus. Such initiatives by leaders from the minority community and political leaders from the party of the majority community look superficial and hence politically motivated. These efforts lack the honesty involved in establishing an overlapping consensus as a response to the universal moral need involving the common people from both sides: the minority and majority. In fact, those who do not see any resolution in such a consensus treat such an overlapping consensus as quite a scandalous illusion. In such a situation, an overlapping consensus in the Indian context remains relevant only at the top as the bottom remains unaffected by such consensus. However, I choose to focus on the politics of overlapping consensus that involves neo-Buddhist and the Hindutva political parties, especially in Maharashtra and Uttar Pradesh. The politics of producing overlapping consensus from the top will also implicate in its explanatory logic not the category of communalism but caste. As I argue, it is caste that defines the relationship between Buddhism and Brahmanical Hinduism. Caste renders the interface between the two almost impossible unless Hinduism unilaterally gobbles up Buddhism into its hegemonic framework. Let us not forget that hegemonic Hinduism did this in its history by projecting the Buddha as the ninth incarnation of Vishnu, the presiding deity of Hinduism.

It is also possible to find such efforts at producing an overlapping consensus as intellectually as well as morally deficient. For example, the neo-Buddhist leaders do not find it necessary to prove that the world vision of Buddhism is good enough to orient the society towards a progressive perpetual peace in society. Comprehensive doctrine like establishing peace does not form the basis of contemporary political alliances. In fact, as Ambedkar has all along proved, Buddhism could provide a better alternative to achieve this end. Neo-Buddhist leaders thus fail to give any strong reason as to why they should go with Hindutva parties in Maharashtra. There is no deep moral argument that motivates these leaders to reach a consensus. Nor does the consensus refer to the reasonable comprehensive view which is the basis of Buddhism. Some of the self-proclaimed neo-Buddhist leaders like R. S. Gawai from Amrawati (who is controlling the Deeksha Bhumi Committee at Nagpur) would not associate with Hindutva leaders. On the other hand, some of the neo-Buddhist leaders at Nagpur were found associating with members of the RSS on the question of nationalism. In fact, these leaders created a situation within which Dalit audiences were made to express their allegiance with the Indian nation. They were seen singing the national anthem at Deeksha Bhumi. Why could the Dalit not be a nationalist outside the Deeksha Bhumi? Clearly, the Hindutva parties are pleased with such conversion of religious places of neo-Buddhism in favour of nationalism. This is ironic as Ambedkar's Buddhism is an idea which transcends national boundaries. However, the Hindutva parties are also ready to undergo a little of what could be termed as moral as well as political pruning to look reasonably decent. This sort of overlapping consensus between the Hindutva parties and the parties claiming to represent the neo-Buddhists has two implications. First, it denies historicity to the Dalit critique of nationalism and, on the other hand, assigns discursive meaning to nationalism so that it can become available to different forces for intersection purposes. Another serious fallout of this overlapping consensus is that it has given prominence to some Dalit leaders at the expense of the million mute common Dalits.

SOME BROAD REFLECTIONS

While the compulsion to gain political power forces parties representing religion to respect the principle of an overlapping consensus, at the same time this consensus may not check the spread of religious homogenization of certain social groups like adivasis (tribals) in civil society. The second conclusion that one can draw is that the political compulsion to gain hold of distributive power forces Dalit leaders to deviate from Buddhism as the reasonable comprehensive doctrine for achieving perpetual peace in society. Dalit leaders are not unhappy because they have not been able to use the framework of an overlapping consensus to push forward Buddhism as a comprehensive doctrine. The Hindutva parties, on the other hand, seek tactical separation of rigid Brahmanical Hinduism from the sphere of an overlapping consensus or public sphere. It is not a genuine commitment to the comprehensive doctrine of establishing perpetual peace that motivates the contending parties to produce an overlapping consensus. In fact, it is the narrow conception of finding a regulatory doctrine that motivates these leaders to work out a consensus.

It can also be broadly stated that both the Hindutva and Dalit parties use the idea of an overlapping consensus to capture power in the name of doing good for common Dalits. But, in actual practice, it only ends up helping a few individuals to better their individual positions. Ironically, the framework of parliamentary democracy does provide space for the politics of an overlapping consensus. However, in such a democracy, the poorer Dalits miss the opportunity to use their numbers to counterbalance the advantage of assets that the dominant groups have. It may be recalled that this is what Ambedkar had planned to do. His general strategy was to modify the power of wealth by democratic numbers using democracy to force a more equitable distribution of the fruits of growth. However, the contemporary politics of an overlapping consensus is purely tactical and does not permit such a result to emerge.

◆

PART III
RELIGIOUS EDUCATION

8 EDUCATION IN SECULAR DEMOCRATIC SOCIETIES
The challenge of religious diversity

TNA GHOSH

The focus of this chapter is on religion, education and secularism in diverse societies where multicultures and multi-religions are posing challenges, especially in former monocultural and single-religion societies. From the point of view of education the issue of religion is rather complex because it raises a variety of issues. Questions deal with policy, process, practice and outcome as they relate to religion as a subject that may be taught in schools but also as it impacts the school culture in a variety of ways. Some of these are terms of participation in mandatory school subjects (such as science education in which the theory of evolution may be contradictory to creationism, participation in mixed-gender physical education classes); religious holidays (which may conflict with exam periods); cafeteria food (for example, beef or pork which are forbidden in certain religions and the non-availability of vegetarian, *halal* or kosher food); special attire (such as turbans for Sikhs, the *kippah* for Jews and the *hijab* for Muslim girls); and rituals (for example, the need to pray five times during the day for strictly observant Muslim students). The overall question is: How can education deal with differences in mitigating conflicting viewpoints in multicultural, multi-religious societies?

In a globalized world, religion is gradually being pushed to the periphery in secular modern democracies both in public and private life. Yet, throughout history it has been a source of strength as well as a factor in conflict in both society and politics. Societal institutions such as education have been linked to religion both for their contradictory roles in transmission of religious traditions and dogma, on the one hand, and in fostering peace and knowledge about the 'other', on the other. At the same time, formal education has been a battleground where courts have been asked to adjudicate the boundaries between religion and the state.

EDUCATION

Like religion, the position of education is complex, and it is changing in several ways. The *reach* of education has extended from being confined to the elite towards education for all in order to eradicate illiteracy as a means of reducing inequities in society and compensate for historical injustices. The *focus* in education has moved from access to education (for example, the Education for All movement coordinated by UNESCO) towards equity and quality. In societies with diverse populations, the issue of equity is more complex because the difference is multifaceted and also because 'diversity' refers to deviation from an arbitrary norm.

The *aims* of education have changed from conformity and socialization in the form of cultural transmission (culture, religion, values and knowledge) to critical thinking and socialization (intercultural competencies, knowledge of human rights and values such as democracy and respect for others). The passive recipient of 'knowledge' is now encouraged to be an active learner who constructs his/her knowledge. The *process* has moved from a banking method (where knowledge was 'deposited' to the student's head) to one of questioning and critical reasoning.

CRITICAL PEDAGOGY

Critical pedagogy is a teaching and learning approach that promotes transformative education and empowers students to find agency and voice through *conscientization* or critical consciousness of people's situations as the starting point of their liberatory journey. Largely influenced by the work of Paulo Freire, the Brazilian educator who wrote the *Pedagogy of the Oppressed* (1970), the various approaches to critical pedagogy have in common the understanding that knowledge is political and attempt to understand how power operates in the construction of knowledge. Critical pedagogy is a process of engaging difference, coming to know others and ourselves. It is involved in creating the critical ability to recognize injustice but also to seek justice – to question taken-for-granted assumptions about *quotidian* experiences in our lives. The emphasis is on changing the world and collective action to achieve that.

The challenge in education is for teachers and students to explore together questions about knowledge and power and how they shape differences in people's lives in diverse societies.

DIVERSITY

The overarching concept of diversity as discussed here implies difference not just in terms of religion but also of class, gender, race, ethnicity, culture, language, sexual orientation and other factors. Even though the concept of diversity involves multiple kinds of differences, its connotation has been limited through the construction of specific meanings, so that some differences make a big difference to people, while others do not. Of course, this varies with time and societal context. In India, diversity has tended to focus on caste and class, as well as religion and language differences. In a Canadian context, diversity focuses on differences in ethnicity, culture and race (which is still very much a social construct even though it has no basis in evolutionary biology). In the context of the United States, discussions of diversity have concentrated on racial and cultural differences as well as on religion (American Protestantism). Since 11 September 2001, religious differences have increasingly become important as a marker of diversity, especially in the United States, Canada and parts of Europe. In each case, the difference focused on is outside the hegemonic power structure and on the 'other'.

I understand diversity to mean variability in ideas, structures, values, beliefs and people. Diversity thus includes a spectrum of perspectives derived from multiplicity and multidimensional differences. We are 'diversely different' because of the pluralities of human identity which cut across each other (Sen, 2006: xiv). These pluralities render simple classifications crude and incorrect. It has been pointed out (Pandey, 2010: 62–69) that the notion of diversity has been seen as one of population segments revolving around a centre: the subordinate or subaltern around the dominant or powerful group. This assumes that the range of social and political possibilities – the organizational structure of society – is already defined. But difference is fluid; it appears 'differently in different places' in 'innumerable forms' (ibid.: 6). Diversity is influenced by our various locationalities (historical, global) and positionalities (in terms of race, gender, language, religion, class, sexual orientation, among others), because where and how a person is situated in a society leads him or her to live through a particular set of experiences and to encounter distinctive power relations. For example, people may be positioned by religion and position themselves in and through their religious identity. The intersections of one's positionalities produce different and distinctive experiences. Religious minorities are often identified as racial minorities and experience racism. This happened after the 9/11 attacks when, in the United States (US) for example, Sikhs were killed after being erroneously identified as belonging to the religion of the attackers. Moreover, as feminist theorists have argued, locationality and positionality are not fixed categories but are relational, complex, ever-changing and volatile.

The question is: Who is seen as different and from whom? The attribution of difference is a way of legitimating, normalizing and reinforcing hierarchical power relations. They are expressions of dominance, subordination and hierarchy in social, political and economic power. Caste Hindus are not different in India: Dalits and tribals are. In the US, white Anglo-Saxon Protestant males are not different, but African Americans are, and so are several other groups that have been identified as different at different times in history (ibid.). Similarly, in English Canada, the white Anglo-Saxon Protestant male is not different: French Catholics and visible minorities are. In the province of Québec, the French Catholic male is not different: the anglophone and allophone cultural communities, especially their women, are different.

The school is a microcosm of society and the complexities of difference and diversity are reflected in the social institutions of public education.

SECULARISM

The two concepts – religion and secularism – have both been interpreted in multiple ways at different times and still have different meanings in different cultures. Without going into a philosophical discussion of these concepts, briefly, the word *secular* derives its meaning from its relationship to religion. While the general understanding of the term is a break from religious ideology, it may imply anti-religious sentiments or simply a non-religious stance. *Secularism* is an ideology that requires separation of religion from the state (as well as other areas of public life) and does not necessarily mean exclusion of religion (Taylor, 2007). Secularism could imply opposition to religion but it could also mean neutrality towards religion. Nor does the separation of religion and state alone define secularism, which involves the ideas of equal rights for all citizens and respect for the other. These rights include the right to education and to religious freedom. Human rights imply social inclusion and a common goal because these rights bind us together by virtue of the fact that we are human beings.

RELIGION

Secularism and religion are ways of seeing and conceptualizing the world. The idea of religion is very complex. Not all religions believe in a supernatural being or God. Buddhism, for example, is agnostic. Defining the concept is problematic but, in general, a religion is a system of thought and explains the mysteries of the universe, the purpose of life on earth, and after-life. Religion has played, and continues to play, a significant role in society. All major life events involve religion and religious rituals. Religion and culture are inextricably related and hence the importance of religion to the socialization process in education.

RELIGIOUS FUNDAMENTALISM

In recent times, religion and religious fundamentalism have become major concerns globally because of their links to extremism and terrorism. Educators have argued that religious fundamentalism needs to be addressed in schools, which are important sites for the development of values, attitudes and perspectives.

The concept of fundamentalism has come to denote something negative. The term actually means a return to the fundamentals of a particular ideology. However, its modern popular usage connotes aggressive convictions of traditional ideological or religious beliefs that hold modernization, Westernization or globalization as being responsible for the divergence of religious belief from their interpretation of the original and 'pure' religion. Since these phenomena are equated with secularism, religion and secularism have become competing ideologies. Religious fundamentalism is not confined to any one religious tradition and there are fundamentalists among Christians, Jews and Hindus as there are among Muslims. Fundamentalism is often closely tied to politics and some fundamentalist movements have led to political revolutions (for example, the Iranian revolution).

When a religion or religious identity is threatened, the reaction can be intense. Fear of destruction or obliteration could lead to fundamentalism and further develop into radicalization. Charles Taylor (1994) defines identity as a person's understanding of who she or he is, a fundamental defining characteristic of a human being; how one defines oneself is partly dependent on the recognition, misrecognition or absence of recognition by others. 'Non-recognition or misrecognition can inflict harm, can be a form of oppression, imprisoning someone in a false, distorted and reduced mode of being' (ibid.: 25).

Appleby (2011: 225–47) notes that fundamentalism has a distinct religious logic unlike any other. It is generally an oppositional movement towards the state because it has an envisioned moral order defined by a religious commitment. There are two characteristics to which fundamentalists react: 'Westoxication' or degradation brought about by the indulgent lifestyle of the West and women's liberation or freedom, which they blame for the increase in divorce rates, sexual depravity and crime. Fundamentalists are often people with education, but they set themselves apart from Westoxication by politicizing fundamentals of their doctrine, which they hold as absolute rather than variable.

THE COMPLEX RELATIONSHIP BETWEEN EDUCATION, RELIGION AND SECULARISM

With the global focus on fundamentalism (partly due to an escalation in terrorist acts), the secular and the religious are increasingly seen in binary form. As ideologies, both secularism and religion have particular moral and political agendas. Those who oppose religious teaching in schools do so based on the claim that religions regulate and delimit critical questioning and free speech in schools. In addition, which religion should be taught (and therefore privileged) when the student body is composed of a diversity of religious faiths? On the other hand, secularism, as a discourse, defines the borders of free speech and will necessarily discriminate against those who hold traditional religious values.

Both religion and education have been used to dominate people or keep them subservient. Religion has been used to dominate one group over others and this has been perpetuated through education. For example, religion has been used to justify white domination and superiority not only for colonizing countries but also for stealing from, enslaving and oppressing the native populations in the Americas. Education has been used either to perpetuate the theory of white superiority or deny slaves (particularly in the US) as well as women (in many societies) access to knowledge, just as it has played, and continues to play, an important role in maintaining the power structure in society. Another example is the history textbook controversy in India where fundamentalist forces have attempted to transform history as a narrative of Hindu religious nationalism whenever it has been possible.

Initially, secularism was a response to domination by the church in Europe as in Québec. It was a response to institutionalized religious domination. Now the imperative in Western countries is immigration, resulting in religious diversity that demands special attention to the equality of treatment and freedom of religious expression. This requires the de-confessionalization of the state and an emphasis on individual rights. For example, France, where the separation of the church and state has taken on a militant form of *laïcité*, derives its national identity from secularism that is now an opposition to immigrants in general, and Islam as a religion in particular.

In India, the centuries-old deep diversity of the population in terms of religions and culture/language/customs and so forth depends on communal harmony and respect for other religions and cultures. Not only is India representative of every religion in the world, it is the source of several religions, and 'Hinduism', which is inclusive, is itself different things to different groups. At Independence, secularism was declared to be a pillar of Indian democracy through which religious diversity could not only be managed but also be legitimized. So, secularism in this case is not an absence of religion (agnostic view) but rather a pluralistic ideology implying equality of, and respect for, all religions, and not their eradication (e.g. in China). Its purpose is equal treatment of all its citizens. Some critics of the Indian variant of secularism have called it Majoritarianism (Upadhyay, 2007), in which the Hindu majority is said to be privileged; some others (Nandy, 1998: 321–44) have rejected it as a Western concept and not suitable for India. And yet, secularization, as a process that transcends religious differences, appears to be the best solution to prevent potential dangers resulting from increasing religious and other divisions.

The practice of religion often has less to do with religious belief than with collective ritual and its social aspects. In that sense, the majority religion, by default, assumes importance and this is particularly so when religion is eradicated rather than equally treated. The present controversy over the Québec Charter of Values, which bans all religious symbols for public servants and in public institutions such as educational and medical establishments, nevertheless maintains that the cross in the National Assembly (Christian symbol) will remain because it is part of history (it was put up in 1938). The majority religion is Catholicism and when religious symbols are banned in public offices the majority religion nonetheless prevails. There is no attempt, for example, to change street names that are named after Christian saints nor is there any willingness to remove a large cross from the top of La Montagne in Montreal. Christmas and Easter will continue to be national holidays. These are all part of the 'tradition' of Québec. Although Québec was the first Canadian province to have a Charter of Rights and Freedoms (1975) that includes freedom of religion, the separatist party in power, in an attempt to consolidate support for its nationalist agenda, has proposed the safeguard of 'Québec' values. This is to be done by proscribing religious apparel that just happens to affect other religious groups where women (primarily the Muslim headscarf) and men (Sikh turbans and the Jewish kippah) are negatively affected. A large-sized cross is not to be worn, but this is irrelevant given that no one other than priests would wear large crosses. The proposed Charter affects men and women in educational institutions greatly and sparked off an intense debate in Québec society.

Since the happenings of 9/11, issues of religion and secularism have come to the forefront. On the one hand, Islam and religious fundamentalism have been the focus of much angst in North America as well as in Europe. A distorted understanding of multiculturalism (which is secular) and multicultural education (which, in its essence, is critical pedagogy) have come under attack by conservatives for being open to multicultures and religions, a move that is blamed for terrorist attacks and protests. On the other hand, Christian fundamentalists, such as the American religious right, have attacked secularism, multiculturalism and multicultural education as moving away from the fundamental values of Christianity. In education, one major point of contention has been in the realm of religion and science and several states have attempted to ban the study of evolution.

Secularism is viewed as being antithetical to religion. Educators and policy-makers must deal with questions as to whether secularism will lead to resistance towards religious fundamentalism and inhibit extremism. Keeping in mind that knowledge is political and that public schooling is one of the most important social institutions, should religious schools be funded by the state (public funds), particularly in religiously diverse societies? What should the place of religion be in the school curricula?

Using public funds to support religious schools is not universal. There are several models worldwide: some countries simply stay out of the business of providing religious education. In the US, the Establishment Clause of the First Amendment to the Constitution prohibits advocating of religion over atheism, or favouring one religion over another. This has been interpreted to mean no religious education in public schools and prohibiting school prayer. In India, Article 27 of the Constitution rules out religion in public schools although religious schools may be partially funded. Religion is separated from the state to provide religious liberty to allow all religions to flourish. Education is a concurrent subject in India and states have power over several aspects of education. Several states have Madrassa School Boards and there has been widespread controversy over government funding for the modernization of madrassas in India.

In Canada, where education is a provincial responsibility, education's role has been highly controversial. The two colonial governments, English and French, set up Protestant and Catholic systems which became enshrined as a confessional system at the time of Confederation in the British North America Act of 1867. While Ontario and Québec followed the confessional system, provinces varied in their adoption of religion in public schools, and some like British Columbia set up a non-sectarian system, while others still have a confessional system. However, due to the principle of separation of church and state, all educational systems have become increasingly secularized. Currently, Canada has a very religiously diverse society and there are varying degrees to which religion is taught in the education systems of the provinces. Some systems do not allow the teaching *of* religion, but allow teaching *about* religion.

The French province of Québec, which is largely Catholic, changed to a linguistic system through a Constitutional amendment as recently as 1997. Religious instruction is prohibited in public schools but a programme on Ethics and Religious Culture is mandatory in all schools, including private and religious schools that receive public funding. In this programme, the idea is to teach, not preach, about world religions. Both in India and Canada, financial aid is provided to schools run by religious organizations on a non-discriminatory basis. In the US, while it is unconstitutional to use public money for religious schools the voucher system allows parents to use public money to the pay for private, mostly religious schools.

Pedagogically, the issue is the imposition of religion on impressionable minds. Teaching religion can be very contentious, especially in multi-religious societies where parents worry about which values are being inculcated. It may even prevent development of respect for other religions. Moreover, teaching about a single religion is likely to prevent young people from exercising religious choices because of the mandatory nature of school subjects, and religious liberty is an important right in a democracy. It may also encourage narrow-mindedness and homogeneity rather than diversity. Religious instruction could lead to the marginalization of minority religions.

THE SCHOOL, CONTROVERSIAL ISSUES, CLASHES BETWEEN SCIENCE AND RELIGION

Science and religion have different roles in society and have different ways of knowing and understanding the world. They are based on different aspects of human experience. Scientific explanations of the natural world are based on empirical evidence, whereas religious explanations are based on faith and usually involve supernatural forces. Science cannot investigate the supernatural, but it does modify or even discard theories that produce conflicting evidence

(National Research Council, 2008). Religion, on the other hand, interprets revelatory knowledge or the scriptures but does not change them.

Increasingly, the issues in science and religion are overlapping in the modern world and schools have to deal with how to reconcile them. An example is the subject of creation and evolution. This has been hotly debated because often the origins of the human species are explained in religions, and scientific explanations clash with literal religious meanings. In countries around the world, the courts have had to pronounce judgement on the topic, and legislation either forbids the teaching of one or the other: creationism/intelligent design or evolution. The US Supreme Court has ruled in several cases that the teaching of creationism in public schools (as opposed to evolution) is unconstitutional and violates the First Amendment Establishment Clause, which prohibits the state from advancing any religion. Some religious leaders have attempted to be inclusive and reinterpreted their religious teachings to accommodate scientific theories of evolution.

Critical pedagogy respects diversity, but recognizes certain cultural beliefs as dehumanizing, and religious ideology (as opposed to spirituality), when pitted against scientific evidence, must be avoided. That is not to say that science has not been used to justify dehumanizing practices. In that sense, the way science has been used is not neutral, but attempts must be made to relate science to the everyday life experiences of students and further the cause of humanization. Critical theory means being critical and, therefore, questions and research are an integral part of the pedagogical process.

A related question is whether there is a contradiction between critical pedagogy (or education defined as conscientization) and religious teachings, especially in revelatory religions.

A crucial issue facing religious education in contemporary times is the issue of identity and legitimacy. It is about curriculum politics. The trend is to talk about religion objectively rather than on subjective terms of belief, so as to retain a neutral attitude towards a rich variety of beliefs, and to develop respect for different belief systems. Religion is not spiritualty, nor is spirituality a monopoly of organized belief systems. Furthermore, there is a difference between 'understanding religion' (detached knowledge) and 'religious understanding' (emotional response to beliefs and practices) (Cox, 1983).

Critical pedagogy examines teachers' and students' religious affiliations and challenges their positionalities vis-à-vis their beliefs. Critical education is about challenging views that are taken for granted. So, questioning religious concepts that are taken for granted is an essential component of critical education.

Critical education challenges and questions the politics of religion. Education is never neutral – it is political. Critical education is about privileging and problematizing student experience, but the emphasis has been on issues of race, class and gender – not as much on religion and religious identifications – although religion intersects with all these categories and influences the development of identities. The lack of attention to religion in critical education is particularly surprising given the importance of religion in Paulo Freire's early life.

Given that the school is a site where values and attitudes develop and students spend a large part of their early lives in the education system, an important question is: Can education fight religious fundamentalism?

Very few studies have dealt with education and its relationship with the spread of religious fundamentalism in the West. A few European educators have looked at religious fundamentalism, extremism and radicalization in relation to education. Some scholars in North America have noted that fundamental schools are the fastest-growing segment of US private education, but there are no studies as yet that look into the possible role of education in combating fundamentalism and radicalization. In India, some studies on education and fundamentalism are related to the history textbook crises during the time when the Janata Party and the Bhartiya Janata Party were in power.

While globalization has caused a convergence in models and goals of public education as well as in educational policy and practice worldwide, there has been an increase in fundamentalist beliefs that is likely a resistance to post-modern society. According to convergence theorists, a worldwide isomorphic process with standardization of beliefs, practices and policies has penetrated all institutions (including education) despite contextual and historical differences in countries. Divergence theorists focus on the pressures on the local identities and cultures brought about by convergence. The consequences result in anomie, and social groups react differently either by eventually converging or actively rejecting imposed conditions. One such response to the pressures of convergence is the divergence and reinforcement of an idealized tradition. And therein lies a paradox: the integration of the beliefs of different populations into the educational system would indicate divergence from the world-culture model. On the other hand, strict adherence to secular principles by restricting other religious cultures, as in France, is convergence. This creates tensions and a crisis for public education.

In his book *Identity and Violence* (2006), Sen points out that faith must not be monolithic and all-consuming. Religious identities should not override other identities – particularly one's identification as a human being. He further argues that when religious schools promote singular affiliations they can be a source of conflict for those who do not have an affiliation. He sees the denial of multiple identities as a fundamental cause of increasingly belligerent modes of self-expression in the world.

How do we deal with belligerent and oppositional students and their points of view? Teachers are likely to be unprepared to deal with student resistance based on religious belief. The discourse on fundamentalism is becoming increasingly prominent because it is often driven by alienation and critique of Western/modern moral values.

Goodburn (1998) points out that the absence of discussion about students' religious backgrounds and beliefs when discussing gender, race, class and so on, can result in 'othering' a student. Fundamentalist students provide diversity in the classroom. Teachers should not panic when differentness manifests itself in the form of fundamentalist ideas. It would be a contradiction to embrace diversity, but forbid its public expression.

Because knowledge in critical pedagogy is seen as inherently political, students should be given spaces to have diverse ideas even if they are extreme until such time as they are able to question and discuss them so that their experiences lead them to reconceptualize extreme views. Students with fundamentalist views must be given the opportunity to engage in counter-hegemonic discourse and practices daily in the classroom because they must get the opportunity to 'read the world through the word' as Freire suggested: through critical literacy, which enables the understanding of the word through the lenses of one's personal world. This will prevent the student from being delegitimized, alienated or challenged on a daily basis. Students need to examine more critically how they negotiate their beliefs when confronted with alternatives so as to engage in more critical dialogue.

Using their religious beliefs as a site for analysis, teachers might be able to see how the oppositional culture and resistance grows through students' life experiences. Students with fundamentalist ideas see the world from different points. The point is not necessarily to change their ideas, but to come to a mutual understanding of each other's position – a respect for different discourse so that they can learn to value and negotiate others' differences. They can move beyond the rhetoric of opposition and defiance to relate through secularism in an increasingly complex world. After all, education involves preparing students as well as teachers to be challenged and enriched by alternative perspectives.

THE IMPACT OF RELIGION ON THE EDUCATION OF GIRLS AND WOMEN

Since women more than men are expected to carry forward the cultural and ritualistic tradition of a group, the impact of religion on girls and women should be of interest to educators. Scholars have analysed the educational implications of religious influences on the socialization of girls and women. The religion and culture nexus is complex and the socialization of girls and boys is rooted in religious ideologies (rituals, custom and institutions) that provide the values and norms for socialization.

In India, although there is considerable diversity even among Hindus, all religious groups have adopted some cultural practices that are similar. They have been influenced by ideas of patriarchy, morality, purity based on religious rituals and customs and, most importantly, by the need to preserve male honour, which hinges exclusively on female chastity. These values of socialization have restricted the movement of girls by segregating them and limiting them from access to social and physical space. Discrimination is not limited to access and is extended in treatment and the daily experiences in the classroom and school culture in overt and covert forms (hidden curriculum). These have prevented women from having education, especially in the subjects that will provide employment in a knowledge economy, and limited their life chances by restraining other possibilities.

In Western societies, women have also been restricted through religion, culture and socialization. Although women in Western societies now enjoy much greater freedom and opportunities and have achieved great success in many fields, they are nevertheless still struggling to strike a balance between work and personal life. In newly multicultural societies the influx of more traditional female socialization practices have been a source of conflict in the schools where home and school cultures clash. This is more so because critical education questions the female role as inferior to that of males and *conscientizes* females to their oppressive situations while opening their awareness to wider horizons.

CONCLUSION

There is a tension between religion and secularism in education in multicultural societies. On the one hand, secularism is a characteristic of global scientific culture and modern democracies must give freedom of religion to all groups. On the other hand, even if the state is separate from the church, people continue to be religious. As a matter of fact, the more globalization pushes religion behind, the more there is a demand for religion among those whose identities are threatened. An education that inculcates respect for religious diversity rather than the eradication of religion will grant equal treatment to citizens as a necessary, even if not a sufficient, condition if peace is to be achieved and maintained.

◆

REFERENCES

Appleby, R. S. 2011. 'Rethinking Fundamentalism in a Secular Age', in Craig Calhoun, Mark Juergensmeyer and Jonathan Van Antwerpen (eds.), *Rethinking Secularism*. New York: Oxford University Press.

Cox, E. 1983. 'Understanding Religion and Religious Understanding', *British Journal of Religious Education*, 6(1): 3–13.

Freire, P. 1970. *Pedagogy of the Oppressed*. New York: Continuum Press.

Goodburn, A. M. 1998. 'It's a Question of Faith: Discourses of Fundamentalism and Critical Pedagogy in the Writing Classroom', Faculty Publication, Department of English, Paper 17. Lincoln: University of Nebraska.

Nandy, A. 1998. 'The Politics of Secularism and the Recovery of Religious Tolerance', in Rajeev Bhargava (ed.), *Secularism and Its Critics*. Delhi: Oxford University Press.

National Research Council. 2008. *Science, Evolution, and Creationism*. Washington: The National Academies Press.

Pandey, G. 2010. 'Politics of Difference: Reflections on Dalit and African American Struggles', *Economic and Political Weekly*, 45, 8–14 May.

Sen, A. 2006. *Identity and Violence: The Illusion of Destiny*. New York: W. W. Norton.

Taylor, C. 1994. 'The Politics of Recognition', in D. Goldberg (ed.), *Multiculturalism: A Critical Reader*. Cambridge, MA: Blackwell.

———. 2007. *A Secular Age*. Cambridge: Harvard University Press.

Upadhyay, P. C. 2007. *The Politics of Indian Secularism*. New Delhi: Cambridge University Press.

◆◆

9 A CULTURAL AND DIALOGIC APPROACH TO RELIGIOUS EDUCATION

SOLANGE
LEFEBVRE

NEW ETHICS AND RELIGIOUS CULTURE PROGRAMMES IN QUÉBEC

I had never considered myself a practitioner of yoga until just recently, when a new health club opened near my home and offered several courses. For some reason, this time I became a veritable amateur yogi, seduced by yoga's allure. Perhaps the gods were preparing me for my first voyage to India. I must also mention, especially in the context of the bitterly cold Canadian winters, the benefits of Bikram Yoga, or 'hot yoga', were exponential. During a session that was animated by a yogi of Indian origin, I was struck by a number of aspects. For one, the entire group listened to Indian music in rapture. Following a number of spiritual words and translations of a number of the Sanskrit mantras by the yogi, the session concluded with a resounding group 'Om' as we contemplated a large image hanging on the wall: Buddha meditating in a garden. Living in Québec, where people are often sensitive to public expressions of religion, I could see that Buddhism and yoga were working well. In fact, more and more in Canada, we find statues of Buddha and some Indian gods in gardens, restaurants, bathrooms, businesses and households. And on this subject, we rarely see a shade of controversy.

This short anecdote helps us broach a number of themes relevant to the subject of religious education. During antiquity, for example, could we imagine a religion, or spiritual tradition, finding followers if it did not refer to revered local divinities, or pertinent philosophies and myths? The colonial and imperial histories that followed no doubt exerted their influence, especially in the wake of political alliances or the conversions of local leaders and populations.

Modernity then established new modes through which to diffuse information, resulting in the further differentiation of the spheres (i.e. one of the many definitions of secularization), and examined whether investment in social missions, hospitals or education guaranteed a central role for religion in Western societies and elsewhere. This indicator has been questioned by advanced modern societies: what other forms of mediation remain apart from religion and spirituality? In my opinion, the most notable resource for this kind of discourse is culture.

A religion can exert a great deal of influence through the standpoint of its relationship with culture: from this perspective, yoga represents the 'success story' of Hinduism. The practice represents a topic for discussion in all textbooks developed in the wake of the new Ethics and Religious Culture programme that was established in Québec in 2008 for all private and public schools. Its conceptualizers have often insisted that the programme should focus on cultural expressions of religion. We might therefore assume more attention gets placed on religions and spiritualties that have had the most marked impact on culture; that is indeed the case.

A SHORT HISTORY OF A HYBRID MODEL OF EDUCATION

In Canada, Article 93 of the 1867 Constitution Act granted provincial legislative authority in the field of education to Protestant and Catholic churches. To date, only the provinces of Newfoundland and Québec (Article 93A, 1997) have requested amendments to the article. Rather than affirm neutrality, secularism or *laïcité*, we immediately find forms of abstentions and recognition – sometimes explicit, at other times implicit – that reaffirm the traditions of the historical Christian majority. With no official state religion, there are few statements of collaboration in the provincial texts regarding certain specific issues, such as health, in which the Christian churches and a number of other religious groups play more or less formal roles in the process. The abstention followed what we refer to as the 'dis-establishment of the United and Anglican Church' of the first half of the nineteenth century. Following David Martin, Van Die has suggested that contrary to the United States, religion has functioned as a kind of informal institution or 'shadow establishment' (2001: 7). While religions remain only peripherally established in the affairs of the state, they nevertheless play influential public roles.

In the province of Québec, the 1960s marked the grand period of institutional laicization within the social services, health and education sectors. In 1961, the Royal Commission's inquiry into the subject of teaching in the province of Québec proposed a number of important reforms. The state of the education system at the time was summarized as follows:

> So far, one of the hallmarks of the Québec school system is that all public education, with the exception of technical and vocational school, is mandatorily denominational, of either Catholic or Protestant inspiration. It is in the private sector, also largely denominational, that we find a number of non-denominational or multi-denominational educational institutions. On the French side, even higher education is fully administered by Catholic institutions. This sectarian character of public education has accorded quite well with a society that is relatively homogeneous from a religious point of view, the vast majority of the population being either Catholic or Protestant. As for Jewish people, the most significant minority group, they were accommodated by Protestant schools; a number of them have, however, created in Montreal and the suburbs sizable networks of private Jewish schools. But today religious pluralism is ever-growing (Rapport de la Commission royale d'enquête, 1966: para. 59).

At the heart of the bilingual and bi-denominational system, with francophones being generally Catholic and anglophones, Protestant, but with a significant Irish Catholic contingent, the Royal Commission's inquiry offered a realm of new possibilities. As in other countries that foster denominational frameworks for education, the first openness to diversity consists of offering non-denominational course options, in the simple form of an exemption. In the Protestant system, an alternative course on the philosophy and morals of diverse religious traditions could be prescribed as a replacement or supplement to religious education (Barré, 2009; Lefebvre and Barré, 2010). Catholic schools allowed a student to be excused from religious education on the request of the parent or guardian. The student could then enrol in a course related to natural morality instead. A religious studies course also appeared on a number of course schedules within the Catholic school, rather than catechism, at the discretion of the institutions (Gouvernement du Québec, 1967: 3661–62).

In 1968, the Catholic Education Service of the Ministry of Education started to reflect on an eventual reform of religious education that would include an overview of religious culture. To this end, secondary school teachers began to experiment with pedagogical materials in religious culture until 1974 (Ouellet, 1985: 315). In accordance with the right to be exempted from denominational religious education, a number of culturally oriented approaches to moral and religious instruction emerged, particularly in secondary schools. That same year, after reviewing the findings, the Catholic Committee supported the implementation of these kinds of culturally oriented, previously experimental courses. Despite its success, in 1981, this programme was abandoned for administrative reasons.

Between 1975 and 1982, three important charters paved the way for secularization of the public school system: the Québec and Canadian Charters of Rights and Freedoms (1975; 1982) and the Charter of the French Language (1977). These documents not only recommend that the state implement frameworks to engender respect for freedom of conscience and religion in general, but the Charter of the French Language also helped initiate larger attendance of students who were the children of recent immigrants in French schools; this demographic had heretofore preferred anglophone schools not only for linguistics reasons but also for the more pluralist education provided by Protestant schools.

In 1983, the exemption regime was replaced by an option regime in which moral instruction became officially open, while denominational moral and religious instruction continued at all scholastic levels. The new option regime did not, however, offer the perfect solution: i.e., the complex administrative process that yanked students from classrooms to form more or less marginal groups within the context of schools, viewed as a form of discrimination, created resentment among certain people (Cadrin-Pelletier, 2005: 97). Finally, with regard to the content for courses in the Catholic system, it is only as of 1991 that religious diversity emerged as a given for elementary students. Prior to this change, only senior year courses broached the subject of religious diversity.

Subsequently, an official discourse ensued in favour of non-denominational schools in which all students could enrol in religious culture programmes as an option (Bélanger, 2012). For example, in one section in the Report *Le défi d'une réussite de qualité* (*The Challenge of Achieving Quality*) that addresses the secularization of schools and respect for freedom and diversity, le Conseil supérieur de l'éducation supported the idea of an optional cultural programme, one that has already been explored in the 1970s. The report envisions the programme as follows:

> At once moral and religious, this approach to teaching could include three broad domains: major questions and ethical reflections; knowledge of the ethical and religious heritage of Québec society, knowledge of the major religious traditions (Conseil supérieur de l' éducation, 1993: 69, my translation).

In the years to follow, the broader lines of this recommendation would fall into effect.

Against a backdrop of perpetual debate,[1] the 1995 Estates General on Education represents the next significant collective discussion on the subject of denominational schools (Les États généraux sur l'éducation, 1995). Both the exposé of the situation and the summary of the consultations reported a division, within the population in general and the Commission itself, on the subject of whether to maintain the denominational system or to instate a non-denominational approach to education. The final report, however, utilized neither neutrality nor laïcité as concepts. The Commission highlighted the pursuit of a non-denominational school system as one of ten immediate priority areas:

> Achieve the separation of Church and State. There no longer remained a reason, other than historical attachment, to dragoon a system of education that privileged particular denominations. In this regard, a rather general consensus exists as to the transformation of denominational school boards into linguistic school boards. Denominational structures appear as an anachronism and prevent educational institutions of the Francophone majority to fulfil their mission to integrate all students and the institutions of the English-speaking minority to control their schools in accordance with their rights. We must, therefore, go back to the start in order to untie the original knot. In this regard, a sizeable movement bolstered

the repeal or at least modification of Article 93 in the Canadian Constitution (ibid.: Section 2.9, my translation).

The final report advocated that the churches take complete responsibility for 'Christian education to be conducted in more appropriate locations than public schools so that the State can stop assuming the costs for this education'. The report, moreover, endorsed the development of a value-based education through the elaboration of teaching materials focused on the cultural aspects of religion and the offering of a civil education course.

From 1997, a number of reforms were launched that are well known in the literature on religion in schools. Briefly in 1997, the governor general of Canada repealed Article 93 of the Canadian Constitution for the province of Québec. In 1998, overhauling the previous denominational system, the school boards became organized around linguistic lines. The year 1999 saw the publication of the report of the Committee for the Study of Religion in Schools that was presided over by Jean-Pierre Proulx, and a subsequent parliamentary consultation committee. In 2000, the eventual termination of all denominational courses was announced in preparation for the 2008 introduction of the Ethics and Religious Culture programme in both the public and private school systems. In 2001, a spiritual animation and community engagement service was established in secondary schools, thereby replacing Catholic and Protestant pastoral animation.

THE NEW PROGRAMME

The process that led to the implementation of the new Ethics and Religious Culture programme bears a number of intriguing details. Experts were consulted in addition to influential social figures and religious groups. The double dimension of the Ethics and Religious Culture programme raised many multifaceted discussions. On the one hand, even the association of ethics and religion in the context of the same course provoked opposition. On the other hand, discussions also highlighted the asymmetry of the two fields, especially with regard to demonstrating certain 'competencies' in the dialogues regarded as central to the programme.[2]

With regard to the combination of ethics and religious culture in a single programme, one might surmise a reflection of the exemptions and options regimes of the 1960s, under various guises, of which a number of examples have already been presented. But the decision to maintain both subjects together has engendered controversy for a fundamental epistemological reason most notably distinguished by Daniel Weinstock. Weinstock has criticized the amalgamation of ethics and religion and insists on an a priori independence of ethics (2006). The report of the Committee for the Study of Religion in Schools, of which Weinstock was a member, also advocated this approach (Proulx, 1999).

Yet certain continuity prevails. The preamble of the programme has explicitly addressed this challenge by insisting on the irreducibility of ethics to one particular religion or worldview: 'While maintaining their specificity, both the ethics and the religious culture areas of instruction grant a common place to the practice of dialogue and share the same objectives: the recognition of others and the pursuit of the common good' (Ministère de l'Éducation, du Loisir et du Sport, 2008a; Rondeau, 2008). Moreover, the ethical side acknowledges that ethical references could draw on either religious or secular worldviews or diverse other criteria.

THE EPISTEMOLOGICAL APPROACH

The relative objectification of religion in the new programme also represents a major topic of debate. The concerns that have arisen in the context of the British debates, especially in the work of Robert Jackson have, in turn, influenced the evolution in Québec in a number of ways, but particularly on the subject of how to account for the spiritual development of children. The study, related to the future cultural approach to teaching religions that accompanied the Proulx report, addresses the question of the contribution to spiritual development as follows. First, the report acknowledges that this pedagogical approach raises a number of concerns, the bulk of which hinge on the delicate role conferred to the teacher and the misgivings that it might incite in parents who face the possibility that their children may be influenced by a teacher with convictions contrary to their own (Comité sur l'éducation au phénomène religieux, 1998: 13). This anxiety has been acknowledged in the new Ethics and Religious Culture programme as it states: 'The goal is neither to accompany students on a spiritual quest, nor to present the history of doctrines and religions, nor to promote some new common religious doctrine aimed at replacing specific beliefs' (Ministère de l'Éducation, du Loisir et du Sport, 2008a: ii).

In Québec, we have nevertheless avoided promoting an approach to religion in the same vein as France with its focus on religious fact (being kept at a distance from the individual). In the interest of clarifying this point, the diverse recommendations produced by the Committee on Religious Affairs count amongst the most explicit. In 2004, the committee proposed a path that represented a clear departure from the approach followed in France, described thus: 'An apprehension of diverse historical objectifications of religious phenomena, to better comprehend the evolution of societies as well as the artistic, literary, and architectural expressions religion has engendered' (Comité sur les affaires religieuses, 2004: 9). The committee argued that this French approach would toil to achieve consensus in Québec as it would have to overcome a certain established habit in public schools, namely a tradition that never really approached the subject of religion from a strictly historical and cultural point of view (ibid.).

During the process of approving the programme, the Government of Québec entrusted the Committee on Religious Affairs with the mandate of consulting religious groups, experts and organizations on the subject of the programme slated for introduction from 1 September 2006. In its report, the Committee recalled the most litigious points contained in previous versions that seemed to be amended for the most recent version. Many of the groups and individuals that were consulted expressed concern that the term 'phenomena' indicated implicit objectification of the religious sphere. The committee noted an improvement to the previous version as the concept of religious experience was included and integrated into the programme:

> Knowledge of these aspects will enable students to grasp, according to their age, the experiential, historical, doctrinal, moral, ritualistic, literary, artistic, social and political dimensions of religion (Ministère de l'Éducation, du Loisir et du Sport, 2008a: 1).

In addition, the theme of religious experience is intended to be studied at the secondary school level.

A PHENOMENOLOGICAL OR TRADITIONAL APPROACH?

Content development for religious culture aptly expresses the tension between the fragmentary analysis of multiple religious phenomena, their links and paying attention to the internal dynamic of unique religious traditions. Two main points pertain to this subject. The developmental stages emphasized the Christian, Jewish and First Nations' traditions by focusing on their historical importance within Québec's borders. Preceding the criticism that this approach risks transmitting a particular religious framework, the approach was eschewed to make room for the presentation of diverse religious phenomena – rites, holy days, tales – that are evident in the many traditions represented in Québec. This movement is of utmost importance as it marks a shift away from a more linear approach to religions.

Among its recommendations from 2007, the Committee for Religious Affairs recalls the fact that criticism has been expressed on this subject by several consultants. They expressed their concern that religious traditions were being compartmentalized and that the content being presented lacked a connection with the believer's experience. For this reason, the Committee proposed the introduction of a systematic perspective of religions that integrates both the historical and experiential dimensions of religions during the last phase of secondary level education. In this regard, the programmes propose the following principal themes: 'Religions over time, existential questions, religious experience and religious references in art and culture' (Ministère de l'éducation, du losir et du sport, 2008a: 21).

We can also contemplate one final remark regarding the content. The hundred-page proposal outlines the content in about two or three pages per grade; this approach keeps the requirements rather unrestricted and permits variations between teaching manuals. Fundamental elements in the structuring, however, constitute a surprising constraint, as for example, the supposed association of stories, rites and rules during the high school freshman year, namely that students 'become aware that stories, rites and rules are often interwoven and that they constitute key elements of religious traditions' (Ministère de l'Éducation, du Loisir et du Sport, 2008a: 32). I had the opportunity to work on a few of these manuals, and this aspect was particularly problematic for Hinduism, since it does not relate myths and religious rituals so closely. But it was explained that this approach could not be applied to all religions. In religious studies, this point represents an overgeneralization. For one, not all religious traditions rely strictly on stories and rites; building a ternary logic based on this assumption is thus problematic. Simply stated, no manual or textbook on religion proposes such a structure. Future analysis of these manuals will demonstrate how editors and experts have been able to surmount these kinds of difficulties.

In my view, the option of an approach focused on themes or phenomena represents a challenge in scope. How can we avoid cultivating an overly spontaneous comparativism in teachers whose training consists of, at best, one year of university courses on religions? If all religions contain birth rites, symbols, leadership and places of worship, these points of reference carry fundamentally differing meanings with each tradition, which was the main critique addressed to Mircea Eliade's (1958) comparative work.

LEGAL DEBATES: THE PRETENCE OF NEUTRALITY

The programme has instigated a political debate in Québec; a number of neo-nationalists have interpreted the programme as an effort to promote multiculturalism. In this regard, the legal cases are most demonstrative. The pretence of neutrality signified the bone of contention (Gravel and Lefebvre, 2012). Since 2008, two cases that contested the new Ethics and Religious Culture programme appeared before the tribunals. The first judgement, in 2009, rendered by the Supreme Court of Québec, favours the provincial government's decision and goes against the parents who requested an exemption from the mandatory course (*S.L. c. Commission scolaire Des Chênes*, 2009, QCCS 3875). In the name of freedom of conscience and religion, the parents, practicing Catholics, argued that the programme bears a serious prejudice, namely that the claim of neutrality was only pretence and that the programme exposed students to a relativism that could be a source of confusion. Moreover, the parents argued that the Ethics and Religious Culture programme would impede their own capacity to transmit their faith tradition to their children. The Supreme Court recently supported the original verdict (*S.L. c. Commission scolaire des Chênes*, 2012, CSC 7). The judgement recognized religious neutrality as a current perspective adopted by a number of Western states as a legitimate angle from which to manage a free space in which citizens with diverse beliefs can exercise their individual rights.

The Supreme Court of Canada's reaffirmation of this decision also bore great weight in the Québec Court of Appeal case involving a private English-Catholic school, Loyola High School, which had previously succeeded in the Superior Court. In its letter to the Minister of Education that was cited in the judgement, the school also attacked the pretence of neutrality. Loyola had proposed that alongside the clear identification of the diverse religious perspectives presented in the course content, the College would present the section on Catholic ethics in greater depth. The letter also declares that the approach of neutrality proposed by the Ethics and Religious Culture programme was quite problematic in theory, because it implies a moral relativism that contradicted the convictions of various people and religions, including Catholicism, and that the notion of neutrality was illusory and impossible to achieve in practice. In fact, the high school also maintained that identifying one's position honestly represented a more objective approach than the pursuit of a notion of neutrality that could never really be attained (*Loyola High School c. Courchesne*, 2010, QCCS 2631, para. 38).

The original judgement by the Superior Court provided Loyola with the option to teach religious culture from a Catholic, rather than secular, perspective. On 4 December 2012, the Québec Court of Appeals overturned the Superior Court's verdict. Seven mentions of neutrality occurred. The judgement advocates the adoption of a policy of neutrality (para. 11). It cites Loyola's position to the effect that the neutrality of the programme is illusory (para. 17). It endorses the objectives of neutrality and objectivity pursued by the Minister of Education (para. 74). It refers to neutrality in the public sphere as recommended by the Supreme Court of Canada in the preceding judgement on the Ethics and Religious Culture Programme as an important challenge (para. 180, para. 13). Notably, as the judgement mentions the concept of laïcité twice, in reference to the favourable judgement for Loyola and the title of the Proulx report, neutrality remains the preferred and dominant judicial concept (Lefebvre, 2012).

CONCLUSION

The identification of the principal discussions surrounding the new Ethics and Religious Culture programme has enabled the identification of four primary sources of tension. Even though the history of the course options that have been offered since the 1960s can explain their association, the fact that ethics and religion are united has not been received with unanimous approval. Second, intense discussions ensued concerning the more or less disconnected epistemological relationship with the question of religion. Third, the two prominent approaches to the study of religion (paying attention to the internal coherence of traditions or focusing on the constitutive elements of traditions, such as rites, authorities and the writings of its founders) have not succeeded in rallying complete favour for their articulation in the programme. Finally, the neutrality of the programme has become a legal issue, contested by a set of parents and a Catholic high school. The judgements have ultimately not decided in favour of denominational religious education in Québec schools.

The development of a common programme for ethics and religious culture in Québec represents the product of progressive evolution. The decision breaks from the educational structures of a major portion of Western countries – apart from France – that continue to provide denominational options. Worth highlighting is the density of the resources that contributed to the establishment of the new programmes and manuals: editors, advisory committees, forums and reviewers. Two problems persist with relation to efficient implementation: teacher training and the production of manuals and pedagogical materials. Educational reforms oriented towards learning situations bear further challenges and considerable difficulties.

We can highlight the strength of the content in terms of the objects and things (*mots et choses*) associated with religions. The manuals that have already been approved by the minister present considerable content on diverse themes; for example, religious heritage and art history. In some respects, the requirements of their production have also advanced the research. For example, prior to these reforms, First Nations spirituality had not been systematically included and expanded in curricula. The following years present a rich opportunity for analysis on all of the aforementioned points (Bousquet and Crépeau, 2012).

Moreover, contrary to subjects such as mathematics for which teachers rely on established knowledge, religion represents a shared cultural location that is continually reinterpreted. We all possess preconceptions of religion. The media and products of popular culture also circulate varying information on the subject. Training teachers appears to be the key issue, alongside realistic pedagogical and ministerial orientations.

Since the events of 11 September 2001 and the advent of judicial debates in Québec and France related to the display of religious signs and symbols, an emphasis has been placed on the idea of 'living together'. For this reason, the latest report on the place of religion in the public sphere of Québec issued by the Consultation Commission on Accommodation Practices Related to Cultural Differences and presided over by Gérard Bouchard and Charles Taylor (2008) unequivocally supports the new Ethics and Religious Culture programme. The report opposes the restrictive laïcité of France and recommends an open and liberal laïcité for Québec, the constituent elements of which are: the importance of spiritual life for many citizens, the importance of protecting freedom of conscience and religion, the reaffirmation of the choice not to marginalize students who wear religious signs and symbols in school, in addition to the necessity of a religious culture course that recognizes religious phenomena and the importance of 'living together'. This position represents a crucial approval of the newly instituted programme that is under observation. For the moment, the debates around the programme have largely subsided. We also know that in some instances, the mandatory nature of the course has been informally contested by certain schools that have placed less importance on the course, or those who have substituted it with another option.

◆

NOTES

1. On the history of religious education in Québec, see Cadrin-Pelletier (2005) and Charland (2004).
2. The concept of 'competence', which has just been introduced, is based on the educational reform of 2001. Recent educational reforms in Québec have

introduced various requirements related to teaching: certain 'competencies' are among them. The new programme is thus defined along the lines of certain competencies in the three directions: (a) reflecting on ethical questions; (b) manifesting a comprehension of religious phenomena; (c) practicing dialogue.

REFERENCES

Barré, Caroline. 2009. *Le dialogue dans le programme scolaire d'éthique et de culture religieuse. Débats, bilan et prospective*, dissertation. Montréal: Faculty of Theology and Religious Studies, Université de Montréal.

Bélanger, Liette. 2012. 'La commission royale d'enquête sur l'enseignement dans la province de Québec, un changement capital', *Site Observatoire des religions*. Montréal: Faculty of Theology and Religious Studies, Université de Montréal (CRCS, CRC-IPG). http://www.observatoiredesreligions.ca.

Bouchard Gérard and Charles Taylor. 2008. 'Building the Future: A Time for Reconciliation'. Commission de Consultation sur les pratiques d'accommodement reliées aux différences culturelles. Québec: Québec Government Printing Office.

Bousquet, Marie-Pierre and Robert R. Crépeau. 2012. *Dynamiques religieuses des autochtones des Amériques (Religious Dynamics of Indigenous People of the Americas)*. Paris: Karthala.

Cadrin-Pelletier, Christine. 2005. 'L'éducation à la diversité religieuse dans le système scolaire québécois', in Solange Lefebvre (ed.), *La religion dans la sphère publique*. Montréal: Presses de l'Université de Montréal, pp. 92–114.

Charland, Jean-Pierre. 2004. *Histoire de l'éducation au Québec, De l'ombre du clocher à l'économie du savoir*. Saint-Laurent: Éditions du Renouveau pédagogique Inc.

Comité sur les affaires religieuses. 2004. *Éduquer à la religion à l'école : enjeux actuels et piste d'avenir*. Avis au ministre de l'Éducation. Québec: Gouvernement du Québec, Ministère de l'Éducation.

———. 2007. *Le programme d'études Éthique et culture religieuse*, Avis à la ministre de l'Éducation, du Loisir et du Sport. Québec: Gouvernement du Québec, Ministère de l'Éducation, du Loisir et du Sport.

Comité sur l'éducation au phénomène religieux. 1998. *L'enseignement culturel des religions. Principes directeurs et conditions d'implantation*. Québec: Ministère de l'Éducation, Groupe de travail sur la place de la religion à l'école.

Conseil supérieur de l'éducation. 1993. *Le défi d'une réussite de qualité, Rapport annuel 1992–1993 sur l'état et les besoins de l'éducation*. Québec: Gouvernement du Québec.

Eliade, Mircea. 1958. *Patterns in Comparative Religion*. New York: Sheed & Ward, Inc.

Gouvernement du Québec. 1967. *Gazette officielle du Québec, n° 24, 99ᵉ année, 17 juin 1967. Arrêté en conseil 1481 concernant l'approbation des règlements numéros 1, 2 et 3 du comité catholique du Conseil supérieur de l'éducation*. Québec.

Gravel, Stéphanie and Solange Lefebvre. 2012. 'Impartialité et neutralité autour du programme québécois Éthique et culture religieuse', in Mireille Estivalèzes and S. Lefebvre (eds.), *Le programme d'éthique et culture religieuse: De l'exigeante conciliation entre le soi, l'autre et le nous*. Québec: Presses de l'Université Laval, pp. 191–213.

Lefebvre, Solange. 2012. 'L'approche québécoise, entre laïcité et sécularité', in Mireille Estivalèzes and S. Lefebvre (eds.), *Le programme d'éthique et culture religieuse: De l'exigeante conciliation entre le soi, l'autre et le nous*. Québec: Presses de l'Université Laval, pp. 85–110.

Lefebvre, Solange and Caroline Barré. 2010. 'Le nouveau programme d'éthique et de culture religieuse au Québec : contexte, défis et tensions', in Marie McAndrew, Micheline Milot and Amina Triki-Yamani (eds.), *L'école et la diversité. Perspectives comparées*. Québec: Presses de l'Université Laval, pp. 91–103.

Les États généraux sur l'éducation. 1995. *Exposé de la situation*, chapter 9; and *Rénover notre système d'éducation. Dix chantiers prioritaires. Rapport final de la Commission des états généraux sur l'éducation*. Québec: Gouvernement du Québec, http://www.mels.gouv.qc.ca/etat-gen/rapfinal/tmat.htm (accessed 15 December 2012).

Ministère de l'Éducation, du Loisir et du Sport. 2008a. *Programmes Éthique et culture religieuse, primaire et secondaire*, Québec: Gouvernement du Québec.

———. 2008b. *Éthique et culture religieuse, Situation d'apprentissage et d'évaluation, L'accueil d'un être unique*, 1er cycle du primaire, Culture religieuse et dialogue. Working Paper, dated 9 September.

Ouellet, Fernand. 1985. *L'étude des religions dans les écoles. L'expérience américaine, anglaise et canadienne*. Waterloo: Wilfrid Laurier University Press.

Proulx, Jean-Pierre. 1999. *Groupe de travail sur la place de la religion à l'école, Laïcité et religions. Perspective nouvelle pour l'école québécoise*. Québec: Ministère de l'Éducation.

Rapport de la Commission royale d'enquête sur l'enseignement dans la province de Québec. 1966. v. 4. Tome 3. *L'administration de l'enseignement-A*, Québec: Ministère de l'éducation.

Rondeau, Dany. 2008. 'Comprendre le phénomène religieux: condition d'une éthique pluraliste', in Jean-Pierre Béland and Pierre Lebuis (eds.), *Les défis de la formation à l'éthique et à la culture religieuse*. Québec: PUL, pp. 73–92.

Van Die, Marguerite. 2001. 'Introduction', *Religion and Public Life in Canada. Historical and Comparative Perspective*. Toronto: University of Toronto Press, p. 7.

Weinstock, Daniel. 2006. 'Un cours d'éthique et de culture religieuse, prochain épisode d'un malentendu?', in Fernand Ouellet (ed.), *Quelle formation pour l'enseignement de l'éthique à l'école?* Québec: PUL, pp. 187–96.

◆◆

10 RELIGIOUS EDUCATION IN A SECULAR STATE*

RAJEEV
BHARGAVA

Should religious education be available in schools funded by the state? It is obvious that in theocracies and in states that establish religion, all schools must get state funding to impart religious education. The issue of whether or not this should be done will never arise in such states. But in secular states, this question is important and urgent. Therefore, I raise it here, although I deal with it contextually, as it presents itself in India, as well as from a particular angle, the perspective of normative political theory.

What do I mean by religious education? Should religious education be available in modern societies in any kind of school? By religious education is meant a deeper, more thorough understanding of the cumulative tradition of a particular religion, and by cumulative tradition is meant the historic deposit of the past religious life of the community in question: temples, scriptures, theological and philosophical systems, dance patterns, legal and social institutions, moral codes, myths and so on, anything that can be transmitted from one person or generation to another, and that even a scholar (an outsider) can grasp more or less objectively (Cantwell Smith, 1991: 156–57).

Education *in* the cumulative tradition of a particular religion is different from education about it. Education in religion is part of the larger process of religious instruction, the whole purpose of which is to initiate the child into a faith or to strengthen it if she already has it. Education about the cumulative tradition may be possessed even by the outsider. Hence, the phrase 'religious education' is ambiguous between education *in* (religious instruction) and education *of* the cumulative tradition of a religion.

With this clarified, let us ask: Should religious education be available in any kind of school? For those who hold the mainstream Enlightenment view of religion (or, at least, one version of it), all religious education is religious instruction and, quite simply, religion is a storehouse of superstition and obscurantism, inculcates blind acceptance of authority and undermines any capacity for independent thought. The true function of education, in this view, is to impart both a sense of individual autonomy (critical thinking, the independence of thought) and the core value of citizenship (openness, the capacity to deliberate and to listen to others, reasonableness, the respect for difference, solidarity, a sense of justice, inclusiveness and accommodation), features believed to be central to a secular vision. Religious education, it is claimed, undermines both. Thus, subscribers to this view – the hard secularists – argue that religious education must not be part of the curriculum of any school, public or private. Rather, there must be one common school which provides only secular education to believers and non-believers.

This view is unrealistic, over-simple and one-sided because, undeniably, humans have an interest in relating to something beyond themselves, which for many means relating to God or some God-like entity. They do so in different ways and this manifests itself as individual belief and feeling as well as social practice in the public domain. Furthermore, religions constitute cumulative traditions (ibid.: 154–69) and are a source of the identity of many people. Yet to accept all of this does not endorse the view held by dogmatic believers who wish all children to be sent to one common school that provides only, or predominantly, religious education. (Religious education here is once again equated with religious instruction.) This view is found in theocracies and in states with established religions and is generally forgetful or neglectful of the oppression, injustice and violence of these traditions. So, we must steer a middle course. No doubt, citizenship and individual autonomy are important, but it does not follow that all parents in any society would want schools to build only good citizens for the future. I am grateful to Jeff Spinner-Halev for helpful discussion on this issue. Parents might have a strong commitment to their identity as citizens and may wish to transmit this commitment to their children, but they may also have other equally strong commitments, including religious convictions. Parents may wish to transform their children into believers as much as they might wish that they became citizens. Therefore, they would be keen to pass on these convictions to their children.

But why can't this transmission take place at home? Why must we depend for this on institutions of civil society? One reason is that parents may wish this transmission to be enduring, which is not possible without formal and systematic training, and may not themselves have the time and qualities required for such training. Second, the religious tradition in question may be so rich that it can be taught only by institutions much larger than the family. Once the value of limited religious education in schools is accepted, we are still left with the question: which type of school? Is it to be conducted in common state-run schools, as part of, or in addition to, secular education, or in separate schools run by religious communities on their own? And should these separate schools be not merely run, but also funded by religious communities?

In the Constituent Assembly, the case against religious instruction in state schools was made on four grounds. First, the financial cost of providing such an education is borne by citizens who do not benefit from it. In an egalitarian and democratic society, public funds raised by taxes must not be utilized for the benefit of any particular religious community. Thus, consider a school established by a District Board that gives religious instruction in Hinduism on the ground that a majority of students in the area are Hindus. This violates the principle mentioned earlier because it requires that children of Muslims and other religious communities not attending religious instruction in Hinduism would nonetheless pay for this instruction. But why should they carry this unfair burden? The cost of religious instruction must be borne by the religious community itself. As K. T. Shah (1999: 877–78) put it, all the funds for the provision of religious education must be supplied by the community that desires it, not by everyone. Since state schools are publicly funded, religious education must remain a wholly private affair.

But what if the state provides education not in one but in all religions? Several arguments were put forward in the Assembly against this proposal. First, as Shah argued, in a liberal, pluralist and democratic society, secular education frequently conflicts with specialized religious instructions. Although Shah did not elaborate his reasons for this view, they were not hard to discern. To begin with, religious instruction usually teaches students obedience, but not the art of questioning. Moreover, it frequently inculcates insulation from the rest of the political community. The boundaries of religious and politically liberal communities do not always coincide. Loyalty to one may conflict with loyalty to another. These limitations obstruct the growth of students into good citizens of a free, democratic society. It is the function of the state to educate children to become good citizens and discourage anything that undermines this process. A state may allow the presence of schools that are detrimental to the value of citizenship, but surely it cannot permit this to occur in educational sites that belong to it!

Second, a point made by B.R. Ambedkar: Given that many religions claim that their teachings are the only right path for salvation, social peace and harmony are bound to be disturbed when doctrinal controversies are brought into the public domain (ibid.: 883–84). Social peace is possible only if all religions publicly declare that they do not have the monopoly over ultimate truth or are publicly silent on this matter. Since religions that believe that they have the monopoly over ultimate truth cannot publicly deny it, the most that can be expected from them is that they do not publicly assert this belief, but remain silent. This means that the doctrines of such religions must not be brought into the public domain. It follows that instruction in these religions should not be permitted in publicly funded institutions. Further, given a commitment to egalitarianism, it follows that no religious community should be given the right to religious instruction in state-aided institutions.

A third related objection came from those who feared that religious instruction exacerbates communalism. K. T. Shah wanted the article concerning religious instruction to be framed keeping in mind not sects and denominations, as they might exist in some ideal world, but as they really are. Actually existing sects and denominations frequently forget the basic truth of all religion, he argued, and 'exalt their own particular brand as any advertiser in the market lauds his own wares' (ibid.: 877). Renuka Ray argued that religion 'had been exploited and prostituted in the country and has led to the worst horrors that could be perpetrated in the name of religion' (ibid.: 878). Similarly, R. K. Sidhwa, a Parsi member, argued that

> the religious books of the various communities are translated by various authors in a manner that has really brought disgrace to

religion. The authors have translated the beautiful original phrases to suit their own political ends with the result that today, on religious grounds, the country has broken into various pieces (ibid.: 906).

Therefore, 'under existing circumstances, there should be no religious education provided in any educational institution which receives state aid' (ibid.). Sidhwa, pointing out several instances of the preaching of communal hatred in the name of religion, argued that unless the meaning of religious education is specified in the Constitution, the same hateful religious education may be taught. The Constitution cannot give people 'the freedom to teach religion in any manner they like' (ibid.).

A fourth practical difficulty was raised by several people. In a multi-religious society, it is physically impossible for the state to make provisions for the teaching of all religions. Under these circumstances, the only solution is to avoid religious instruction in state-aided schools. Finally, there was an argument propelled simply by an anti-majoritarian impulse. For instance, most Sikh members supported a total ban on religious instruction in educational institutions maintained wholly out of state funds, because they feared that this inevitably favoured the religion of larger communities. Indeed, some wanted the ban to be extended to the media (ibid.).

It appears, then, that in a pluralist and democratic society only common schools should be supported by the taxpayer's money. All right, it might be said, religious teaching should neither be altogether banned from all schools nor be permitted in state schools, but can we allow *some* public funding for privately run schools with religious affiliation? At first sight, it appears, the correct answer is to reply in the negative. After all, arguments against public funding of religiously affiliated schools are similar to arguments against religious education in state-run schools. If it is impermissible for state-run schools to provide religious education, how can it be proper for states to give financial support for religious education in private schools? Would an affirmative answer here not imply an exaggerated sense of the power of states to cause grave harm and a correspondingly lower estimate of the power of private institutions to do so? If the object of our concern is the threat to liberal and democratic values, then we must attend to the source of this threat, whatever that might be. If religiously affiliated private schools undermine liberal and democratic values, then ways must be found to discourage them to the same degree, in much the same manner as we might wish to prevent states that pose a similar threat. If so, should a secular state not intervene in these institutions? Should it not discourage them by refusing to publicly fund them? This kind of argument, however, proves, at best, that religiously affiliated schools and state schools do not deserve public support to the same degree, not that they do not deserve any support whatsoever. To arrive at this conclusion, we must show these arguments to be so strong or invincible that they rule out even a disproportionately small public funding of private, religiously affiliated schools. For instance, it must also be shown that religiously affiliated schools always violate liberal and democratic values.

Therefore, does any justification exist for even partial funding of separate, religiously affiliated schools? The answer to this question depends, as I said, on the assessment of arguments against religious education. Consider first the argument from unfair burden. This argument is sound if funding is provided to schools run by one religious community, but loses at least some of its force if it is given to schools run by all religious communities. Moreover, this argument assumes that separate schools impart only religious education. This is almost always not the case. Most educational institutions run by a religious community teach much more than religion, which remains only a fraction of the overall curricula, and in many schools is not its dominant feature. Should financial support not be given to the secular part of education in such schools? If religious communities had originally set up schools to teach their respective religions, and if secular education is publicly funded, would it not place an unfair burden on religious communities if they were also to support secular education in their schools? Why, for instance, should a school lose public funding for science just because it holds a few classes for the purpose of teaching religion? It is not illegitimate for taxpayers to pay for good-quality secular education in all schools. In any case, others are unfairly burdened only when denied entry to such institutions. If admitted, and if they can partake equally of its non-religious curricula, then they, more or less, pay for something from which they clearly benefit. The unfairness of the burden is also considerably lessened if those who study in such schools or colleges are exempt from instruction in the dominant religion of these institutions.

Perhaps an element of unfairness continues to persist if public grants are given to some, but not to other, religious communities; but, if available on a non-preferential basis to all religious communities, then nothing much remains of the argument that the partial funding of educational institutions run by religious communities imposes an unfair burden on other citizens of a society.

What about the argument that majoritarianism may be fuelled when educational institutions that impart religious instruction are funded by the state? Given its dominance in civil society, is it unlikely that the majority religious community will hog large chunks of state funds for its own educational institutions? If so, will state funding not help the majority community? However, there is an equally good argument that, without the partial funding of educational institutions of minority communities, the majority will benefit at the expense of minorities. If a particular religious community dominates a society, then it does not need public funds or specially created religion-centred schools to ensure community boundaries. When the majority of students and teachers come from the same religion, then the ethos of most public schools will be that of the majority. In such situations, where the dominant ethos is permeated by the culture or religion of the majority, the minorities may feel estranged, may feel as misfits. To avoid this feeling of alienation, they may wish to assimilate. On the other hand, if there are state-supported, religiously affiliated schools, they may be able to more easily maintain their community identity. If so, state funding is likely to benefit the minority community. A majority religious community may successfully run its educational institutions without support from the state but, given its relative marginalization in civil society, a minority religious community may, on its own, not be able to sustain its schools and colleges. In India, Article 26 may be hollow without Article 30(2). Thus, the argument from majoritarianism against partial funding of educational institutions of religious communities is not compelling.

A second argument for religious education is grounded in a peculiar feature of Hinduism. The very distinction between religion, philosophy and culture makes no sense in Hinduism. Therefore, taking religion out of public education would mean virtually excluding Indian culture and civilization. In this context, Ambedkar made an interesting distinction between religious instruction and religious education and argued in favour of religious education. When asked if institutions, where the Vedas, the Smrithis, the Gita and the Upanishads are taught and maintained wholly out of state funds, would be shut down once the Constitution came into force, Dr. Ambedkar replied that there was a distinction between religious instruction and religious study. Religious instruction means the teaching of dogma. Religious study or religious education is different (religious study must imply that we also question dogma because all education implies possible critique, i.e., the critical questioning of anything under scrutiny) (ibid.: 885). The implication was clear. The critical study of religious texts is not only permissible but must be positively encouraged.

It appears then, that, given some important qualifications, partial funding to separate, religiously affiliated schools must be granted. This still leaves us with one problem, however. State schools, on our model, do not teach religions. Private schools, on the other hand, must teach religion and teach it in the right way, for example, without deriding other religions, but they do not teach *other* religions. If so, we are in a situation where no school imparts proper inter-religious education, necessary for inter-religious understanding and eventually, civic friendship. Is this a justifiable state of affairs? It is pertinent here to mention that not much validity resides in the claim that teaching religions in schools invariably leads to violent communal conflicts. Ismail's point in the Constituent Assembly that communalism is exacerbated only because people misunderstand each other's religion overshoots its aim but is not entirely mistaken (ibid.: 875). Although some religious conflicts could arise only because we properly understand the religion of others, others are intensified instead by false propaganda, stereotyping and caricature. Proper teaching of different religions assists in dispelling these and diffuses tension between religious groups. It should do so as much by minimizing prejudice as by helping us see the futility of trite answers, such as all religions are essentially the same.

Second, inter-religious education is crucial because just and peaceful societies cannot be built either without persons of faith or when people of different faiths clash with one another. Nor can they be built any longer by foolishly persevering with the belief that all religions, other than one's own, are wrong, by the domination of one's own faith. They can be built only when diverse groups of believers and non-believers can come to effective mutual understanding, accommodation and acceptance. Third, what is needed today is not just that Muslims or Hindus or Christians be good Muslims, Hindus and Christians only in their respective religious communities, but rather that they be good Muslims, Hindus or Christians in a world where other intelligent and sensitive people are not Hindus or Muslims or Christians (Cantwell Smith, 1965). This is possible only with sensible multi-religious education.

It might be argued here that this problem can be overcome if children from different religious backgrounds meet one another, as they do in state-run schools, and learn that ways of thinking and being exist other than the one taught by their parents. They may even learn to respect other ways of life and thought. Besides, this diversity need not be restricted to public schools. It may be encouraged in religiously affiliated schools if these schools are also thrown open to children from other religions, as they are in India. Though less than in schools run wholly by the state, this diversity may still be good enough to encourage inter-religious toleration and this may in turn help civic friendship and values of citizenship. Religiously affiliated schools too may encourage people to listen to one another, to negotiate and compromise with one another. Yet, up to now, a school only incidentally provides an arena for inter-religious toleration. It does not address the issue of inter-religious education, of properly learning about other religions.

So, we do need multi-religious education. This still leaves us with the question: What is the proper site of inter-religious education? Should state-run schools provide inter-religious education or should they keep away from all types of religious education, but make it a condition of public funding that private, religiously affiliated schools give education not only in their own religion but in other religions as well? I do not think it is fair to expect separate, private schools to do this job. The whole point of keeping them separate is to give them the opportunity to initiate children into beliefs and practices associated with a particular faith. To expect them to do otherwise is to expect them to make a paradigm shift – a rather impossible expectation. So, my own view is the following:

(a) To procure public funding, separate, religiously affiliated schools must meet the following minimum conditions:

    (i) They must accord with general standards of national curricula.

    (ii) They must not discriminate on grounds of religion in their policy of admission.

    (iii) They must not compel children to attend instruction in the religion of the community that runs the school.

    (iv) They must not foster negative stereotypes of other religions.

(b) The state should itself undertake the important task of providing inter-religious education.

At this stage, another objection might be raised. Should a secular state commit itself to multi-religious education? Does a state remain secular when it undertakes religious education in any form? Is there a significant difference between education in one religion and education in many? This is yet another issue that dominated the assembly debates. Several members worried that a state that provides multi-religious education may compromise its secular character. However, this worry is unfounded. It stems from wrongly equating the secular character of states with one particular manifestation of it. This point needs elaboration.[1]

It is a commonplace that political secularism means the separation of state and religion. But to unpack the metaphor of separation and to grasp what is really at issue here, we must see separation in terms of a possible disconnection at three distinct levels. A state may be disconnected from religion at the level of ends (first-level), at the level of institutions (second-level) and the level of law and public policy (third-level). A secular state is distinguished from theocracies and states with established states by a primary, first-level disconnection. A secular state has free-standing ends, either substantially, if not always completely, disconnected from the ends of religion or conceivable without a connection with them. States with established religions have something in common with secular states – at least a partial institutional disconnection.

But secular states go further in the direction of disconnection; they break away completely. They withdraw favours or privileges that established churches had earlier taken for granted. Finally, a state may be disconnected from religion even at the level of law and public policy. When it disconnects at this third level as well, it excludes religion altogether from every form of state activity. Such a state maintains a policy of strict or absolute separation. In this incarnation, it typifies a hysterical Brahmanical attitude: religion is untouchable, so any contact with it contaminates secularist purity. Secularism here becomes a doctrine of political taboo; it prohibits the state to come into contact with religious activities. Such a view proposes that religious and political institutions live as strangers to each other, at best with benign, respectful indifference. When a state is disconnected from religion at all three levels in this particular way, then we may say that a 'wall of separation' has been erected between the two. In this conception of secularism as a wall of separation, religion must be outside the purview of the state and, in this sense, must be privatized. Now this conception of a secular state, in which religion is disconnected from the state at all three levels, is not the only available conception of a secular state. A state can be secular if it disconnects itself from religion at the first two levels, but is connected at the third level: in short, when, instead of excluding religion at the third level, it keeps a principled distance from it. The policy of principled distance entails a flexible approach on the question of inclusion/exclusion, engagement/disengagement, intervention/abstention, dependent on the context, nature or current state of relevant religions. It accepts a disconnection between state and religion at the level of ends and institutions but does not make a fetish of it at the third level of policy and law.

Principled distance is premised, therefore, on the idea that a state that has secular ends and is institutionally separated from the church, or some church-like entity, may engage with religion at the level of law and social policy. This engagement must be governed by principles undergirding a secular state, i.e., principles that flow from a commitment to the values mentioned previously. Thus, even religion may be included, or equality, or any other value integral to secularism. For example, citizens may support a coercive law of the state purely grounded in a religious rationale if this law is compatible with freedom or equality. Or a state may grant aid to religious institutions, or may itself provide multi-religious education if it promotes equality or fraternity. Since a third-level disconnection is not constitutive of secular states, a state does not lose its secular character if it aids religiously affiliated schools or provides multi-religious education. I have argued that under some circumstances, a secular state may directly provide multi-religious education. I am not here claiming, of course, that this is the only function of schools run by states. This would be an absurd claim and more in line with states with established religions than with secular states. Rather, my proposal is that multi- or inter-religious education can, and, in some circumstances, must be an integral part of the larger project of secular education by the state.

I end this chapter with one more proposal and a hope. The proposal is that there must be some form of cooperation between state-run or recognized common schools and separate, religiously affiliated private schools. This cooperation is essential because each type of school serves an important social or public purpose. Separate religious schools make children fluent in their own religions and enable them to sustain and renew their particular religious traditions. Common schools make children fluent in a language that helps them understand the economic, political and social forces affecting their lives and to be articulate about them in the public sphere. A programme of inter-religious education in common schools can teach them a language to engage each other, respectfully and reverentially, across different religious traditions. But how might this cooperation work? Two possibilities come immediately to mind: one which was discussed in, and discarded by, the Constituent Assembly. The first allows students to attend public schools in the morning and religiously affiliated schools in the afternoon. Although the split-day programme fosters ideals of inclusion and diversity, and for some is perhaps a better option than state funding for religiously affiliated schools, it places an undue burden on students. A good alternative is that children who wish to get religious education attend religiously affiliated schools at the primary and secondary levels and a common school at the senior level. This helps them to secure the benefits of both, without unduly burdening them with an unbearably heavy schedule at the primary and secondary levels.

My hope is that one day we will discard the form of multi-religious education that, in the current context, I have endorsed.

In the present form, multi-religious education means learning about a religion that is one's own and then, secondarily, learning about religions that are not one's own, which belong to others. However, this idea of separate religious systems, to which each of us owe distinct allegiance, is not a natural idea, as Wilfred Cantwell Smith, the great historian of comparative religions, so brilliantly showed. Asian faiths – the great faiths of the East – are not and can become religions only with cataclysmic distortion. It is well known that in the recent past a person in parts of rural India could easily be both a Hindu and a Muslim. Even today, and I must be corrected if I am mistaken here – a single Chinese may be, and usually is, 'a Confucian, a Buddhist and a Taoist'. This may baffle many for it is difficult for us to imagine how a single person can belong to three different religions. But, as Cantwell Smith reminds us, this perplexity arises from an inappropriate imposition of the concept of a religious system on what really are three rich and complex traditions of thought. These schools of thought have been cherished for centuries in China. Their teachings are available and everyone partakes of them, but what each person does with them is entirely up to him. (Take the case of political thought and theory. As a student of political thought, I cherish the thought of Plato, Aristotle, Locke, Burke, Rousseau, Marx, Gandhi and Ambedkar, but I do not necessarily become an ideologically committed Lockean, or Burkean, or even Gandhian, as I do so. I embrace a part of their thought, without swallowing the whole. Nor do I feel the need to build a closed community around each tradition of thinking.) One day, I hope it will be possible for each one of us to partake of the rich traditions of the Jains, the Buddhists, the several communities that fall under the umbrella of the Hindus, the Muslims, the Jews, the Christians, as well of the many indigenous peoples, without the compulsive need to publicly display that we belong first and foremost to only one of these.

◆

*This chapter is based largely on Rajeev Bhargava (2010).

NOTE

1. See Rajeev Bhargava (2009).

REFERENCES

Bhargava, Rajeev. 2010. 'Secular State and Religious Education: The Debate in India', in *The Promise of India's Secular Democracy*. Delhi: Oxford University Press.

———. 2009. 'Political Secularism: Why It Is Needed and What Can Be Learnt from Its Indian Version', in Geoffrey Brahm Levey and Tariq Modood (eds.), *Secularism, Religion and Multicultural Citizenship*. Cambridge: Cambridge University Press, pp. 82–109.

Cantwell Smith, Wilfred. 1991. *The Meaning and End of Religion*. Minneapolis: Fortress Press.

———. 1965. *Modernization of a Traditional Society*. Delhi: Asia Publishing House.

Shah, K. T. 1999. *Constituent Assembly Debates*, Vol. VII, 8 December 1948, Lok Sabha Secretariat, New Delhi, pp. 877–78.

Spinner-Halev, Jeff. 2000. Surviving Diversity: Religion and Democratic Citizenship. Baltimore: Johns Hopkins University Press.

11 TEACHING 'RELIGION' AND 'PHILOSOPHY' IN INDIA

SONIA SIKKA

I t is a truism that in social contexts involving diversity, living together well across differences is aided by accurate and comprehensive knowledge of one another. Difference alone need not be a source of hostility and mistrust between groups, but when combined with ignorance, it functions to produce the kinds of social situations in which hatred and violence thrive. Admittedly, it would be hard to deny that, in India and elsewhere, there are actors who benefit from and actively promote attitudes of conflict between communities marked by difference of various sorts. There are also many who take positive pleasure in aggression towards others, and indeed in the very process of positioning people as 'others'. It would, therefore, be naïve to suppose that inter-group conflict is exclusively a result of inadequate knowledge. Still, we do generally believe, and legitimately so, that getting to know the truth about one another at least helps to counter prejudices and negative stereotypes, to build respect for difference, and to recognize the humanity of the other.

There would seem to be no reason a priori to exclude religious differences from this general case. In contexts containing religious diversity, therefore, one might fairly suppose that harmony between religious groups would be aided by better public knowledge about the varying beliefs and practices of these groups, delivered in an unbiased and respectful spirit. If promoting social harmony is a legitimate aim of the state, which surely it is, it follows that providing public education on this subject is a sensible and permissible state action. Yet in India, unlike, for instance, the United Kingdom, commitment to political secularism has meant excluding the teaching of religion from publicly funded educational institutions. As we know, however, thanks to the labours of many recent historians of the subject, 'secularism' can take many forms, adapting to the particular needs and realities of the various nations in which some version of it has evolved, and continues to evolve. Consequently, there is no single, principled answer to the question of whether secularism as such is compatible with the provision of state-funded education. Rather, to answer the question, one has to examine the likely benefits and hazards of providing such an education, given the concrete circumstances of a given nation. Addressing this point, Rajeev Bhargava draws a distinction between 'education *in* the cumulative tradition of a particular religion' and 'education about it', where the former seeks to initiate a child into a faith or to strengthen it, while the latter is available even to an outsider (2010: 302). Whereas public schools cannot be in the business of promoting a particular faith, Bhargava argues, the state not only can but should provide inter-religious education about religion (ibid.: 311).

There are certainly powerful arguments to be made in favour of providing non-sectarian, objective and critical public education about religion in a nation like India. Not least amongst these is the fact that political and religious actors with questionable agendas often seek to manipulate the sentiments of religious communities, and on balance, public ignorance helps rather than hinders their endeavours. Martha Nussbaum alludes to this problem in *The Clash Within*, suggesting that the absence of public education in post-independence India, while grounded in understandable fears rooted in the massive communal violence that accompanied Partition, has created conditions in which narrowly communal religious ideologies can flourish (2007: 178). More recently, in *Not for Profit: Why Democracy Needs the Humanities*, Nussbaum laments the fact that 'the study of comparative religion and the history of religions is not an academic subject in Indian universities' (2010: 131), leaving people more vulnerable to propaganda fostering religious violence (ibid.: 142).

The situation vis-à-vis the academic study of religion in India is not quite as dire as it may look at first, at least in terms of research and programmes of studies on offer to students (the relative prestige and popularity of these programmes is another matter). While religious studies does not exist as a separate field of study in

India, the subject of religion is researched, and courses on it are offered to students in a number of other humanities and social science departments, such as history, sociology, philosophy and literature. With respect to my own discipline – philosophy – it is worth mentioning reforms instituted in 2008 to programmes offered by the Department of Philosophy and Religion at Visva-Bharati University. These now include B.A. and M.A. options on comparative religion, the content of which is explicitly modelled on religious studies programmes in Canada, covering the study of different religious traditions as well as a variety of approaches to the analysis of religion. To note another example, the Philosophy Department at the University of Mumbai offers certificate and degree programmes in Jainology and Vedanta, with affiliated colleges integrating the study of religious texts into some of their courses. The extent of academic study and the teaching of religion in India certainly does remain modest, however, considering the importance of religion itself in India's past and present, and the potential benefits of education in this field warrant its expansion.

At the same time, designing and implementing the delivery of such education involves numerous challenges, and the options carry with them potential drawbacks. One of these is especially acute in the case of India, given the nature of what are now commonly identified as its 'religious' traditions. The problem is intimated in Bhargava's hope 'that one day we will discard the form of multi-religious education that, in the current context, I have endorsed' (Bhargava, 2010: 313). This statement, surprising at first glance, is inspired by Wilfred Cantwell Smith's thesis that, in Bhargava's words, the 'idea of separate religious systems to which each of us owe distinct allegiance is not a natural idea', but an invention of the modern West and largely inappropriate to the character of Asian faiths (ibid.: 313). Bhargava hopes that just as it is possible to cherish the ideas of a range of political thinkers without being ideologically committed to any one of them, so it might one day be possible to partake of different religious traditions in the same spirit (ibid.: 314).

Bhargava presents this hope in terms of a proposal for first teaching 'religions' in the conventional manner as systems of allegiance and then going beyond this way of relating to religion. But the problem is that the former method of organizing the study of religion may work against the latter aim. I argue in this chapter that the discipline of philosophy can play a special role in mitigating this difficulty. Wilfred Cantwell Smith was on to something important in his genealogy of the concept of religion, I believe, and his analysis does have special relevance to the case of India. In light of that analysis, I wish to address a specific question: How should we conceptualize the fact that within classical Indian intellectual traditions, 'religion' is not distinguished from 'philosophy'? My aim in raising this question is not merely to provide greater conceptual and historical clarification but rather to make a normative claim, with implications for teaching Indian traditions of philosophy/religion. There is, I suggest, a valuable element in the relation to 'religious' subjects that exists in contexts containing no concept of 'religion' in the modern sense. This element is lost in the transition to a situation where people imagine – and thereby make it true – that there *are* religions, understood on the Western, largely Christian, model as communities of faith. While Smith valorizes 'faith' in opposition to 'religion', this notion of 'faith' is still rooted in Abrahamic religious traditions, and prepares the way for a self-reflexive relation to beliefs of a certain kind that places these beliefs outside the arena of critical reflection and debate. When approached in a certain manner, Indian traditions offer an alternative to precisely this relation.

THE CONCEPT OF RELIGION

Over the past few decades, a considerable body of scholarship has emerged problematizing the category of religion. This scholarship challenges the assumption that the term 'religion' properly names a perennial feature of human cultures over the course of their history, proposing instead that the concept is a modern Western construction. Ground zero for this line of critical analysis is Wilfred Cantwell Smith's *The Meaning and End of Religion*, in which he took issue with the contemporary custom of thinking that:

> there is in human life and society something distinctive called 'religion'; and that this phenomenon is found on earth at present in a variety of minor forms, chiefly among outlying or eccentric peoples, and in a half-dozen or so major forms. Each of these major forms is also called 'a religion', and each one has a name: Christianity, Buddhism, Hinduism, and so on (1991: 15).

Since then, many scholars have criticized this idea of religion and the way it functions in the production of academic as well as popular and political discourses. In relation to India, one line of argument has been that there is actually no such thing as a 'religion' in India. Indigenous Indian traditions, it is often pointed out, have no word corresponding to 'religion', and until the colonial encounter the inhabitants of the subcontinent did not separate what we now call the 'religious' sphere of activity from other aspects of society and culture.[1]

Scholars have also sought to trace the ways in which 'Hinduism', in particular, is originally a colonial construction, taken up in the project of Hindu nationalism (Bloch *et al.*, 2010; Dalmia, 1997). Their studies point out, for instance, that there was in India no such thing as a religion called 'Hinduism' prior to the importation of Western, and especially Christian, ideas of 'religion'. Even if 'invention' may be too strong a term, Hinduism, as a distinct religion defined by a determinate set of beliefs and practices, came into being as a result of, and in interaction with, the political and institutional requirements imposed upon India by various colonial discourses (Pennington, 2005). Through such processes, this new identity took shape in contradistinction to 'other' Indian religions – Buddhism, Sikhism and Jainism – and in opposition to Islam. These religious identities continue to be constructed, moreover, both in India and abroad, as part of a process of 'religion-making' that had its roots in colonial mappings, but now follows diverse trajectories under a variety of motivations and pressures (King, 2011; Ludden, 2005; Mandair, 2011; Zavos *et al.*, 2012). An implication of such analyses is that the historical construction of these religious identities laid the basis for the hostility and conflict between religious communities that has been such a pronounced feature of the subcontinent's modern history, and for the brand of Hindu nationalism that still defines itself in antagonistic relation to Islam.

Although these points about the construction of distinct Indian 'religions' are well-taken, some of the more radical claims made by those who argue that there is no such thing as religion in India are open to debate. It is true that classical Indian languages contain no term that can be properly translated as 'religion', and no concept precisely corresponding to this one. Still, insofar as pre-modern Indian traditions do relate themselves to supra-mundane issues – to questions about life after death, heaven and gods, for instance – they recognizably address phenomena covered by the modern concept of 'religion'. Granted, that concept is heavily shaped by the character of Christianity, and one should be careful not to impose the Christian model of religion on other traditions. But as Pennington argues, one can accept that 'there are myriad ways in which Hindu and Christian traditions differ in the character and content of their normative models', while rejecting the view that 'religion is now so ossified and monothetic a concept that it cannot accommodate a careful elaboration of these significant differences' (2005: 15).

It is also important to be aware of the reductionist assumptions behind many recent critiques of the concept of religion generally, with which some analyses questioning the concept in relation to India are connected. Authors like Timothy Fitzgerald (2000) and Russell McCutcheon (2001), for instance, argue against the usefulness of the category of religion on the grounds that there is no special domain of experience captured by it. This claim involves the view that religion is reducible to other categories of analysis – sociological, political and cultural – that it is not grounded in any unique form of experience, and that the purportedly objective scholarly outsider is in a better position to understand it than are the insiders who comprise its faithful adherents. Maya Warrier points out, against such assumptions, that there exist also 'critical insiders', that religion has its own rationality, and that scholarly approaches are themselves far from value-neutral, 'deriving from such disparate sources as scientism, secular or liberal humanism, feminism, cosmopolitanism, Marxism and postmodernism' (2012: 47).

That said, one should not underestimate the significance of analyses drawing attention to the constructed character of the current concept of religion, and to the fact that this concept did not exist in pre-modern and non-Western societies. The latter point is especially important, and in ways that remain under-thematized and under-explored. Cultural phenomena that we now consider to be religious may well have existed in, for instance, ancient India, but it does make a difference if they were not conceived under a category that would separate them into spheres distinct from, say, philosophy, science and politics. It also makes a difference if they did not conform to a notion of religion whose character and components are based on Protestant Christianity. Perhaps most importantly, it makes a difference if individuals, communities and traditions that would, from a modern Western perspective, be positioned as 'religious' did not *relate* themselves to a concept of religion as a fixed body of belief defining the identities of different religious communities.

This observation lies at the heart of Smith's critique of the concept of religion in *The Meaning and End of Religion*, which was certainly not reductive. In his account of the historical emergence of this concept, Smith notes that the Latin adjective *religiosus* had more to do with 'a quality of men's lives or a coloring of the world that they perceive than . . . some independent substance or entity' (1991: 20). At a certain point within the history of Christianity, a different conception begins to take shape, he argues, involving 'a new notion of boundaries . . . a *religio* of one set of people, clearly and radically distinct from the *religions* of others' (ibid.: 27). Eventually, there arose the idea of '"the" Christian religion', where this means a certain 'system of beliefs and practices, considered as a system, irrespective of whether or not they elicited in the human heart a genuine fear and love for God' (ibid.: 39).

Smith is clearly making an evaluative rather than exclusively descriptive point regarding the change from religion as piety to 'religion' as a system of belief. He views this historical development as a decline, saying at one point: 'I have come to feel that, in some ways, it is probably easier to be religious without the concept; that the notion of religion can become an enemy to piety . . . one might almost say that the concern of the religious man is with God; the concern of the observer is with religion' (ibid.: 19). Thus, Smith assumes that *being* religious involves some unique element having to do with a relation to God. The subject matter of the study of religion is therefore not in doubt for him, and it is a subject he addresses with obvious sympathy. This aspect of his analysis is sharply rejected by some of the authors I mentioned earlier, who follow Smith in analysing 'religion' as a historically constructed concept, but take that analysis in a different direction. For Smith, 'personal faith', which he defines as 'an inner religious experience or involvement of a particular person; the impingement on him of the transcendent, putative or real' (ibid.: 156), is essential to being religious. Critics of the category such as McCutcheon and Fitzgerald, on the other hand, see this stance as endorsing the view that religion is *sui generis*, involving a unique form of experience that cannot be explained in terms of non-religious concepts.

However one judges this issue of piety or personal experience, I want to focus on another point that Smith's historical account helps to isolate: namely, the development of a kind of self-reflexivity about 'religion' as a system of belief as a well as a community of membership. Smith observes, for instance, that

> in the Bhagavad Gita, when Krishna the Lord, previously disguised as Arjuna's charioteer, has led Arjuna to a point where he is capable of receiving a divine revelation, he does not reveal 'Hinduism' to him, but reveals Himself, a personal God (ibid.: 128).

What people listening to this narrative related to then, was not a religion called 'Hinduism', but Krishna, God, reality, death, fate, duty and whatever other themes may be addressed in the verses in question. What are the implications of this fact? One frequently noted point in this regard is that there was no unity to what we have come to call 'Hinduism' at the time such narratives were composed, and over the history of their retelling and being written down until the advent of Western colonialism. More radically, though, Smith's analysis suggests that not only is the text not about 'Hinduism', but it is not about 'religion' at all. It does not address its audience as members of a 'religion', nor do they see themselves in this way. They are focused rather on Krishna and whatever else the text is about – and it is *not* about 'religion' in the modern sense.

RELIGION AND PHILOSOPHY IN INDIA

But why does this matter, one might ask? Nonetheless, can we not stand back and identify the concerns raised in the text as 'religious' in that they have to do with a god and supermundane matters, even if no concept of religion is being used? Can a certain phenomenon not exist in a culture, even if there is no concept for it? After all, whether or not all phenomena counting as 'religious' in some sense posit gods or other supernatural beings, this narrative certainly does, and the positing of such beings clearly belongs to the domain of what we now term 'religion'. The passages in the Bhagavad Gita, where Krishna reveals his true form to Arjuna deal with the nature, power and activity of a divine being who is responsible for all that exists and who is presumed to exist. What reason would we have, then, for hesitating to call this a 'religious' narrative?

Yet the Bhagavad Gita is not 'only' identified as a religious text within contemporary academic disciplines; it is 'also' considered to be a philosophical one. Discussion of at least some parts or aspects of the Gita is included in many Western textbooks on Indian philosophy. This is partly because some of the subjects treated in the text – the nature of reality, the self, ethics, knowledge – fall within the disciplinary borders of modern Western philosophy. It is not subject matter alone, however, that distinguishes philosophy from other aspects of culture, and from religion and theology in particular; it is also method or approach. Aquinas's arguments for the existence of God are considered as philosophy because they are *arguments*. They give reasons, and they do not rest on appeal to supernatural experience or to an authoritative text that is supposed to be revealed by God. Alternatively, using categories evolved within the Western tradition, they count as 'natural' rather than 'revealed' theology.

Smith rightly points out, however, that 'a differentiation between religion and philosophy is palpably out of place for the history of India' (ibid.: 92). That no such distinction is made in the Bhagavad Gita does not mean merely that the narrative contains what we would now distinguish as religious and philosophical elements but does not recognize them as such. It means that its authors and listeners do not distinguish a special set of beliefs as belonging to the category of 'religion', regarding these as, for example, a matter of 'faith' in the sense of something revealed and to be taken on trust. Krishna does 'reveal' his true form to Arjuna, who is then being granted an extraordinary vision of the truth of things, but this does not lead to the Gita being considered a revealed text in the way the Bible is for Christianity, or the Qur'an for Islam. What we have here is not 'religion' as a distinct sphere of existence involving a special way of believing, but a description of how things are, along with views about how one gets to know how things are, and how one should think and act, given that this is how things are.

When schools we now identify as 'Buddhist' took issue with views we now associate with 'Hinduism' – for instance, with the idea of the self as a single, unitary reality – they were not defining themselves as belonging to a 'religion' distinct from Hinduism. They were taking issue with certain claims about the self and reality among their contemporaries, arguing that these claims are false. The differing positions among the schools have implications for how one should think and live, in order to achieve the best kind of life or the highest goal of life. These are translated into monastic codes in cases where such a form of life is recommended. The resulting groups are not 'communities of faith' on the Christian model, and they do not distinguish themselves from one another as separate religions. But they do distinguish themselves from one another in *some* fashion. A late Upanishadic text includes 'juggleries of the non-self doctrine' in its list of teachings that lead astray, exhorting 'those who are bound for a heavenly world' not to live amongst those who are not. Furthermore, the latter group includes all those who do not know 'the difference between knowledge and ignorance' where that means not knowing the Vedas, since 'what is set out in the Vedas is truth' (Roebuck, 2003: 385–7). It might seem that one can speak quite accurately, in retrospect, of different 'religions' to describe this situation, and even of 'faith', since at least one of the groups in question accepts the authority of a particular text. But it matters that this Upanishad does not relate itself to anything conceived as 'religion', and does not issue a call to faith on behalf of that religion. It expresses broad disagreement with a variety of groups who are thought to hold false views and engage in bad practices, where the question of the authority of the Vedas is a crucial part of the disagreement.

What I am trying to stress is that the orientation here is not towards *the content of a religion* but towards the world, reality, life, knowledge, matters about which people held divergent beliefs, on the basis of which they adopted different paths of life and action. Judging by the historical evidence, there were many variations in position regarding such matters within the classical Indian traditions now studied as 'philosophy' and 'religion', as one would expect when people disagree in their struggles to determine the truth about how things are and to live in accordance with their understanding of that truth. It is hardly surprising if many of these positions cannot be easily classified as either 'Hindu' or 'Buddhist', or if one finds among them common and overlapping elements.

The idea of 'faith' provides an especially poor lens through which to view the multiplicity of these positions or the manner in which they are arrived at and held. The late philosopher of religion John Hick makes this point in relation to Smith's analysis, which he mainly judges positively, noting that '"faith" is a term that is more at home in the Semitic than in the Indian family of traditions' (Hick, 1985: 29). Smith does attempt to separate the concept of 'faith' from that of 'belief', acknowledging 'the peculiarity of the place given to belief in Christian history' (1991: 180) and its consequent inappropriateness as a defining feature of all religious groups. However, it is very difficult, and perhaps impossible, to remove all connotations of 'belief', along with trust in authority, from the term 'faith'. Furthermore, Smith's own understanding of faith as a personal act before God – 'My faith is an act that I make, myself, naked before God' (ibid.: 191) – seems equally out of place in relation to some of the traditions he is seeking to cover in his account, including Indian ones.

In fact, I would argue that one of the most serious problems with conceiving of Indian traditions as 'religions' is precisely that the term 'religion' has become largely synonymous with 'faith'. Faith, moreover, tends to be defined in terms of the various 'others' of reason. Richard Dawkins captures this well when he interprets 'religion' as meaning 'some combination of authority, revelation, tradition and scripture' (1997: 397). This understanding of 'religion' is rooted in the specificities of Western history, with its patterns of conflict between religion and science, and its formulation of an Enlightenment ideal of reason conceived in terms of freedom from ecclesiastical and other forms of authority. As a result of this history, making appeal to 'authority, revelation, tradition and scripture' is indeed what it means to be 'religious'. And making appeal to an established set of these elements is what it means to belong to a given religion, to be a Christian, or a Muslim. But the historical context that produced these ideas of 'religion', and in explicit opposition to 'philosophy' as a discipline that is supposed to rely on reason, is not the context that produced the Indian traditions now classified as, for instance, Hindu or Buddhist or Jain. When these traditions are viewed through the lens of a modern Western idea of religion, or are compelled and incited actually to conform themselves to such an idea, as they have been by various modern and colonial processes,[2] their original way of engaging with their subject matters is radically transformed. And I want to suggest that something valuable is lost in this transformation, namely, the possibility of negotiating 'religion' (for lack of a better term) in a manner that does not involve commitment to a circumscribed body of belief and practice and does not move within the Western antithesis between faith and reason.

Approaching the matter from another direction, it is equally inappropriate, as Richard King points out, to view Indian *philosophical* traditions through a version of this antithesis, 'the "mystical" versus the "rational"' (1999: 24). This dichotomy is often employed within Western discourses to characterize, and dismiss, Indian philosophy. King rightly questions the idea of the 'mystical' as a way of describing European as well as Indian thinkers, noting that 'many of those figures who are frequently described as mystics, such as Plotinus, Augustine, Meister Eckhart, Nagarjuna and Sankara have produced intellectual systems and literary works of a highly sophisticated and erudite nature' (ibid.: 25). Moreover, it is far from clear what 'rational' is supposed to mean when the 'mystical' is defined as 'irrational' or 'non-rational' (ibid.: 25). Are claims about *atman* and *anatta* within Indian philosophical traditions, for instance, properly described as 'mystical', and in what sense? In many cases, the debates around these concepts involve rational argument of a sort that is readily recognizable within Western philosophy, but they also involve observation and experience. If these observations and experiences require mental disciplines that focus attention away from its usual objects, or involve a stilling of ordinary forms of desire, does that make the resulting insight 'mystical'? Do such experiences have anything genuinely in common with reports of extraordinary visions or divine revelations that would warrant lumping all of these phenomena into the same category? I believe the answer is no, in which case describing these aspects of Indian thought as 'mystical' is at best unilluminating and at worst distorting.

In making these points, I am agreeing with the numerous scholars who have problematized the category of 'religion' in application to India, and who have argued that in a sense there is no such thing within indigenous, pre-modern Indian traditions. But I am doing so in order to make the point that those traditions express a distinctive possibility that is worth preserving. They embody a way of relating to questions and aspects of reality that have become the province of 'religion', but that were once addressed without being conceived as 'religious' in the modern Western sense – as situating a person within a community of believers, for example, or as resting on a fixed body of revealed or otherwise authoritative discourse. The proper question in relation to these traditions is not to what religion do they belong? It is, rather, what do they claim, and why, and what sort of life do they recommend?

Studying and teaching Indian 'philosophy' (also for lack of a better term) can help to keep this possibility alive and can be at the same time a way of engaging with 'religion' that counters, or at least offers an alternative to, the interpretation of religion as a fixed body of doctrine, ritual and practice defining the identity of a given community. A condition for accomplishing these goals, however, is that one not assume the modern Western categories of 'philosophy' and 'religion' in one's approach to Indian traditions within academic disciplines. That would mean, for one thing, respecting the reflective, critical and debate-oriented approach to issues that is a hallmark of the original traditions. Genuinely preserving this methodology necessitates not merely tracing and describing the original ideas and debates but also relating them to contemporary ways of formulating philosophical, theological, moral and existential questions. At the same time, one must be careful not to lose what is distinctively valuable about Indian traditions in a rush to excise from them elements deemed to be 'religious' or 'spiritual' or 'mystical', under the pressure of current Western conceptions of philosophy that are themselves questionably narrow. Sue Hamilton raises this concern in *Indian Philosophy: A Very Short Introduction*. Like King, she argues against the tendency, among Western philosophers, to dismiss Indian philosophy for being, allegedly, '"mystical," "magical", and anything but rational' (2001: 139). But she also suggests that perhaps the time has come to go beyond such defensive gestures to build appreciation for those features of Indian philosophy that differentiate it from its modern Western counterparts: a concern with how to live, for instance, and what Hamilton describes as 'an attempt to understand the true nature of reality in terms of an inner or spiritual quest' (ibid.: 1).

One way of stating the difference is to say, as Hamilton herself does, that 'what Westerners call religion and philosophy are combined in India' (ibid.: 1). I have tried to highlight one reason why speaking of 'religion' at all in relation to these traditions is problematic. Having said that, however, in a country like India, where religion – and now in very modern incarnations – is potentially divisive and a source of significant violence and social disharmony, it is important that academic institutions impart knowledge about the subject, of an objective and non-confessional sort. As Bhargava argues, providing such education is not incompatible with a commitment to political secularism. But determining how to structure delivery of such knowledge is no easy task, and it requires sensitivity to both the current social and political realities of Indian religion, and to its historical differences from modern Western formations of religion. Against the construction, since the colonial period, of rigid, mutually distinct and often opposed, religious communities in India, many scholars have underlined the dynamic, porous and plural nature of Indian traditions in its more distant pasts. In so doing, they have focused not only, and not primarily, on the intellectual and literate levels of discourse that I have been discussing but also on everyday forms of worship, ritual and practice: pilgrimage sites, prayers, songs and festivals, symbols, customs and deities.

A problem with the academic study and teaching of 'religion', however, is that if it proceeds through a framework that employs the modern Western concept of religion, it will naturally tend to structure its subject by dividing it into the study of various 'religions', seeking to understand and communicate the content of these discrete bodies of belief and practices. Clearly, the very process of doing so distorts, and potentially transforms, the nature of those 'religious' traditions which once did not operate as discrete systems of that sort, and which are often held up as salutary alternatives to the hostile groupings called into being later on. In the case of these alternative patterns of religiosity, one cannot even speak accurately of borrowing or syncretism, since these conceptions require the existence of communities that see themselves as distinct and as, in the first place, bounded by the bodies of belief and practice that constitute their identities.

In relation to this problem, too, philosophy departments in India can play an important role in delivering an appropriate academic study of religion, because they are able, in principle, to study, teach and discuss Indian traditions of thought without freezing them into mutually distinct 'religions'. Of course, religion is not only philosophy and theology, and I recognize that the mainly Sanskrit literary traditions that form the corpus of Indian philosophy are very far from encompassing the whole of Indian religion. Still, the fluidity and openness that scholars trace among local religious traditions is also reflected, I believe, at the level of many of these intellectual traditions. For this reason and others, such traditions contain valuable resources for thinking about religion – or, perhaps better, for thinking about ourselves and the world *without* thinking about 'religion'.

CONCLUSION

At the end of his essay on religious education in India, Bhargava writes:

> one day, I hope it will be possible for each one of us to partake of the rich traditions of the Jains, the Buddhists, the several communities that fall under the umbrella of Hindus, the Muslims, the Jews, the Christians, as well as of the many indigenous peoples without the compulsive need to publicly display that we belong first and foremost to only one of these (2010: 314).

I have been suggesting that a philosophical approach to Indian traditions can help in developing the relation towards the ideas contained in various traditions that Bhargava is hoping for here. This would be an approach that engages with topics and claims without drawing the sort of boundaries that constitute 'religions'.

Religion is, however, not merely a set of ideas, and there are also important differences between religions and political theories. These differences limit the analogy Bhargava uses in articulating the possibility of a non-dogmatic and non-identitarian approach to traditions. Religions also involve practices – prayer and meditation, rituals of worship and sacrifice – as well as patterns of symbolic forms that are wholly absent in thought traditions like political theory. It might be possible for an individual to adopt some of these practices on her own, selecting those she thinks are right and good from the traditions of various communities. This does happen, as when individuals incorporate meditative practices into their lives without adopting a religious identity or changing the one they already have. But in many, perhaps most, cases religious practices involve shared activity, where the act of performing these activities with others is essential to their meaning and value. It is hard to imagine a purely individual practice of Hajj or Dussehra or Mass, and that is not how pilgrimages, festivals and rites have traditionally been performed. Participation in such practices inevitably places individuals within intergenerational communities. To be sure, such participation does not require in all cases that a person be a member of only one 'religion'. Witness the example of certain shrines in India that are visited by people with differing religious identities. It is inevitable, though, that people will form themselves into groups with common religious practices that can be distinguished, to one degree or another, from those of other groups. It will then be natural that membership in one or more of these groups is, in the first place, inherited rather than chosen, and understandable if people feel ties of loyalty and a sense of belonging to the religious identity of their parents and ancestors.

In addition, religious life is mediated by sets of interconnected and culturally embedded symbols. While religious symbols are not wholly wedded to given cultures (if they were, a symbol like the cross could not have travelled all over the world), they are also not free-floating. Their significance is constituted, at least in part, by their location within densely textured patterns of meaning. Culture and history play an important role in shaping these patterns, to which rituals and practice are also connected. In short, religion is more than a system of thought, and religious identities overlap with ethnic and cultural ones. These features of religion link this aspect of culture to community identity in a different and much stronger fashion than is the case for political theory or, for that matter, what is commonly understood as philosophy. They also make it possible to maintain a deep pluralism about certain dimensions of religion, of a sort that is not tenable for ideas asserted in propositional form as truth claims.

Yet religion does also involve beliefs and assertions of truth, to which its practices and rituals are related in complex ways. Bhargava's proposal points to the possibility of a critical and reflective approach to this component of religion. 'Religion' should not become equivalent to uncritical endorsement of a set of beliefs, where, as an individual, one can only choose wholesale between the sets that are on offer as 'religions', donning one of these as defining who she is as a religious person. To say this is not to propose a 'cafeteria' model of religion, as if, should one choose to reject a belief or practice within a given religious tradition, this means choosing what one likes in terms of tastes and convenience. Only those who define religions as bodies of belief in which one has faith can see the matter in this way. Such a view supposes that reasoning, reflection, observation and critique are all foreign to 'religion', so that the beliefs and practices of a religion are decided either by obedience to authority or, when religion is fading, by personal taste. It would be sad if this view of what it means to be religious comes to prevail. Engagement with Indian traditions in their original spirit fosters an alternative way of relating to what we have come to regard as religious subjects. It can thereby help to counteract the twin dangers of religion's becoming equivalent to the acceptance of doctrines on grounds other than reason on the one hand, or, on the other, purely a matter of identity, the content reduced to the status of a symbolic marker of no greater significance than the colours in a nation's flag.

◆

NOTES

1. Versions of this argument have been made by Dubuisson (2003: esp. pp. 64–65; 92; 100–101); Balagangadhara (2005), among others; cf. also Nongbri (2013).

2. There are many case studies of this process in relation to Indian religious communities. For two examples, see Mayaram (2000) and Vallely (2014).

REFERENCES

Balagangadhara, S. N. 2005. '*The Heathen in his Blindness': Asia, the West and the Dynamic of Religion.* 2nd revised edition. Leiden: E. J. Brill.

Bhargava, Rajeev. 2010. 'Secular States and Religious Education', in Rajeev Bhargava, *The Promise of India's Secular Democracy*, Chapter 12. New Delhi: Oxford University Press.

Bloch, Esther, Marianne Keppens and Rajaram Hegde. 2010. *Rethinking Religion in India: The Colonial Construction of Hinduism.* London: Routledge.

Dalmia, Vasudha. 1997. *The Nationalization of Hindu Traditions.* Delhi: Oxford University Press.

Dawkins, Richard. 1997. 'Obscurantism to the Rescue', *The Quarterly Review of Biology*, 72(4): 397–99.

Dressler, Markus and Arvind-Pal S. Mandair (eds.). 2011. *Secularism and Religion-Making.* New York: Oxford University Press.

Dubuisson, Daniel. 2003. *The Western Construction of Religions: Myths, Knowledge and Ideology.* Trans. William Sayers. Baltimore: John Hopkins University Press.

Fitzgerald, Timothy. 2000. *The Ideology of Religious Studies*. New York: Oxford University Press.

Hamilton, Sue. 2001. *Indian Philosophy: A Very Short Introduction*. Oxford: Oxford University Press.

Hick, John. 1985. *Problems of Religious Pluralism*. London: Macmillan.

King, Richard. 1999. *Orientalism and Religion: Postcolonial Theory, India and 'The Mystic East'*. New York: Routledge.

———. 2011. 'Imagining Religions in India: Colonialism and the Mapping of South Asian History and Culture', in Markus Dressler and Arvind-Pal S. Mandair (eds.), *Secularism and Religion-Making*. New York: Oxford University Press, pp. 37–61.

Ludden, David (ed.). 2005. *Making India Hindu: Religion, Community, and the Politics of Democracy in India*. 2nd edition. Delhi: Oxford University Press.

Mandair, Arvind-Pal S. 2011. 'Traditions of Violence: Secularism and Religion-Making in the Discourses of Sikh Nationalism', in Markus Dressler and Arvind-Pal S. Mandair (eds.), *Secularism and Religion-Making*. New York: Oxford University Press, pp. 62–86.

Mayaram, Shail. 2000. *Resisting Regimes: Myth, Memory and the Shaping of a Muslim Identity*. Delhi: Oxford University Press.

McCutcheon, Russell T. 2001. *Critics Not Caretakers: Redescribing the Public Study of Religion*. Albany: SUNY Press.

Nongbri, Brent. 2013. *Before Religion: A History of a Modern Concept*. New Haven: Yale University Press.

Nussbaum, Martha. 2007. *The Clash Within: Democracy, Religious Violence, and India's Future*. Cambridge: Harvard University Press.

———. 2010. *Not for Profit: Why Democracy Needs the Humanities*. Princeton: Princeton University Press.

Pennington, Brian K. 2005. *Was Hinduism Invented? Britons, Indians, and the Colonial Construction of Religion*. New York: 2005.

Roebuck, Valerie (ed.) 2003. 'Maitri Upanishad VII', in *The Upanishads*. Revised edition. Translated by author. London: Penguin, pp. 385–7.

Smith, Wilfrid Cantwell. 1991. *The Meaning and End of Religion*. Foreword by John Hick. Minneapolis: Fortress Press.

Vallely, Anne. 2014. 'The Difference "Difference" Makes: Jainism, Religious Pluralism and Identity Politics', in Sonia Sikka and Lori Beaman (eds.), *Multiculturalism and Religious Identity: Canada and India*. Montreal: McGill-Queen's University Press.

Warrier, Maya. 2012. 'Engaging the 'Practitioner': Boundary Politics in the Academic Study of Hinduism', in John Zavos, Pralay Kanungo, Deepa S. Reddy, Maya Warrier and Raymond Brady Williams (eds.), *Public Hinduisms*. Delhi: Sage, pp. 45–54.

Zavos, John, Pralay Kanungo, Deepa S. Reddy, Maya Warrier, Raymond Brady Williams (eds.). 2012. *Public Hinduisms*. Delhi: Sage.

◆◆

PART IV
INTERROGATING LIBERAL SOLUTIONS

12 DIVERSITY, SECULARISM AND RELIGIOUS TOLERATION

ASHWANI KUMAR
PEETUSH

DEEP DIFFERENCES: NON-LIBERAL, NON-SECULAR SOCIETIES

As an international legal or political principle of justice, I have difficulty with the idea that secularism is the only legitimate manner in which a society or nation may organize itself and that all traditional non-liberal forms of governance are necessarily, a priori, anti-liberal and unjust. I am not entirely convinced that secularism conceived of as, to use Thomas Jefferson's (1802) words, 'a wall of separation' is an absolute requirement for all nations and peoples everywhere, an inevitable legal rung on the ladder of modernity. Although, when I say this, I have in mind the various and sophisticated indigenous forms of governance around the globe, rather than the subcontinent of India. Indeed, I contend that, given the remarkable pluralism of India, some model of secularism, conceived of as an overlapping consensus between comprehensive doctrines and values, as opposed to a merely political consensus, such as that of John Rawls, is absolutely necessary.

To be clear, following a Hegelian intuition, it seems to me that difference does not always entail opposition. Because a community does not organize itself according to legal, liberal principles of justice, such as a wall of separation between church and state, does not mean that it does not have moral and ethical standards against various abuses, such as rape, murder, torture, genocide or slavery. It does not mean that such a society does not have respect for the life, integrity and basic well-being of its members, or positive duties to help those in need or ideals such as compassion, care, trust, loyalty, respect and fairness. How a society articulates, legally institutionalizes and metaphysically justifies such prohibitions and prescriptions may vary from context to context and it is natural and advantageous that they do so, as Jacques Maritain had once argued in the context of human rights in 1948. Values, norms and legal structures that resonate within cultural traditions are bound to be more successful than those that do not. In a culturally diverse world, I urge that the key is to arrive at an agreement on basic ethical standards, such as freedom from discrimination, and assuring the basic necessities of life, such as food, shelter and clothing, without being overly concerned about what justifies these. As the brilliant Sarvepalli Radhakrishnan once argued (1955), and as Gadamer (Pantham, 1992), and James Tully (1995) follow, the purpose of such an agreement is not uniformity in diversity, but rather, unity in diversity (a phrase that is often heard in India).

The importance of this insight has been recognized by the United Nations as a matter of international justice. According to the 'Declaration on the Granting of Independence to Colonial Countries and Peoples' (adopted in 1960), formerly colonized peoples have a right to self-determination, which means a legitimate claim to pursue their social, economic and cultural interests. In this regard, in the context of a theory of international law, Rawls makes a very similar argument (1999). I contend that Rawls's theory of international justice provides the best theoretical architecture, for liberals, to not only tolerate and put up with non-liberal non-Euro-Western peoples, but in fact recognize and respect them as decent societies.[1] Rawls contends that a non-liberal peoples, in the sense of a peoples based around substantive or religious doctrines, ought to be considered acceptable and decent as long as such societies protect their members from the grossest infringements, or what he calls urgent human rights. These are:

> . . . the right to life (to the means of subsistence and security); to liberty (to freedom from slavery, serfdom, and forced occupation, and to a sufficient measure of liberty of conscience to ensure freedom of religion and thought); to property (personal property); and to formal equality as expressed by the natural rules of justice (that is, that similar cases be treated similarly) (ibid.: 65).

Such a society ought to be respected (not simply tolerated) as an acceptable form of social organization. Now, freedom of conscience in such a society may not be as extensive as in a liberal society; Rawls goes so far as to assert that religious perspectives may dominate state policy and perhaps governmental positions may only be open to members of the state religion. Such a society remains in good standing for Rawls as long as members of other religions can practise their faith (or non-faith) without any threat or persecution. As an example, Rawls considers a hypothetical religious Islamic state and argues that such a state may be considered an acceptable form of polity that ought to be respected and recognized, as long as this state could protect the right of non-Muslims (whether they be religious or not).

Moreover, Rawls argues that to conflate human rights with the schedule of extensive individual rights in a liberal democracy is a mistake. Human rights, for Rawls, need to be approached as a special or urgent subset of such rights, those without which human beings, arguably, simply cannot flourish. I would argue though, against Rawls, that the exact nature of this subset needs to be open to intercultural dialogue, discussion and argumentation, and not simply drawn from Western consensus.

Others provide similar arguments. Graham Walker (1997) contends that, historically, as well as conceptually, liberalism does not equal constitutionalism, even though most liberals make this conflation. Historically, constitutionalism came first and seeks as its object to fetter political power. Indeed, as long as a society has norms and institutions, constitutionally enshrined, that can protect its members from the arbitrary abuse of political power, there is no reason why such a society should not be treated with respect. Because a society is not liberal or secular does not mean that it is mob-rule, grounded in the arbitrary abuse of political power.

Now, I think the Aboriginal peoples of Canada are a good example of non-liberal societies that ought to be recognized and respected. Although such cultures are certainly not unchanging and monolithic, many Aboriginal spokespersons in Canada argue that their communities revolve around various pervasive constellations of ideas that continue to animate the lives of their communities. Many spokespersons continually emphasize that they demand self-determination because they seek self-definition. And, they emphasize that integral to this demand is being able to promote some of their traditional spiritual self-understandings in their institutions. It involves being able to, for example, freely teach their children, in their public educational systems, about their distinct spiritual relationship to the land,[2] without fear from the liberal secular majority that Aboriginal nations are somehow planning to violate basic human rights.

DIVERSITY, SECULARISM AND RELIGIOUS TOLERANCE

Am I enlisting theocracy as a viable political option for India? Certainly not. My point was that I do not see why such nations are in principle (and some in practice) unjust. My intuitions are largely based on indigenous forms of governance in Canada and from what I understand about various episodes in India's history, such as Aśoka's or Akbar's India; my intuitions are certainly not based on current Islamic theocratic states, many of which have little regard for the rule of law, or human rights, or gender equality or the rights of non-Muslims. Of course, there are critical differences between the Aboriginal nations in Canada and the subcontinent of India. The Aboriginal population of Canada is approximately 1.6 million, with various 600 recognized bands. And importantly, they continue to share a cluster of various conceptions of the good and continue to resist forced assimilation into liberal secular society. India, on the other hand, is one of the most heterogeneous nations in the world. It contains more than one-sixth of the world's population (1.24 billion, 17.5 per cent) and is extraordinarily diverse, both religiously and linguistically. At the time of the 2001 Census, India had approximately 800 million Hindus, 140 million Muslims (the third-largest Muslim population in the world), 24 million Christians, 20 million Sikhs, 10 million Buddhists, 4 million Jains, about 6 million of other persuasions (such as Zoroastrians, Jews and Bahai) and 700,000 others for which religion was not stated. This is not to mention linguistic diversity, which includes Hindi, Bengali, Telugu, Marathi, Tamil, Urdu, Gujarati, Kanada and even Sanskrit, among others.

In such diverse circumstances people need to find some schema for living together, which is not simply based on the distribution of power, a modus vivendi. One of the challenges in an environment where religion seems so pervasive is that religious doctrines and consequent practices tend to be exclusivist. This is not true of religion alone, however. Most comprehensive doctrines and practices, including political, as well as scientific, are often exclusivist. They claim to have the road to truth – the only road – and provide the adherent with an ethics of the good life that flows from such truth, and the means to achieve enlightenment, salvation and the true meaning of the good. Given that there is more than one such doctrine, and given that these are incompatible, it has the potential for disastrous conflict, especially if difference is coupled with social, economic and legal inequality. This is not a new problem for India, but something that Indian civilization has had to cope with long before the wars within Christianity in Europe and the consequent development of liberal secularism as a political solution.

One route out of this potential conflict is to find resources internal to one's own traditions, texts and doctrines that allow one to deal with, explain and cope with such differences and diversity of perspectives, theologically or philosophically. But liberal secularism purposes a different route. It is the route that Nehru, who thought of religion as a vestige of primitive and savage thinking, had in mind for India. That is, when doctrinal differences exist, we agree to put these aside in our dealings, we agree to disagree on certain core issues and leave it at that. Ashis Nandy (1998, 2004) and T. N. Madan (1998) contend that this version of liberal secularism as a wall of separation is both unfair and unrealistic, and thus unstable, in the context of India. It is unfair because it infringes on the equal rights of religious citizens; it places an unequal burden on the part of the believer to privatize her beliefs, something that is not asked of the non-believer. The religious have to simply be silent about their beliefs and practices and put up with differences in the public domain, while stewing in their personal lives and the lives of their communities. This seems particularly unrealistic in India, given the pervasive and constitutive nature of religious identity in this context.

In this regard, Madan argues that South Asia's major religious traditions, Hinduism, Buddhism, Islam and Sikhism are 'totalising' in character. They are, in an important sense, all consuming and encompassing of every aspect of a follower's life. Whereas in Western Christian traditions one may make a conceptual divide between the sacred and the profane, such is not readily an accepted distinction in Indian traditions. Indeed, secularism in Europe arose not simply because of the wars of one religion, but partly because of this internal conceptual and theological hermeneutic, which allowed one to separate God from the mundane world. Protestant Christianity provided the transcendental conditions without which individualism and the secular state could not have thrived.

But even though traditional Indian self-understandings may not be grounded in such a distinction, it does not mean that religious tolerance, and furthermore, respect, has not been, and is not, an important value in India. On the contrary, Nandy argues that toleration and respect and peaceful cohabitation for ordinary villagers in India are grounded in comprehensive religious doctrines. Although I cannot detail the arguments here,[3] I would suggest we need to explore grounding toleration and respect in doctrines such as *Anekāntavāda* of the Jains, or the Buddhist ideal of *Pratītyasamutpāda,* or the Advaitic conception Self or *Ātman.* That is, rather than attempting to artificially graft the Western idea of secularism as a solution to religious factions, we should rather look to indigenous resources that resonate at a deeper level with the majority of the population, and which have worked for thousands of years. There are good examples of this in Indian history: Aśoka, Akbar, Kabir and Gandhi. Nandy contends that 'to go to an Indian village to teach tolerance through secularism is a form of obscene arrogance to which I do not want to be party' (2004). Tolerance and respect in India cannot be predicated upon an abstract legal notion of liberal citizenship, especially when such conceptions of self and agency have little resonance with peoples' deeply held beliefs, self-understandings, religions and philosophies about the world. Yet there are grassroots versions of tolerance and respect by which people have lived together, side by side, for thousands of years. This is the alternate terrain on which we should attempt to build a stronger foundation for tolerance and seek to broaden inter-religious dialogue.

Let me ask: Is this picture not unrealistically too optimistic? This is especially so in the context of the rise of Hindu nationalism, Islamic fundamentalism and new forms of global terrorism. Let us look more closely.

MODERNITY AND RELIGION AS A POLITICAL TOOL

One of the interesting claims made by Nandy, Partha Chatterjee (1998) and Amartya Sen (1998) is that religious extremism and violence in India has increased since post-independence. Nandy interprets this as a consequence of modernity and the product of liberalism itself. Chatterjee offers an interesting analysis of current Hindu nationalist movements. What we might, prima facie, think of as theocratic movements appear but the opposite. Unlike the older Hindu national movements such as the Hindu *Mahāsabhā,* the new political conception of the *Hindutva* movement rests on mostly a purely political platform. Apart from a few lone voices, the Hindutva campaign does not seek to ground theocratic institutions or conformity to Vedic texts and injunctions, or seek a place for religious institutions in the judiciary, or compulsory religious education, or censorship of science in the name of religion or any such things – usually. On the contrary, it attempts to set itself apart from most current Islamic fundamentalist movements or various such strains in other religions. It distinguishes itself apart from such movements as the voice of reason and progress, often calling its opponents 'pseudo-secularists'. Indeed, one sometimes wishes that perhaps the Hindutva movement was actually 'religious', that they took to heart the readily available sources of tolerance and compassion within Hindu traditions.

Nandy interprets this as the instrumentalization of religion for the use of political power, which is made possible by modernity, secularization and the privatization of the religious realm. He makes a distinction between religion as faith, piety and a way of life and religion as a political ideology.

On the face of it, I see something odd about this distinction. It seems to me that most religions are, by their very nature, political in an important sense, or at least, ethical, in that they provide a blueprint of what the good life is and ethical moral standards by which to achieve this. But, perhaps one can defend Nandy's distinction by arguing that in religion as faith, one's political outlook flows out from one's religious values, whereas in religion as ideology, religion is but a mere tool for the use of ends which do not have anything to do with the substantive content of the particular religion.

The really dangerous men, according to Nandy, are those who don the guise of believing in the public realm but are actually non-believers in their private lives. These are the Sāvarkars and the Jinnahs, who used religion as a means to mobilize the masses to achieve various political ends.

What does liberal secularism have to do with this? In one sense, it purportedly creates the conditions by which the religious are disenfranchized from the legal and political process. They become a voiceless entity wrapped in social isolation. The state tells them what is constitutive of their sense of self that has no relevance in public life. Given the dominance of religion and the often poor economic conditions of many in India, we have a powder keg waiting to be lit. The Hindu nationalist now has the means to achieve his political ends. The Muslim and other such minorities are the perfect target, a common enemy upon whom to foist displaced feelings of anger and resentment, linked to an internal sense of inferiority for not being able to match up to the Nehruvian secular ideal. On the other hand, by resting on this wall of separation ideal, the secular state lacks the power to use the rich substantive ethical and moral discourse developed in India, since it is supposed to be neutral with regard to such discourse (the moral, after all, is also a part of the private realm on the liberal picture). Nandy argues that the neutral public realm is anything but neutral; it privileges the discourse of the so-called rationality and science (of course, interpreted philosophically in terms of scientific realism) as the common ground around which to gather reasons and public justifications, however impotent such a discourse may be in the face of ethical terror.

Although I think there is an important point here, I believe that Nandy misses something crucial. I think it is right to notice that liberal critics of religion simply too often point to the Ayatollah Khomeinis and Bin Ladens of the world, as somehow representative of the true essence of where religion will eventually lead us – especially when discussing the non-Euro–Western world – thus providing a false dichotomy between 'us and them'. And, it is true that the Gandhis and Martin Luther Kings and accounts of the powerful force of various religious doctrines in the service of justice and non-discrimination are conveniently left out. Often missing, too, is the fact that secular regimes can and have been as unjust and murderous, if not more (e.g. Stalin, Hitler, Saddam Hussein, the current Chinese government, various episodes in American history).

I think that one can grant all of this, but still argue that the Nandian position itself suffers from an over-generalized idealism. It is true enough that religion has been, and is, of great good. But it cannot be denied that it has led to oppression, and importantly, an oppression that cannot be simply pushed under the rug and attributed to religion becoming an ideology and no longer piety, in the Nandian sense. It is with much Brahmanical piety that one may turn to the Ṛgveda to find a justification for the caste system, or perhaps, some other religious doctrine; for example, to deny women alimony after three months on the basis of Islamic law, as was in the case of Shah Bano.

And, this is where the secularist liberal will attempt to push the non-secularist. The argument might go something like this: it is true that perhaps the liberal doctrine has been used as an oppressive instrument by some, but there is nothing inherent in the concept of liberal individual freedom and equality that is unjust. That is, there are only hypocrites who pretend to be liberals (or Marxists) for that matter. But, in the case of religion, the doctrinal content is often simply itself unjust. That is, it is not that Muslims are being hypocrites and not living up to the true spirit of the Koran, but that the Koran itself, at least parts of it, provide unjust guidance, for example, with regard to the treatment of women and non-Muslims. The same kind of objection can be made of the Upaniṣads, or the Bible, with regard to, for example, the treatment of homosexuals, women, atheists and so on.

I do not think that this objection can be taken lightly, and I think that Nandy does not provide an adequate response by pointing to religion as piety and as ideology. This only fuels the fire of suspicion of secularism. I believe one needs to admit that it is true that there are things in such texts that are indeed problematic, unethical and outright unjust. But one can retort, on the other hand, that there are also many aspects of such traditions that are as admirable and even ethically groundbreaking. Indeed, they have provided the groundwork for where we are now. For example, one might argue that the ideal of equality in the Western tradition is in part made possible because of its Judeo-Christian roots, that of equality under the eyes of God. One can argue that the Advaitic unity of the Absolute inherent in each can also potentially provide such an interpretive foundation, one that Gandhi often emphasized in his struggle against caste. The ideal of individual freedom and autonomy, to live one's life according to one's conscience, also has religious roots in the individualism of Protestant Christianity. The ideal of the earth as intrinsically good is currently being taught to us by various indigenous spiritual traditions around the world.

Let me make a stronger point, though. The objection that, in the case of liberalism, injustice is always simply a matter of hypocrisy, as opposed to the case of religion, where the oppression results from internal doctrinal injustice, is itself problematic. This assumes somehow that concepts such as individual freedom, autonomy, self, property and so on, are a given – that is, they are seen as existing in some pure Platonic and analytic realm, with exact mathematical set-theoretical boundaries and with certitude. Concepts such as these are certainly not axiomatic or a given. A cursory reflection of political history in the West alone should free one from such a delusion. For example, even now, many liberals argue among themselves about various interpretations of 'individual freedom', and what exactly this idea means. Left liberals staunchly argue that the libertarian conception of freedom is empty and serves to justify the severest of economic inequalities and injustice. Here, it is the manner in which we define the concept of freedom itself that leads to oppression and social injustice. So, it is not that somehow we are not living up to intrinsically just principles (being hypocrites) but that the principles themselves are abstract enough that various formulations can lead to oppressive practices.

Nor would I argue that somehow the discourse of 'science and rationality', the neutral and unquestionable modern-day trump card, is somehow free from ethical scrutiny, as Hiroshima and Nagasaki certainly showed us.

The point is that I do not believe that religion alone provides a unique breeding ground for extremism and violence. I think the Nandian thesis is right in an important sense, although it is not adequately defended by Nandy. Most doctrines, religious or otherwise, with enough ingenuity, can be used in the service of oppression and injustice.

I would urge that we need to remember that religious traditions speak with a multiplicity of voices, with an internal plurality of contest and critique, often composed through historical struggles and battles between the powerful and the disenfranchized, embedded in iniquitous hegemonic relationships between the dominant and vulnerable. This leaves one in the position of having to interpret and argue, in an attempt to provide a coherent story, to put text and tradition in their best possible ethical light. There is no raw text, so to speak, no uninterpreted pure raw datum that we can call the Bible, the Koran or the Gītā. Interpretation is part and parcel of the very enterprise of religion and spirituality. Ideas and concepts have histories. While ideas may be perennial in an important sense, we always make them our own, we see them uniquely through our eyes, in the worlds in which we find ourselves. Sometimes, we may simply have to abandon parts of our traditions that we can no longer defend to ourselves or to others. I do not see this as something necessarily to lament. Cultures and religions and philosophies are dynamic processes that change from the inside, from internal protest, and, often from the outside as well, through debate, dialogue and mutual understanding. In fact, as Sonia Sikka has argued in this volume, such change is ironically stultified by the liberal privatization of religion, where it can no longer be debated or critically examined in the public sphere, thereby leaving it vulnerable in the hands of extremists.

SECULARISM AS OVERLAPPING CONSENSUS: COMPREHENSIVE NOT POLITICAL

As such, I think secularism in India should be seen as an overlapping consensus, although my version is different from that of Rawls. The Rawlsian liberal secularist doctrine arises as a purely political ideal with its associated notion of public reason, but, on the Indian model, I would urge, overlapping consensus emerges as essentially comprehensive in nature and does not deny the importance of religious or philosophical justification in public reason. As such, I think that there is a critical difference between the Indian overlapping consensus and the political version defended by Rawls. I think that the best formulation of Indian secularism that I have come across is from Sarvapalli Radhakrishnan, a philosopher and former president of the Union of India:

> When India is said to be a secular state, it does not mean we reject the reality of an unseen spirit of the relevance of religion to life or that we exalt irreligion. It does not mean that secularism itself becomes a positive religion or that the state assumes divine prerogatives. Though faith in the Supreme is the basic principle of the Indian tradition, the Indian State will not identify itself

with or be controlled by any particular religion. We hold that no one religion should be accorded special privileges in national life or international relations for that would be a violation of the basic principles of democracy and contrary to the best interests of religion and government . . . . No group of citizens shall arrogate to itself rights and privileges which it denies to others. No person should suffer any from of disability or discrimination because of his religion but all alike should be free to share the fullest degree in the common life. This is the basic principle involved in the separation of Church and State. The religious impartiality of the Indian state is not to be confused with secularism or atheism. Secularism as here defined is in accordance with the ancient religious traditions of India. It tries to build up a fellowship of believers, not by subordinating individual qualities to the group mind but by bringing them into harmony with each other. The dynamic fellowship is based on the principle of diversity in unity which alone has the quality of creativeness (1955: 202).

On the Indian model then, state neutrality is interpreted as equal or an even-handed treatment of religions – the state does not favour one over the other and recognizes the importance of religion in the life of each citizen. Rajeev Bhargava has explored these ideas in detail in many of his works (see, for example, Bhargava 2010). This view of secularism is unlike the case of France, where secularism has been interpreted on a complete wall of separation model, where religion ought to play no part in the political or the public sphere of life (thus forbidding the *hijab* in public school on such a basis). On the Indian approach then, religious identity is something that is accepted as a part of the constitutive identity of citizens, and the manifestation of such an identity is accepted as an integral part of the public sphere, rooted in the historical and political self-understandings of the subcontinent.

As Radhakrishnan argued, such a model of secularism is more rooted in the historical and political self-understandings of the subcontinent. Indeed, Amartya Sen, in defending the idea that individual freedom and human rights are particularly Western, often brings up tolerance and diversity in the case of Aśoka and Akbar (1999). But, he consistently fails to mention that tolerance for both Aśoka and Akbar were hardly liberal secular values, justified on the basis of individual freedom. Their justifications were entirely dependent on religious perspectives. Aśoka's view was an instantiation of Buddhist principles and values, whereas Akbar's tolerance was derived from Islam. As well, of course, Gandhi's political resistance to British colonialism was deeply rooted in Hinduism and Jainism, as well as other religious influences from Christianity.

In one sense, I want to say that such various movements in India were an overlapping consensus of sorts. I qualify this with 'of sorts' because I believe that there are key differences from Rawls's. Overlapping consensus on the Rawlsian model is limited to the realm of the political conception of justice, as opposed to a comprehensive notion. We attempt to agree on a range of principles that have limited application to the 'economic, social and political institutions of a society', without any recourse to discussing any substantive comprehensive reasons for why we are agreeing on such principles.[4] In fact, for Rawls, offering substantive doctrines in the political domain is a violation of public reason itself. I believe that there are a number of problems with this model of public reason.

Indeed, I am arguing that the very notion of what one considers limited and hence political or extensive and comprehensive is itself intricately related to one's viewpoint, contrary to what Rawls thinks. For example, according to Rawls, the 'political' and 'normative' conception of a person is conceived of as having two moral powers: the capacity for a sense of justice and the capacity for a conception of the good (1993: 18–19). This excludes not only the severely disabled and the elderly but also other sentient beings. But how is this not a 'comprehensive' view? From whose perspective does it, as Rawls says, 'involve no particular metaphysical doctrine about the nature of persons' (ibid.: 29). This is certainly not so from various Buddhist, Hindu or Jain perspectives, where the basic unit of moral and political consideration includes other sentient beings. From such perspectives a restriction of this notion to include only human beings itself constitutes a comprehensive and hence deeply metaphysical doctrine, something which Rawls thinks he avoids. As such, it seems to me that the Rawlsian insistence on the distinction between the political and comprehensive and the idea of barring the former from the public is problematic. Ultimately, it is grounded in a search for a view from nowhere, some form of universal neutrality that cannot be attained in principle or in practice. Metaphysical doctrines always sneak in through the back door, whether one likes it or not. In this case, to insist on such a distinction is to unwittingly privilege and legitimate dominant forms of discourse while silencing others.

I think that the distinction between the political and comprehensive does not foster or further intercultural understanding. It is true that various communities may differ in their justifications for the ways in which they ground various political concepts, and differ in such a way that makes a Rawlsian political agreement necessary (as opposed to comprehensive agreement), but I see this as a fall-back position. Why assume it as the ideal? Why not hope for more? The discussion of substantial reasons in the public domain, apart from furthering understanding among communities as to why they do what they do, has the hope of transformation of one's own self-understanding, which can ultimately lead to a fusion of horizons. In such a fusion, our standards change and grow, to encompass the views of the other, and ultimately offer a stronger agreement from which to tackle various mutual challenges. I know that such a fusion is not always possible or even likely, but, at least, even when it is not forthcoming and even if we could never share justifications, we can at least attempt to truly understand the other. This makes such a dialogue more than worthwhile; indeed, in a world where extremists feed off of misunderstandings and caricatures of the other, such a dialogue is indispensable.

◆

NOTES

1. See Rawls (1999). He remarks that 'if liberal peoples require that all societies be liberal and subject those that are not to politically enforced sanctions, then decent non-liberal peoples . . . will be denied a due measure of respect by liberal peoples' and that this 'argues for preserving significant room for the idea of a people's self-determination' (p. 61). On the other hand, Rawls's respect for non-liberal societies is muted by some of his other comments, e.g., 'when offered due respect by liberal peoples, a non-liberal society may be more likely, over time, to recognize the advantages of liberal institutions and take steps toward becoming liberal on its own' (p. 62).

2. See Gunn Allen (1979: 191). 'We are the land. To the best of my understanding, that is the fundamental idea embodied in Native American life and cultures. . . . More than remembered, the earth is the mind of the people as we are the mind of the earth. The land is not really the place (separate from ourselves) where

we act out the drama of our isolate destinies. It is not a means of survival, a setting for our affairs, a resource on which we draw in order to keep our own act functioning. It is not the ever-present "Other" which supplies us with a sense of "I". It is rather a part of our being, dynamic, significant, real. It is ourselves, in as real a sense as such notion as "ego", "libido" or social network, in a sense more real than any conceptualisation or abstraction about the nature of human being can ever be. The land is not an image in our eyes but rather it is as truly an integral aspect of our being as we are of its being. . . . Nor is this relationship one of mere "affinity" for the earth. It is not a matter of being "close to nature". The relation is more one of identity, in the mathematical sense, than of affinity. The Earth is, in a very real sense, the same as ourself (or selves)'.

3. See Peetush (2015) and Peetush (forthcoming) for detailed arguments regarding the project of grounding human rights and toleration in various Indian traditions.

4. See Rawls (1993: 13). The supposed distinction between a political and comprehensive conception of justice rests on the idea that the former is more limited in terms of scope and applies only to the basic economic, social and political structure of a society. In contrast, a comprehensive doctrine applies to and includes wider reaching subjects that deal with, for instance, 'what is of value in human life, and ideals of personal character'.

REFERENCES

Bhargava, Rajeev. 2010. *The Promise of India's Secular Democracy*. New Delhi: Oxford University Press.

Chatterjee, Partha. 1998. 'Secularism and Tolerance', in Rajeev Bhargava (ed.), *Secularism and Its Critics*. New Delhi: Oxford University Press.

Gunn Allen, Paula. 1980. 'Iyani: It Goes This Way', in G. Hobson (ed.), *The Remembered Earth: An Anthology of Contemporary American Indian Literature*. Albuquerque: University of New Mexico Press.

Jefferson, Thomas. 1802. 'Letter to the Danbury Baptists', http://www.loc.gov/loc/lcib/9806/danpre.html (accessed 10 November 2013).

Madan, T. N. 1998. 'Secularism in Its Place', in Rajeev Bhargava (ed.), *Secularism and Its Critics*. New Delhi: Oxford University Press.

Maritain, Jacques. 1948. 'Introduction', in a symposium edited by UNESCO, *Human Rights: Comments and Interpretations*. http://unesdoc.unesco.org/images/0015/001550/155042eb.pdf (accessed 18 May 2010).

Nandy, Ashis. 1998. 'The Politics of Secularism and the Recovery of Religious Toleration', in Rajeev Bhargava (ed.), *Secularism and Its Critics*. New Delhi: Oxford University Press.

———. 2004. 'A Billion Gandhis', *Outlook India*. 21 June.

Pantham, Thomas. 1992. 'Some Dimensions of the Universality of Philosophical Hermeneutics: A Conversation with Hans-Georg Gadamer', *Journal of Indian Council of Philosophical Research*, 9: 123–35.

Peetush, Ashwani. 2015. 'Human Rights and Political Toleration in India: Multiplicity, Self, and Interconnectedness', in Ashwani Peetush and Jay Drydyk (eds.), *Human Rights: India and the West*, ed. New Delhi: Oxford University Press.

Peetush, Ashwani. Forthcoming. 'The Ethics of Radical Equality: Vivekananda and Radhakrishnan's Neo-Hinduism as a form of Spiritual Liberalism' in Shyam Ranganathan (ed.), *The Bloomsbury Research Handbook of Indian Ethics*. London: Bloomsbury Press.

Radhakrishnan, Sarvepalli. 1955. *Recovery of Faith*. New York: Harper and Brothers Publishers.

Rawls, John. 1993. *Political Liberalism*. New York: Columbia University Press.

———.1999. *The Law of Peoples: With the Idea of Public Reason Revisited*. Cambridge, MA: Harvard University Press.

Sen, Amartya. 1998. 'Secularism and its Discontents', in Rajeev Bhargava (ed.), *Secularism and its Critics*. New Delhi: Oxford University Press.

———. 1999. 'Human Rights and Economic Achievements', in Joanne R. Bauer and Daniel A. Bell (eds.), *The East Asian Challenge for Human Rights*. New York: Cambridge University Press.

Tully, James. 1995. *Strange Multiplicity: Constitutionalism in an Age of Diversity*. Cambridge: Cambridge University Press.

Walker, Graham. 1997. 'The Idea of Nonliberal Constitutionalism', in Ian Shapiro and Will Kymlicka (eds.), *Ethnicity and Group Rights*. New York: New York University Press, pp. 154–84.

◆◆

13 RELIGIOUS DIVERSITY AND THE DEVOUT

BINDU PURI

FOUR CHALLENGING QUESTIONS

It is the element of *praxis* (the 'living with') which makes religious diversity a problem that demands urgent – conceptual and practical – attention in a liberal, democratic society. The argument of this chapter is located in the context of such a society. There are two sites where the question of praxis becomes especially critical to the problem of religious diversity in a plural, democratic, liberal society. The first is the site of governance. Although the conditions of governance in plural, liberal democracies are based on the consent of the citizen, it is governmental institutions which make it practically possible for citizens to live together peacefully. The sites of governance lay down policies and laws which regulate the nature of the interactions between citizens belonging to diverse religious communities. The central terms of such interactions are: secularism (understood as a position calling for the separation of the church and state); equal/equitable, differential treatment to different religions; respecting the religious liberty of individual citizens; and promoting religious diversity.

The second site of the praxis associated with religious diversity is the life of the believer and the conflicting other. The believer has faith in her religious beliefs and confronts opposing 'others' who have different beliefs. However, to believe (for the believer) means that she accepts her beliefs as providing legitimate grounds for action, or refraining from it. There are consequences of the believer acting on the grounds of her religious beliefs. Primarily, it is the believer who must bear such consequences. However, there are also non-believing 'others' who have to bear the consequences of the believer's beliefs/ practices. These non-believing others may think that the beliefs whose consequences they have to bear are false, wrong or even evil.

◆◆◆

FOUR QUESTIONS CENTRAL TO THE PROBLEM OF RELIGIOUS DIVERSITY

This chapter proposes that there are four axes central to a discussion about living with religious diversity in a liberal democracy:

1. Living peacefully with religious diversity – principled agreement, modus vivendi or an overlapping consensus?

How is one to solve the problem of living with religious diversity? The minimal answer seems to be that citizens must arrive at some agreement on a conception of justice so that they can live together peacefully. However, on expansion, this answer involves a critical choice between the grounds of the agreement – do the citizens agree to set up a stable and just society based upon a modus vivendi or upon a principled agreement on the essentials of their diverse conceptions of the good?

2. The question of sources – certainty or moderate scepticism/ indifference?

This is a question about the sort of epistemological stance which defines tolerance to religious diversity. Is the individual citizen's tolerance of religiously diverse others coming from a position of the believer *qua* one who is certain about religious truth; or the sceptic, at best moderately sceptical, and at worst positively indifferent to religion?

In a sense, the next two questions emerge from this:

3. The primacy of reason and scepticism in liberalism leads one to ask: Can there be a liberal yet religious citizen of faith?

Given that liberalism has a good case for solving the problem, one may note that despite internal divisions all liberals share a belief in the primacy of reason. Since reason cannot work in matters of faith, tolerance is recommended by liberals. In that sense, moderate scepticism is a part of liberal thinking about religion. This might raise another important question. Can the religious believer *qua* believer be a liberal?

4. Can there be any reasons for the believer *qua* believer to respect dissenting religious others?

It is important to recognize that in a religiously diverse democratic society there is not only actual disagreement but possible rational disagreement between 'epistemic peers' (Audi, 2012: 233). How can a person of faith, certain of the truth of her religious beliefs, respond to a persistent disagreement with a conflicting but apparent epistemic peer? Can there be any argument in support of tolerating diversity that addresses itself to the faith of the believer? To me this might be the most important axis for discussion, given that in the world we inhabit very many people are not disinterested observers of religious diversity. Some are certain about their religious beliefs. To such persons this question might matter.

◆◆◆

PRAXIS: PRINCIPLED AGREEMENT, MODUS VIVENDI OR JOHN RAWLS'S OVERLAPPING CONSENSUS

To return to the first axis of this discussion: How is one to solve the problem of living with religious diversity in a plural yet liberal, democratic society? It seems clear that in a liberal democracy, characterized by a reasonable pluralism of comprehensive religious doctrines, it might be possible to establish a stable society on the basis of an agreement on a conception of justice. Such an agreement can apparently take two forms – principled agreement on the essentials of diverse conceptions of the good or, alternatively, a modus vivendi agreed upon for mutual advantage. Rawls believes that there can be a third kind of agreement among citizens, which can provide a more stable basis of social unity. This is an agreement which takes the form of an overlapping consensus of diverse conceptions of the good on a purely political conception of justice, which is itself non-comprehensive. Together, these three kinds of agreement can provide possible answers to the problem posed by the need to live together peacefully in a situation of religious diversity.

Principled agreement can be the outcome of an agreement on the essentials of different religions. However (quite independently of liberal scepticism), such an agreement on the essentials of diverse and opposing religious beliefs often becomes practically difficult to sustain in a world increasingly characterized by both reasonable and unreasonable comprehensive religious pluralisms. Given the primacy of reason, there appear to be compelling grounds why liberal epistemology must rule out the possibilities of principled agreement. There might, then, be a great case for liberalism grounded on a modus vivendi. This is, in fact, borne out by the early history of European liberalism. In the classical world (particularly the European), post the Reformation, tolerance was a disaster for the citizen of faith, but in the nature of a modus vivendi it was preferable to unending civil war. The late Judith Shklar (1998) spoke of the liberalism of fear represented by Montaigne and Montesquieu and described as born of the cruelties of the religious civil war.

However, the problem with a modus vivendi is that it provides an unstable basis for social unity. By its very nature, modus vivendi can only take the form of a consensus/truce based on reciprocal advantage. Any party to such a truce/agreement, which grows in strength, can (and will) overthrow such a consensus if it is no longer perceived to be advantageous. The stability of a conception of justice, which is backed by a modus vivendi between diverse comprehensive conceptions of the good might, therefore, be practically precarious.

This appears to be the point where John Rawls (2005) proposes that there can be a third axis – an overlapping consensus of comprehensive conceptions of the good on principles belonging to a purely political and non-comprehensive conception of justice. Such a consensus would provide a more stable basis of social unity than a modus vivendi. Rawls makes it clear that the political conception of justice can be acceptable to diverse conceptions of the good precisely because it is not in itself a comprehensive doctrine. He distinguishes between comprehensive and non-comprehensive conceptions and clarifies that his political conception of justice is not even a partially comprehensive doctrine. It '...is a normative (moral) conception with its own intrinsic ideal though not itself a comprehensive doctrine' (ibid.: 13).

If Rawls's overlapping consensus on justice as fairness is to be stable, it must be based on normative considerations that can provide overriding reasons to citizens having conflicting conceptions of the good. However, once Rawls imports normative considerations to support the overlapping consensus on the purely political conception of justice, that conception becomes a comprehensive account of justice. It then competes with rival comprehensive doctrines, in a religiously plural society. Clearly, if justice as fairness is to be the ground of social unity for opposing religious/comprehensive doctrines, it must itself be a non-comprehensive (in Rawls's sense of that term) conception. However, if it is to be non-comprehensive, it might become difficult to differentiate Rawls's conception of the overlapping consensus from a mere modus vivendi.

Since 'what counts is the kind of stability' (ibid.: 142), the stability of the overlapping consensus must be grounded on some normative considerations. Rawls argues that justice as fairness must 'gain the reasoned support of citizens who affirm reasonable although conflicting comprehensive doctrines' (ibid.: 143). On this view, the overlapping consensus can be stable for normative reasons without thereby transforming the conception of justice as fairness into a comprehensive account of the good. Rawls argues that there are 'two aspects of an overlapping consensus – moral object and moral grounds' (ibid.: 148) The object of the consensus,

> the political conception of justice, is itself a moral conception. And second, it is affirmed on moral grounds, that is, it includes conceptions of society and of citizens as persons, as well as principles of justice, and an account of the political virtues through which these principles are embodied in human character and expressed in public life (ibid.: 147).

On this view, citizens who affirm the political conception of justice because they are reasonable can nonetheless 'start from within their own comprehensive view and draw on the religious, philosophical, and moral grounds it provides' (ibid.: 147).

However, the problem comes from the *living with* aspect of religious diversity. Conflict may (and often does) arise between the reasons that comprehensive/religious doctrines provide their believers to support the principles of justice as fairness, and other reasons such doctrines provide believers to reject those principles. Rawls thinks that such conflicts will be resolved because: 'From the point of view of public reason, citizens must vote for the ordering of political values they sincerely think the most reasonable. Otherwise they fail to exercise political power in ways that satisfy the criterion of reciprocity' (ibid.: 479). There are two ways in which Rawls supports the argument that the conception of justice as fairness will be a stable basis of social unity in a plural society: first, by showing that this conception of justice can be arrived at without referring to any conception of the good; and, second, by arguing that citizens would accept this conception as a means to social unity because they are so constituted that they have two moral powers – the powers of being reasonable and of being rational.

Rawls explicitly raises the question which forms the first axis of discussion in this chapter: 'How is it possible that there can be a stable and just society whose free and equal citizens are deeply divided by conflicting and even incommensurable religious, philosophical and moral doctrines?' (ibid.: 13). In terms of his answer, the basic rules of society can be agreed upon without reference to the contents of people's rival conceptions of the good. He uses the devices of the original position and the veil of ignorance to arrive at the two principles of justice which constitute a political and non-comprehensive conception of justice as fairness. In this argument, the agents representing free and equal citizens (who are reasonable and rational) agree upon the principles of justice without reference to any citizen's conception of the good. Such an acceptance derives from the fact that individual citizens are conceived as being not only rational but also reasonable about conflicting 'others'.

It is important to note that if Rawlsian citizens were conceived only as rational, they would simply pursue their individual advantage in a prudent manner. It would then not be possible for Rawls's theory of justice to serve as a more stable basis of social unity than a mere modus vivendi grounded upon the individual pursuit of enlightened self-interest. However, Rawls's argument places significant conceptual reliance on the idea that individual citizens are both reasonable and rational. It may be noted that though Rawls argues that the rational and the reasonable are two distinct powers of individual citizens this distinction has been the subject of much criticism in recent years (Gaus, 1995; Gewirth, 1983; Klosko, 2000; Macedo, 1990; Young, 2005).

It is in his second text that Rawls argues that he is making a distinction between the reasonable and the rational as independent moral powers of persons *qua* citizens. He clarifies that there are two philosophical sources for this distinction – Immanuel Kant and W. M. Sibley. Rawls speaks of the '…two basic aspects of the reasonable as a *virtue*[1] of persons engaged in social cooperation between equals' (Rawls, 2005: 48). He defines the two aspects as follows:

> The first basic aspect of the reasonable then is the willingness to propose fair terms of cooperation and to abide by them provided others do. The second basic aspect, as I review now, is the willingness to recognize the burdens of judgment and to accept their consequences for the use of public reason in directing the legitimate exercise of political power in a constitutional regime (ibid.: 54).

In an important footnote in *Political Liberalism* Rawls explains:

> Knowing that people are rational we do not know the ends they will pursue, only that they will pursue them intelligently. Knowing that people are reasonable where others are concerned, we know that they are willing to govern their conduct by a principle from which they and others can reason in common; and reasonable people take into account the consequences of their actions on others' well being. The disposition to be reasonable is neither derived from nor opposed to the rational but it is incompatible with egoism, as it is related to the disposition to act morally (ibid.: 49).

Clearly, then, the stability of an overlapping consensus on the political conception of justice in a religiously diverse democratic society rests on the individual citizen's disposition to act reasonably. However, it may be noted that this disposition to be reasonable (in Rawls's conception of it) is powerfully contingent on the criterion of reciprocity. Individual citizens act reasonably on the assurance that others will do so as well. This becomes clear when one examines Rawls's argument to support the first aspect of being reasonable. He says that persons/citizens are reasonable when they accept and willingly abide by fair terms of cooperation '…given the assurance that others will likewise do so' (ibid.: 49). Further, according to Rawls,

> The reasonable is an element of the idea of society as a system of fair cooperation and that its fair terms be reasonable for all to accept is

part of its idea of reciprocity. ... the idea of reciprocity lies between the idea of impartiality, which is altruistic (as moved by the general good), and the idea of mutual advantage understood as everyone's being advantaged with respect to one's present or expected situation as things are (ibid.: 50).

Rawls argues that reasonable people

... are not moved by the general good as such but desire for its own sake a social world in which they, as free and equal, can cooperate with others on terms all can accept. They insist that reciprocity should hold within that world so that each benefits along with others (ibid.: 50).

Later in the same text, while discussing his political constructivism, Rawls clarifies that the principles of justice as fairness are established by persons themselves '... in view of what they regard as their reciprocal advantage' (ibid.: 97).

Given that the reasonable (in Rawls's account of it) is conceptually contingent on the ideas of reciprocity and mutual advantage it seems difficult to distinguish being reasonable from being rational/prudent, i.e., from following one's self-interest in an enlightened manner. Yet Rawls needs to maintain that individual citizens living in a plural democracy can be reasonable (as distinct from being only rational) if there is to be a stable, overlapping consensus. It remains difficult to find an adequate differentia to distinguish between the reasonable and the rational in Rawls. W. M. Sibley (1953) had made the distinction between the two terms by arguing that to be reasonable meant to take account of the interests of others *per se*. It may be noted that Sibley had made a critical distinction in this context:

But there is an obvious difference between (1) taking account of the interests of others merely as factors in the situation capable of affecting the promotion of 'my own' interests, where 'my own' interests are opposed to, or at least distinct from, those of others; and (2) taking account of the interests of others as a disinterested, impartial spectator might do, i.e., putting them on a par with my own interests. Any prudent egoist takes account of the interests of others in the first sense. But to take account of their interests in the second sense requires something more than possessing an intellect capable of correctly calculating future consequences. It requires a positively sympathetic disposition toward others, a preparedness to be genuinely concerned with 'their' interests per se, as well as my own, and a preparedness to be 'objective' not in a merely logical, but also in a distinctively moral sense. If I possess this *moral* virtue, I shall then be not merely *rational*, but I shall also be prepared to act, where the interests of others are involved, in a *reasonable* manner as well (ibid.: 557).

While, for Sibley, being reasonable (in contrast to being merely prudent) meant taking account of the interests of others *per se,* Rawls specifies that being reasonable means accepting fair terms of cooperation *given the assurance* that others will do likewise. Rawls's statement of the first aspect of being reasonable seems to reconstruct reasonableness as a moral power of citizens in terms that are hypothetical rather than categorical, perhaps in the following terms: 'Be reasonable – if you can be sure that others will do so as well'. Rawls's reciprocity condition might also make it difficult, in the context of Sibley's argument, to distinguish between the reasonable and the rational. Taking account of the interests of others *on the assurance of reciprocity* seems substantially different from taking account of the interests of others independently of their role in promoting one's own interests. For a prudent man would also take account of the interests of others as conditional on the reciprocal behaviour of such others taking account of his or her own interests. Being reasonable in Rawls then seems to be the outcome of prudence or enlightened self-interest. Consequently, it becomes difficult to understand the difference between being reasonable and being rational in Rawls.

Rawls's overlapping consensus on a political conception of justice was proposed as a stable solution to the problem of social unity in a democracy characterized by conflicting comprehensive accounts of the good. As stated, Rawls believes that religiously diverse citizens will support the political conception of justice because they are reasonable and rational. However, there are two problems with Rawls's argument. Rawls gives individual citizens reasons for being reasonable: reasons such as the assurance that others will also do their part or that cooperative ventures succeed over time. First, giving reasons for being reasonable transforms the *reasonable* into an intellectual virtue and obliterates the distinction between the *reasonable* and the rational. It then becomes difficult to argue that the overlapping consensus is different from (and more stable than) a modus vivendi. The second difficulty is that this argument might lead to circularity. Such circularity is something modern citizens may be familiar with from their experience of life in a pluralistic society. One is reasonable provided others are reasonable. One trusts others if one's faith in their being reasonable is sustained over time and experience. However, every religious other also has similar expectations. He or she will only be reasonable, if he or she has an assurance that the other will also be so. Unless there is an unconditional moment to start the process of being reasonable, the circle will remain a circle and the overlapping consensus will remain a desperate attempt to look for a point of overlap at an intersection of beliefs between circles that go around in self-contained circles. In other words the terms *reasonable* and *trust* will not function in the manner in which Rawls expects that they will. This can be the problem if one looks at moral experience to provide the aspirant the opportunity to grow into the distinction between being moral and being merely interested in one's enlightened self-interest. For unless such moral experience is premised on some unconditional moments in the form of background qualitative distinctions, such experience might simply lead to a circle of reciprocal expectation of moral vis-à-vis merely prudential behaviour from each other in a society of human persons.

This has practical implications for the stability of the overlapping consensus. The viability of Rawls's conception becomes dependent upon those that are subject to its constraints, voluntarily and faithfully, ensuring that their goals and related behaviour adhere to the requirements of the public conception of reasonableness. Shaun P. Young, like George Klosko (2000), notes that this claim is at minimal 'extremely suspect' (Young, 2005: 314). It becomes difficult for Rawls to save the conception of the overlapping consensus from the charge of reciprocal egoism and thereby differentiate it from a modus vivendi. It may be recalled that Rawls believed that the problem with a modus vivendi was that 'its stability is contingent' (Rawls, 2005: 147). He had, therefore, argued specifically against the objection that 'an overlapping consensus is a mere modus vivendi' (ibid.: 145). Yet given the philosophical difficulties of Rawls's distinction between the rational and the reasonable the only possible liberal answer to the problem of living with religious diversity remains a modus vivendi, based on reciprocal advantage.

◆◆◆

LIBERAL REASONS FOR TOLERANCE: UNCERTAINTY AND SCEPTICISM

As far as the second axis is concerned, I see in this discussion certainty versus scepticism. Although the best case for living with religious diversity is the liberal one, it can be argued that liberal reasons for tolerating religiously diverse others can only come from positions of uncertainty or scepticism about religious truths. As such, liberal arguments are not even addressed to religious devouts who believe in religious truths. When liberals try to solve the problem of living with religious diversity, they address themselves to all but the class of persons who need most to be addressed – the men of faith. This could become apparent if one briefly examines at least some of the celebrated liberal arguments for tolerance. Those made by John Stuart Mill and by John Locke are a case in point. Mill, in the meta-inductive argument for tolerance in *On Liberty,* recommends tolerance on account of the fact that we know that we are not infallible about matters that concern us deeply (2006: 24). However, what of the devout believer who feels certain about these matters? Can such a religious person still tolerate dissenting others for the reasons that Mill suggests?

Mill, of course, thinks that the devout believer can – once she recognizes the value of diversity to the search for being progressively confirmed about the grounds of certainties. However, this would mean two things. One, that the person of faith must be modest about her claim to truth and recognize that one has been mistaken about one's convictions in the past. Two, there must be a prior and overriding commitment to a comprehensive liberalism that values autonomy and diversity above the truths of religion. If one considers that it is internal to being religious/part of being religious that one believes in the truths of one's religion, one can understand that religious believers simply might not be able to make such commitments. Consequently, it is difficult for a person of faith to derive tolerance from a liberal position (like Mill's) of moderate scepticism.

Locke has a set of similar arguments for tolerance. In the 1667 essay on toleration he argues that religious beliefs are 'purely speculative opinions' (1997a: 137). Since religious worship 'is a thing wholly between God and ... the individual' such worship 'necessarily produces no action which disturbs the community' (ibid.: 138). In Locke's view, a believer must be tolerant to opposing religious others because religion is not only purely speculative, but being so it is a private affair of a man. Consequently, religious belief is of no consequence in man's relations with his fellow men. In another essay written in 1676, Locke discusses the relationship between reason and revelation. He argues there that faith and revelation can never override the claims of reason for one can never be certain about God's having revealed the truth to us.

> For faith can never convince us of anything that contradicts our knowledge. Because, though faith be founded on the testimony of God (which cannot lie), yet we cannot have an assurance of the truth of it greater than our own knowledge (ibid.: 249).

Locke's arguments simply reinforce the point that, for the liberal, living with religious diversity proceeds from a tolerance that is an inevitable outcome of uncertainty and scepticism about the truths of religion.

◆◆◆

THE RELIGIOUS BELIEVER AND THE EPISTEMIC ABSTINENCE OF A LIBERAL THEORY OF PUBLIC REASON

Moderate scepticism is a part of liberal thinking about religion. Given that this is so, one might well ask if the believer can take liberalism to be a part of his or her religion. This raises issues of what might be involved in having a religious belief.

It seems a part of being religious that the person of faith believes in religious truths. It must be admitted that at least some of these truths influence her conversations with fellow citizens, and indeed her evaluations of the actions of the liberal state as just and unjust.

For example, think of the devout Muslim women who believes that she must wear a *hijab* or a veil. This belief certainly influences her conversations with conflicting others and with the state when it opposes her right to wear the veil. In an essay examining the contemporary philosophical responses of John Rawls and Thomas Nagel to the diversity of ideologies present in plural democratic societies, Joseph Raz (1996) examines the difficulties with the epistemic distance recommended by liberals like Nagel and Rawls. On this view, Nagel and Rawls have argued that 'certain truths should not be taken into account because, though true, they are of an epistemic class unsuited for public life' (Raz, 1996: 61). In this context, Raz argues that for a liberal society 'the social role of justice can be purchased only at the price of epistemic distance' (ibid.: 66). The believer must put aside the question of what she believes to be true in political matters and be guided by the criterion of reciprocity. For the liberals, this is psychologically easy enough for she is sceptical of the truth of religious beliefs, but for the believer this presents a psychological crisis – the word of God/religious belief versus the need to live peacefully with those who deny God's word/truth. One may recall that Rawls had argued that '...in public reason ideas of truth or right based on comprehensive doctrines are replaced by an idea of the politically reasonable addressed to citizens "as citizens"' (Rawls, 2005: 481).

Rawls states that the believer can deal with the crisis of conflict between religious truths and the opposing religious beliefs of conflicting others by taking recourse to a conception of public reason, which is not concerned with truth but only with reciprocity. Thomas Nagel has offered an argument which he presents as an attempt to capture the sound intuitions advocated by Rawls among others. Like Rawls's own arguments, Nagel's argument also rests on the advocacy of epistemic abstinence. In his view 'true liberalism' requires that 'a limit somehow be drawn to appeals to *the truth* in political argument' (Raz, 1996: 88) The argument rests on Nagel's idea that however justified our convictions be from within, when we look at them from outside 'the appeal to their truth must be seen merely as an appeal to our beliefs, and should be treated as such unless those beliefs can be shown to be justifiable from a more impersonal standpoint....' (Nagel, 1987: 230; quoted in Raz, 1996: 89). The goal of justification according to Nagel is practical – to persuade the reasonable. Nagel admits that to believe in a proposition is to believe it to be true. However, the critical point is that the belief cannot be the believer's reason for thinking that the proposition is true. My belief in a proposition is, *a fortiori*, no reason for others to accept it.

In this connection, Raz argues that to believe involves believing to be true and, thereby, belief is understood as providing grounds for action. To take the case of a religious believer – it is only if the believer can distinguish between believing a proposition and its truth as a ground for accepting it, acting on it, etc., can she be said to have a belief at all. Certainly, the recognition of the possibility of error is a logical prerequisite of the believer's capacity to believe to be true. The believer is aware that to distinguish between belief and true belief she must recognize the possibility of error. However, this does not mean that the believer thereby recognizes that when she holds beliefs 'the appeal to their truth must be seen merely as an appeal to our beliefs...' (Raz, 1996: 90). It is difficult to think that the Muslim woman who believes in the proposition that she must wear a veil knows that this is only an appeal to her belief, distinct from an appeal to the truth of that belief. Surely, that she believes means that she believes that her belief is not erroneous. Consequently, it is difficult to accept Nagel's argument that the religious believer can believe *qua,* make an epistemic commitment to the truth, and yet not let those beliefs count as political reasons because she recognizes that beliefs require justification from an impersonal standpoint before they can be acted upon.

The person of faith who has beliefs recognizes that the truth of those beliefs is the reason for accepting and acting on them. Therefore, she cannot believe and yet be moderately sceptical about the truth of what she believes in as a ground for acting on such belief. It might be difficult for a devout person to be a consistent liberal and practise the sort of epistemic abstinence that liberals advocate.

◆◆◆

ANSWERING QUESTIONS

GANDHIAN AHIMSA: MAKING A CASE FOR THE DEFERENTIAL BELIEVER

Although liberalism might seem to be the best solution to the problem of living with religious diversity, it seems clear that it presents nothing more substantial than a somewhat precarious modus vivendi. Further, liberal scepticism can seriously deter religious persons from accepting liberal arguments for living with conflicting others. Of the various arguments M. K. Gandhi made for living with religious 'others', this section will reconstruct Gandhi's equation of *ahimsa* with truth in terms of the reasons it provided the religious believer to defer to diverse and opposing 'others'. This argument might be an interesting alternative to the prominent liberal arguments.

Like Tagore (and unlike Nehru) Gandhi's reasons for tolerance came from a position of certainty, but he seemed to have had a fairly different understanding of the connection between certainty and tolerance. It has been recently argued by Ananya Vajpeyi (2012: 55) that Gandhi's *Hind Swaraj* presented an epistemological Galilean break for India's dying political tradition. I would like to argue that *Hind Swaraj* and the rest of Gandhi's work presented a Galilean moment in the Western epistemological tradition itself. Gandhi can be reconstructed as having proposed an alternative epistemology – that of engagement with difference through a practice of ahimsa/love as the only means to truth.

Before attempting a philosophical reconstruction of Gandhi's equation of truth and non-violence it seems fair to start by understanding Gandhi's truth. Gandhi appears to have seen individual moral life primarily in terms of a quest for the truth or God. This is essentially a quest which needs to be informed by the practice of the vows (*yamas* and *niyamas),* which are part of the ethical discipline recommended by traditional schools of Indian philosophy. It may be recalled that *satya*/truth was one of the yamas to which Gandhi referred frequently. Therefore, it is possible to argue that Gandhi seems to have used 'truth' in a dual sense. First, as the proper end of human moral endeavour, i.e., as a sort of Aristotelian *telos,* or the good at which individual moral life is properly aimed. Without such a goal or 'end' it might be said that moral life would become episodic and lack the unity which helps to make sense of a good human life. Second, Gandhi also spoke of truth in another sense as one of the 'cardinal virtues' and thereby as an inherent part of the quest for the truth *qua* the good as the transcendent object of all moral endeavour. Gandhi made this distinction explicitly:

For me truth is the sovereign principle, which includes numerous other principles. This truth is not only truthfulness in word, but truthfulness in thought also, and not only the relative truth of our conception, but the Absolute Truth, the Eternal Principle, that is God (Prabhu and Rao, 1967: 42).

In Gandhi's understanding of truth, thought, in terms of a virtue of character, or as the end of the moral /religious life, can only be arrived at by the practice of ahimsa. He makes the connection in the strongest terms:

Ahimsa and truth are so intertwined that it is practically impossible to disentangle and separate them. They are like the two sides of a coin.... (Gandhi, 1968: 219).

Gandhian ahimsa is understood as much more than mere non-injury and it presents a fairly extensive ethical discipline. Gandhi explains: 'In its positive form ahimsa means the largest love, the greatest charity. If I am a follower of ahimsa, I must love my enemy' (Bose, 1948: 157–8). In Gandhi's understanding, the individual religious life was a quest for truth/God. He argues that the progressive realization of truth can only come from the practice of ahimsa as non-violence.

Ahimsa is not the goal. Truth is the goal. But we have no means of realizing truth in human relationships except through the practice of ahimsa. A steadfast pursuit of ahimsa is inevitably bound to truth… (Prabhu and Rao 1967: 118).

Gandhi's equation of truth with non-violence presents the religious believer with an internal route from the love of dissenting others to truth/God. On this account, the only way to arrive at the truth of one's beliefs is to defer to the beliefs and persons of opposing others. One way in which one can philosophically reconstruct Gandhi is simply to think of the impossibility of arriving at the true knowledge of the self or the other without the practice of non-violence as humility, egolessness and love. In support of the Gandhian argument one may note that in an individual moral life the primary source of self-deceptions is the 'dazzling' ego (Murdoch, 1970: 30). As Murdoch suggests, it is the 'fat relentless ego' (ibid.: 51) which entrenches the individual self in 'personal fantasy'. It is the central preoccupation of that ego to show the self in the best possible light and as so dazzling an object that all others seem inevitably to pale in comparison. In that sense, truth or certainty can only come from a suppression of an exaggerated individual sense of self, and from the related freedom from self-deceptions generated by the individual ego: in other words, from the practice of Gandhian ahimsa/non-violence as humility and selflessness. It may be recalled that Gandhi had described ahimsa as 'utter-most selflessness' (Bose, 1948: 155).

Gandhi frequently describes ahimsa as a universal love of all others. Gandhi's use of love in connection with ahimsa is surely significant – for it can be argued that love is an emotion which has the strength to displace the ego from the centrality of self-concern. Once the self is displaced, all self-centred emotions/passions, which obstruct the knowledge of both oneself and others, are also overcome. As the self becomes progressively free of selfish emotions (such as lust, anger, revenge, injustice and hate) it also becomes free of self-deceptions which might be caused by those emotions. Consequently, the self comes progressively closer to the truth of its own beliefs. It may be noted that non-violence effects this transformation, both in the self that practises ahimsa and in the other confronted with it.

This Gandhian understanding of the relationship between truth and ahimsa/non-violence provides the religious believer with an overriding reason to defer to the views of opposing religious others equally as she would to her own religious beliefs. One may recall that Nagel had spoken of the gap between believing and knowing that one's belief could be justified from an impartial standpoint. In Nagel's view, the believer has to recognize that inward conviction requires impartial justification to be a ground for acceptance and action. This gap appears problematic when one considers that for the religious believer to believe means to accept and act on her beliefs as true, and not as mere private convictions. For Gandhi, there is no gap between believing something to be true and considering one's belief as providing legitimate grounds for actions affecting the 'other'. This is because of the Gandhian insistence that actions affecting others must be *ahimsanat*. The religious believer simply cannot arrive at the truth of her beliefs without practising non-violence, in conduct and in thought, by deferring to the opposing beliefs of religious others. What makes Gandhi's position different from that of the liberals is that Gandhian ahimsa as deference does not come from the consciousness of being fallible, but from the recognition that non-violence is the ground of arriving at certainties. Hence, Gandhian tolerance is connected with certainty rather than with liberal scepticism.

One might conclude with the observation that Gandhi's arguments provide the religious believer with good reasons to live peacefully with diverse religious others. These Gandhian reasons can be reconstructed as internal to the individual believer's living of the religious/good human life. In Gandhi's view, it is a part of pursuing truth or God that one is non-violent towards the persons and beliefs of opposing others. This makes the Gandhian position significantly different from the liberal one. Liberal reasons to live peacefully with diverse religious others can be described as external to the believer's living of the religious/good human life. At best, liberal arguments ask the believer to put her religious beliefs aside in political life and, at worst, they demand that she retain a minimal sense of scepticism about her convictions. It can be said that Gandhi made out a better case for living with religious diversity. On the basis of a Gandhian understanding, non-violence is the ground of certainties and, therefore, in a sense, one can only be an ahimsat devout.

◆

NOTE

1. The emphasis is mine.

REFERENCES

Audi, Robert. 2012. 'Religion and Politics', in David Estlund (ed.), *The Oxford Handbook of Political Philosophy*. New York: Oxford University Press.

Bose, N. K. (ed.). 1948. *Selections from Gandhi*. Ahmedabad: The Navajivan Trust.

Gandhi, M. K. 1968. 'From Yeravda Mandir', in *The Selected Works of Mahatma Gandhi Volume VI. The Basic Works*. Ahmedabad: Navajivan Publishing House.

Gaus, Gerald F. 1995. 'The Rational, the Reasonable and Justification', *The Journal of Political Philosophy*, 3(3), pp. 234–58.

Gewirth, Alan. 1983. 'The Rationality of Reasonableness', *Synthese* 57, pp. 225–47.

Klosko, George. 2000. *Democratic Procedures and Liberal Consensus*. Oxford: Oxford University Press.

Locke, John. 1997a. 'An Essay on Toleration', in Mark Goldie (ed.), *Locke Political Essays*. Cambridge, UK: Cambridge University Press.

Locke, John. 1997b. 'Faith and Reason', in Mark Goldie (ed.), *Locke Political Essays*. Cambridge, UK: Cambridge University Press.

Macedo, Stephen. 1990. *Liberal Virtues*. Oxford: Oxford University Press.

Mill, John Stuart. 2006. 'On Liberty', in *On Liberty and the Subjection of Women*. London: Penguin Classics.

Murdoch, Iris. 1970. *The Sovereignty of Good*. New York: Routledge & Kegan Paul.

Nagel, T. 1987. 'Moral Conflict and Political Legitimacy', *Philosophy and Public Affairs*, 16/3 (Summer 1987).

Prabhu, R. K. and U. R. Rao (eds.). 1967. *The Mind of the Mahatma*. Ahmedabad: Navajivan Publishing House.

Rawls, John. 2005. *Political Liberalism*. New York: Columbia University Press.

Raz, Joseph. 1996. 'Facing Diversity: The Case of Epistemic Abstinence', in *Ethics in Public Domain: Essays in the Morality of Law and Politics*. Oxford: Clarendon Press.

Shklar, Judith. 1998. 'The Liberalism of Fear', in Stanley Hoffmann (ed.), *Political Thought and Political Thinkers*. Chicago: University of Chicago Press.

Sibley, W. M. 1953. 'The Rational versus the Reasonable', *Philosophical Review*, 62(October 1953), pp. 554–60.

Vajpeyi, Ananya. 2012. *Righteous Republic: The Political Foundations of Modern India*. Cambridge: Harvard University Press.

Young, Shaun P. 2005. 'The (Un)Reasonableness of Rawlsian Rationality', *South African Journal of Philosophy*, 24(4), pp. 308–20.

◆◆

14 THE INTERNATIONAL POLITICS OF RELIGIOUS FREEDOM

ELIZABETH
SHAKMAN
HURD

In the United States (US), religious freedom is often described as the 'first freedom', a fundamental human right, and a *sine qua non* of modern democratic politics, if not of civilization itself. Americans, we are told, invented and perfected religious freedom. It is ready for export. And exporting it we are. A rapidly escalating number of actors are promoting religious freedom across state boundaries. Some are American, but many are not. Some are state-sponsored, but others are not. Legal guarantees of religious freedom are embedded as riders in trade agreements, in aid packages and in humanitarian projects. Diplomats are taught how to persuade their counterparts to safeguard religious freedom. Foreign policy establishments are formalizing its promotion. The most recent example is Canada, where Prime Minister Stephen Harper announced that his government is creating an Office of Religious Freedom at the Department of Foreign Affairs and International Trade (DFAIT), modelled on the US Office of International Religious Freedom in the Department of State. The European Union is promoting religious freedom in its external affairs programming, adding clauses to bilateral trade agreements with North African and Central Asian trading partners that guarantee a commitment to religious freedom. In Europe, initiatives to train EU diplomats in religious freedom promotion are in the works. Again, the emphasis is on formalizing religious freedom advocacy by public authorities. At the United Nations, the Office of the High Commissioner for Human Rights is in its third decade of promoting religious freedom and has initiated a campaign to combat incitement to religious hatred. This office has a large bureaucracy led by the Special Rapporteur on Freedom of Religion or Belief, appointed by the UN Human Rights Council. It focuses on ensuring state compliance with human rights norms and standards developed over the past 60 years and embodied in declarations such the 1948 Universal Declaration of Human Rights.

The promotion of religious freedom is ubiquitous. And it is not only by evangelicals. An impressive array of institutions and public authorities across the political spectrum, secular and religious, have taken up the cause. Religious freedom is fast becoming a language used to garner international political legitimacy. When the Moroccan Justice and Development Party won the November 2011 parliamentary elections, prominent party member and future Minister of Justice and Liberties Mustafa Ramid underlined the party's commitment to religious freedom: 'We have a progressive approach to Islam. The Islamicisation of Morocco will be achieved only by re-establishing justice and religious freedom' (Mekhennet, 2011).

Over the past two decades, the right to religious freedom has become what Lila Abu-Lughod calls a 'dialect of universality' (2010: 87). Religious freedom is 'being disseminated through international institutions and practices so that it is, to some extent, everywhere – translated, resisted, vernacularised, invoked in political struggles, and made the standard language enforced by power' (ibid.: 85). Like human rights, religious freedom has, in some sense, captured the field of emancipatory possibility. It stands for the good and the right in many difficult and often violent situations. It is easy to be swept up in the collective common sense that guaranteeing religious freedom is what stands between us and pre-modern orders based on tyrannical forms of religious authority that leave women and minorities in the dust. Positioned as the only alternative to these unappealing options, it is hardly surprising that religious freedom projects, pronouncements and policies have gathered such momentum. In all of the excitement surrounding religious freedom as a universal norm – who can be against religious freedom? It is easy to forget that these are political projects that are situated in history and implemented by powerful state and global authorities. It is easy to overlook the fact that religious freedom is a site of politics, even of what Beaman and Sullivan (2013) have recently described as 'religious establishment'. The promotion of religious freedom is not a story of the progressive global dissemination of a universal norm and legal standard. We need to distinguish between an abstract and aspirational state of peaceful religious coexistence and the official practice of promoting religious freedom. While the former is certainly desirable, it is not the case that the latter actually helps to realize it, and, as I will suggest, it may actively impede it.

This chapter steps back from the excitement and the anxiety surrounding the frenzied promotion of religious freedom to explore three paradoxes of religious freedom. I then ask whether the world created by religious freedom is a world we want to live in, drawing on the example of Syria, and then discussing a current lawsuit against one of the US bureaucracies created to promote and protect religious freedom globally. If religious freedom is not the answer, then what other possibilities are there for negotiating across deep lines of social and religious difference? Where might we look to find peaceful coexistence being imagined without religious freedom, as it is commonly understood today?[1]

CRISIS IN SYRIA

Calls for the protection of persecuted Christians in Syria and around the Middle East have been a cornerstone of US and European foreign policy in the wake of the uprisings. There are serious concerns here. But a closer look at how this problem has been framed and the consequences of this framing reveals that, paradoxically, framing the problem in Syria as a crisis of religious freedom may help to *create* the very problems that religious freedom seeks to resolve.[2]

Christian Solidarity International has lobbied President Obama to urge Ban Ki-moon to declare a genocide warning for Christians across the Middle East. Howard Berman of the House Foreign Affairs Committee (HFAC) says that the future of minorities is 'on our agenda as we figure out how to help these countries and their treatment of Christians and other minorities is a "red line" that will affect future aid' (Dorell and Lynch, 2012). Habib Malik of the Lebanese American University calls for Western nations to stand up for the rights of Christians, who, he says, may be cleansed from lands where democratic elections are used to oppress minorities rather than empower them. While this must be done, he says, 'in a way that is not misperceived on the other end, the West should not be cowed'.[3] *USA Today* reports that 'Christians in Syria, where Muslims have risen up against President Bashar Assad, have been subjected to murder, rape and kidnappings in Damascus and rebellious towns'.

The momentum builds. The logic of this story is clear: when 'Muslims rise up against Assad', the result is Christian persecution. But the problem is that the Syrian protests are not captured by the notion of 'Muslims rising up against Assad', just as the protests in Bahrain are not captured by the notion of 'Shi'a rising up against Sunnis'. This is what these regimes want us to believe. For decades, the Assads have relied on the threat of sectarian anarchy lurking just below the surface to justify autocratic rule. When the media, government officials and other public figures frame the revolt not as a popular uprising against a secular autocracy, but as an armed sectarian conflict pitting Sunnis against Alawites and their Shi'ite allies (Iran and Hezbollah), it hardens lines of religious difference. It brings these lines to the surface, accentuates and aggravates them. This makes sectarian violence more likely. It makes the regime's argument that it is the only bulwark against sectarian warfare à la Lebanon and Iraq more plausible. This framing of the conflict energizes categories of religious difference – Christian, Alawite, Sunni – that might not otherwise necessarily define it.

Like people everywhere, however, Syrians hold multiple allegiances, often celebrate diverse traditions, are frequently of mixed backgrounds and do not always fit into the rubric of religious identity demanded by the sectarian assumptions of religious freedom discourse. Left out in the cold, these 'in-between' individuals find themselves in the impossible position of having to make political claims on religious grounds, or having no grounds from which to speak (Castelli, 2007: 684). This process of silencing is the first paradox of religious freedom.

To suggest that conflict stems from a failure to acknowledge the rights of believers conceals the ways in which social divisions cut across sectarian divides. It obscures the ways forward that emerge when the focus is not on beliefs or communities of believers, but rather on shared human needs and visions. The crisis in Syria calls for an approach to protecting human dignity that goes beyond calls for freedom of belief, and that loosens the grip of this construct on the political framing of the conflict.

Of course, the logic of sectarianism extends far beyond Syria. Calls for the protection of persecuted minorities have been a defining feature of the political landscape across the Middle East. A similarly tragic trajectory has taken hold in Bahrain, where an embattled regime challenged by both Shi'a and Sunni dissenters has framed the conflict as sectarian, mobilizing Sunni against Shi'a on the claim that the latter are controlled by a predatory Iran.[4] As Joost Hiltermann (2012) argues:

> by whipping up sectarian sentiments, the [Bahraini] government hopes to change the perception of the conflict from one that pits a popular pro-democracy movement against an authoritarian regime to one of a sectarian struggle between Sunni and Shia, with the strong government needed to maintain order.

In Syria, Bahrain and elsewhere, the everyday realities and ambiguities that shape religious identification cannot be squeezed into the categories of a sectarian logic that is built into claiming and legally enforcing a right to religious freedom. If you don't know who is religious, how would you know who should be freed? Recent scholarship in religious studies is helpful in this regard. As Salomon and Walton argue:

> What makes someone a believer or a member of a faith community and what makes someone not so? What life experiences, confessional commitments, and ritual practices qualify one as an insider, and which prohibit an individual from inclusion? Are 'insider' and 'outsider' categories that we must inhabit permanent[ly] or can we move creatively between them? Most importantly, should scholars [or governments?] attempt to adjudicate these questions of religious identity and belonging, thereby becoming arbiters of orthodoxy? (2012: 406)

Salomon and Walton allude to the complexities of religious affiliation and practice. They acknowledge the difficulties of assigning individuals to the category of believer or non-believer. They allude to the structures of power – the 'arbiters of orthodoxy' – that are involved in deciding who is in and who is out. Official religious freedom advocacy, it seems to me, works in the opposite direction, operating out of a different sensibility. Religious freedom advocates do not question the power of established authorities to make religious designations, but, to the contrary, they look to such authorities to publically adjudicate lines of identity and difference – along the lines of what Linda Woodhead refers to in this volume as 'Olympian' religion. These projects do not seem to question the ability or willingness of everyday people to live according to these religious designations as organized around distinct confessional communities. Instead, they funnel people into one community or the other, fortifying lines of religious difference that otherwise might not be as salient politically, or as divisive socially. So the second paradox of religious freedom promotion is that singling out religion legally and politically from among multiple affiliations held by individuals makes religious difference more politically salient, thereby exacerbating rather than calming social divisions. Advocacy for religious freedom, then, may actually contribute to the violence and discrimination that it purports to cure.

As an example of this politicization, take the current lawsuit pending against the United States Commission on International Religious Freedom (USCIRF).[5] This commission, the bipartisan US government watchdog agency created in 1998 to promote and protect religious freedom abroad, is being sued for religious discrimination in hiring. In 2009, Safiya Ghori-Ahmad, an American lawyer from Arkansas, fluent in Urdu and Hindi, with a master's degree in international development, accepted a USCIRF position as a South Asia policy analyst. The Commission hired her to conduct research on South Asia's human rights and religious freedoms. According to the complaint, four weeks after she had been offered the job, and after she had already left her previous job at the Muslim Public Affairs Council, the offer was rescinded. Instead, she was given a temporary 90-day position that began in late July 2009.

The suit alleges that the Commission withdrew its job offer because Ghori-Ahmad is Muslim. She was told, she says, that the job could not start because of a hiring freeze – but she saw others hired during that same period. Once on the job, according to the suit, her supervisor told her that Commissioner Nina Shea 'would be upset that USCIRF had hired her because she was Muslim and had been affiliated with a Muslim organisation', and then 'suggested ways that Ms. Ghori-Ahmad could limit the negative impression her beliefs and background would create with members of the Commission'. The suit claims that the supervisor recommended that she push back her start date to avoid certain commissioners and 'call in sick' on days when certain commissioners might be in the office, to avoid running into them. This supervisor also allegedly told her to 'downplay her religious affiliation', and 'emphasise that she was a mainstream and moderate Muslim' who 'didn't even cover her hair'. Legal briefs also claim:

> Internal USCIRF email and discussions make clear that Ms Ghori-Ahmad's national origin and religion drove USCIRF's ultimate decision to rescind its job offer. For example, Shea wrote that hiring a Muslim like Ms Ghori-Ahmad to analyse religious freedom in Pakistan would be like 'hiring an IRA activist to research the UK twenty years ago'.

In an open letter to the *Washington Post* in June 2012, Ms. Shea claimed that she did not use the words 'hiring a Muslim'. She countered that:

> the first 13 words of this quote – as is clear in the legal complaint – are not mine.... What is especially problematic are the words 'hiring a Muslim,' which imply that I am a religious bigot ... I voiced opposition to Ms Ghori-Ahmad because of the bias evident in some of her writings.

Yet such a comment would be consistent with Shea's record. The suit describes Shea as 'a long-time vocal critic of Islam as a religion, majority-Muslim countries, and Muslims generally'. She vehemently opposed the Cordoba House/Park 51 project (the so-called Ground Zero Mosque), as did the USCIRF's prominent former commissioner Leonard Leo. A prominent advocate for persecuted Christians, she stated in a 2001 interview, 'I believe that religious freedom is universal ... but at the same time I find that religious freedom is only fully understood in this country – not even in the west, but in this country'. Despite such stances, Shea felt it appropriate to ask whether Ghori-Ahmad's writings and advocacy betrayed a bias.

This is part of a pattern at USCIRF of questioning the motives and patriotism of American Muslims. Most recently, Mitch McConnell appointed M. Zuhdi Jasser as a USCIRF commissioner. Jasser, a practicing Muslim, is an Arizona cardiologist who founded the American Islamic Forum for Democracy, a conservative lobbying group that promotes 'the preservation of the founding principles of the United States Constitution, liberty and freedom, through the separation of mosque and state'. He also served as the narrator in the controversial film, *The Third Jihad*, which alleges a conspiracy of radical Muslims to undermine the United States from within.[6] Why would an agency dedicated to promoting religious freedom abroad discriminate against religious minorities within the United States?

For Shea and her sympathizers, since religious freedom can only be understood by Americans with 'mainstream' beliefs, it can only be extended to 'mainstream' religious Americans. Even American Muslims who present themselves as moderates should have their motives questioned and their records examined. According to the suit, Ms. Shea wrote in an email that Ms. Ghori-Ahmad's profession of tolerance could be dismissed as a sham because it would have been 'really stupid' for her to have revealed what Shea believed must be her real views. Islam, in Shea's mind, equals intolerance, and she was personally committed to exposing this alleged Muslim hypocrisy abroad. This is not religious freedom but a combination of Christian supremacy and flagrant bias against Islam. In this view, 'religious freedom' is anything but a pluralist mission to make the world safe for different ways to be religious; it means, rather, a mission to protect American majority religious interests from perceived threats from minority religious traditions.

The Equal Employment Opportunity Commission finished its investigation of Ghori-Ahmad's case in March 2010, and in May 2010 issued an Acknowledgement and Order according to which both Ghori-Ahmad and USCIRF were allowed to 'obtain certain discovery from each other'. But, according to the complaint, USCIRF refused to produce documents and denied access to the commissioners involved in rescinding Ghori-Ahmad's offer for a permanent job. She then requested a hearing before an administrative judge, who dismissed the case. According to the suit, 'USCIRF – an entity created by Congress to promote religious freedom – argued that it could discriminate against employees without sanction because it was not subject to Title VII of the Civil Rights Act of 1964'. The judge agreed. But subsequent legal reforms sponsored by Senator Dick Durbin (H.R. 2867) made USCIRF subject to the Civil Rights Act. In June 2012, Ghori-Ahmad filed a lawsuit in the federal district court in Washington, alleging that USCIRF had illegally discriminated in hiring on the basis of religion. The suit has been wending its way through complex procedural hurdles; at this moment, it appears that the suit will proceed to trial.

Some within USCIRF were appalled by this treatment of Ghori-Ahmad. Bridget Kustin, a former USCIRF researcher, resigned in protest. Knox Thames, the commission's policy and research director, is quoted in the suit as admitting that Ghori-Ahmad's offer had been retracted because 'certain Commissioners objected to her Muslim faith and affiliation.... He said he was sorry this had happened'. Tom Carter, former communications director for the Commission, told *The Daily Beast* that, 'the Durbin reforms give USCIRF a do-over. Hopefully, the new commissioners will take the opportunity to get it right this time'.

But will they? And, more fundamentally, what would it mean to 'get it right'? The USCIRF needs more than an overhaul. Simply broadening the commission's mandate to clarify that it must protect Muslims or other disfavoured minority religions is not sufficient. Government promotion of religious freedom is, by its very nature, a flawed enterprise because the government inevitably becomes involved in deciding which religions, and which forms of which religions, deserve protection. Any government position on which religions to protect is necessarily tangled in that government's political commitments, interests and biases. Some will counter that the USCIRF can be fixed by appointing 'better' commissioners. After all, none of the commissioners identified in the lawsuit is still serving. Perhaps future Muslim–American job candidates will not be required to write an essay to prove that they are 'objective and unbiased', as was asked of Ghori-Ahmad. But who will determine who the 'right' person is, politically and religiously? Simply asking the question reveals the project's fatal flaw: no commissioner selected by politicians can possibly stand above religious politics. No governmental officer – no government, period – should be taking on the role of religious arbiter, at home or abroad. A commission that promotes 'religious freedom' may be nearly impossible to oppose – and yet it is an inevitably Orwellian project.

Ghori-Ahmad and USCIRF may reach a settlement. If not, this trial will surely become, as *Christianity Today* describes it, 'one of the most ironic in American history, with the congressional commission charged with monitoring religious freedom around the world defending its own employment practices in court' (Grant, 2012).

AFTER RELIGIOUS FREEDOM?

The globalization of religious freedom is not a sign of the victory of rational, peaceful religion over archaic and violent rivals. It is not a sign of the triumph of religion over secularist attempts to run it off the court. There is a more complex story about religious politics to be told about these projects and policies and the bureaucracies conjured up by states and other authorities to implement them. They help to draw lines that publically divide religion from non-religion (increasingly marked as 'culture', as Beaman has argued), differentiate believer from non-believer and mark off one religious community from the next. Religious freedom advocacy does not merely enforce a universal norm, as liberal internationalists would have it. It helps to *create* individual subjects and 'faith communities' for whom choosing and believing in religion are seen as the defining characteristics of what it is to be a modern religious subject. The right to choose to believe (or not), then, becomes the essence of what it means to be free. To achieve this unity in freedom of belief – belief in belief, as it were – across communities of belief (and non-belief), is what it means to have achieved religious freedom (Hurd, 2012).

This particular model of religious freedom empowers religious authorities in positions of power at the expense of dissenters, doubters and those on the margins of community. It may also undermine democracy.[7] And this is a third paradox of religious freedom. The promotion of religious freedom may undermine democracy not because democracy is necessarily secular, but because the hierarchical, institutionalized forms of religion defended by the US bishops, the US Department of State, USCIRF Open Doors, the European Union, the HFAC, Canada's DFAIT and other advocates for religious liberty regulate – and may even eradicate – the potential for non-established, minority, diverse and democratic forms of religion to flourish.

If the problem that religious freedom is meant to solve is to find ways to live together with multidimensional social diversity and difference, then it may be something that has to occur outside of the spaces enacted through legal regulation by public authorities, religious or secular. Take Foucault's notion of freedom. In this image, as William Connolly explains, freedom is 'not reducible to the freedom of subjects; it is at least partly the release of that which does not fit into the molds of subjectivity and normalization'. This leads to a 'conception of rights attached not to the self as subject, but especially to that which is defined by the normalized subject as otherness, as deviating from or falling below or failing to live up to the standards of subjectivity' (Connolly, 1985: 371). Under Foucault's agonistic conception of rights, freedom emerges as a transitory site of resistance or mode of insurrection rather than a form of religious or political discipline imposed by the authorities. Rather than something enforced from on high, it is attached precisely to that which the authorities define as other, unorthodox, dissenting, or 'minoritarian'. An example is the recent campaign by the US Leadership Conference of Women Religious, representing 80 per cent of Catholic nuns in the United States. Women Religious faces disciplinary action by the Vatican, as detailed in the recent 'Doctrinal Assessment of the Leadership Conference of Women Religious'.[8] In Elizabeth Castelli's (2012) reading of this Assessment:

> Religious freedom emerges as nothing more than a mode of shoring up the authority of the Magisterium of the Bishops, not a set of values that shelters and protects the acts of conscience undertaken by Catholic women religious in the United States. Yet ironically, recourse to a robust notion of personal conscience is an unambiguously orthodox position in Catholic theology and a fully justifiable exercise of religious freedom on the part of the nuns.

I have suggested in this chapter that religious freedom structures the field of religious and political possibility such that individuals are compelled to make political claims on religious grounds; it makes religious difference more politically salient and socially divisive; and it empowers central, often majoritarian, authorities at the expense of dissenters, doubters, minorities and those living in the shadows or at the margins of established communities. An alternative, agonistic image of freedom, on the other hand, is by definition not something that can be imposed by a state, church or international organization – or any large, centralized, hierarchical authority. If religious freedom is not something that can be officially promoted, as Sullivan's (2012) 'impossibility' argument persuasively argues,[9] then, we could ask, what are all of these centralized, hierarchical religious and political authorities promoting? In whose name do they speak? Are those empowered by the rise of religious freedom capable of assessing and judging the lives of those they seek to redeem?[10] And if not, who will speak for the other ways of being religious, and being human, that are casualties of the relentless, and at times reckless, drive to globalize religious freedom which is, after all, only one mode of living with religious diversity among others.

◆

NOTES

1. These possibilities are explored in a recent of posts, 'The Politics of Religious Freedom', on *The Immanent Frame*, the Social Science Research Council's online discussion forum on religion and the public sphere: http://blogs.ssrc.org/tif/the-politics-of-religious-freedom/. The series addresses the multiple histories and genealogies of religious freedom and the many contexts in which these histories and genealogies are salient today. It is part of a joint research project, 'The Politics of Religious Freedom: Contested Norms and Local Practices': http://iiss.berkeley.edu/politics-of-religious-freedom/.

2. This section expands upon my post, 'Believing in Religious Freedom', *The Immanent Frame*, 1 March 2012, http://bit.ly/wqmRWT.

3. Quoted in Dorell and Lynch (2012).

4. Hiltermann (2012) observes that 'Sunni-Shia interaction is what defines daily life at the workplace and in many neighborhoods'.

5. See Hurd (2013).

6. See http://therevealer.org/archives/10349.

7. See Sullivan (2012).

8. See the Vatican Congregation for the Doctrine of Faith's 2012 report for more.

9. See Sullivan (2007) for more on this argument.

10. See Abu-Lughod (2011: 255).

REFERENCES

Abu-Lughod, Lila. 2010. 'Against Universals: The Dialects of (Women's) Human Rights and Human Capabilities', in J. Michelle Molina and Donald K. Swearer (eds.), *Rethinking the Human*. Cambridge: Harvard University Press.

———. 2011. 'Anthropology in the Territory of Rights, Islamic, Human, and Otherwise. . .', in Ron Johnston (ed.), *Proceedings of the British Academy, Vol. 167, 200. Lectures*. Oxford: Oxford University Press.

Beaman, Lori G. and Winnifred F. Sullivan (eds). 2013. *Varieties of Religious Establishment*. London: Ashgate.

Castelli, Elizabeth A. 2007. 'Theologizing Human Rights: Christian Activism and the Limits of Religious Freedom', in Michel Feher, Gaëlle Krikorian and Yates McKee (eds.), *Non-Governmental Politics*. New York: Zone Books.

———. 2012. 'The Bishops, the Sisters, and Religious Freedom', *The Immanent Frame*, 16 May, http://blogs.ssrc.org/tif/2012/05/16/the-bishops-the-sisters-and-religious-freedom/.

Connolly, William E. 1985. 'Taylor, Foucault, and Otherness', *Political Theory*, 13(3): 365–76.

Dorell, Oren and Sarah Lynch. 2012. 'Christians Fear Losing Freedoms in Arab Spring Movement', *USA Today*, 31 January, http://usatoday30.usatoday.com/news/religion/story/2012-01-30/arab-spring-christians/52894182/1.

Grant, Tobin. 2012. 'The Story behind One of the Most Ironic Religious Freedom Lawsuits Ever Filed', *Christianity Today*, 26 September, http://www.ctlibrary.com/ct/2012/september-web-only/most-ironic-religious-freedom-lawsuit.html.

Hiltermann, Joost. 2012. 'Bahrain: A New Sectarian Conflict?', *The New York Review of Books Blog*, 8 May, http://www.nybooks.com/blogs/nyrblog/2012/may/08/bahrain-new-sectarian-conflict/.

Hurd, Elizabeth Shakman. 2013. 'Muslims Need Not Apply', *The Boston Review,* 24 January.

———. 2012. 'Believing in Religious Freedom', *The Immanent Frame*, 1 March, http://bit.ly/wqmRWT.

———. 2013. 'Muslims Need Not Apply', *The Boston Review*, 24 January.

Mekhennet, Souad. 2011. 'Moderate Islamist Party Winning Morocco Election', *The New York Times*, 26 November.

Salomon, Noah and Jeremy F. Walton. 2012. 'Religious Criticism, Secular Criticism, and the "Critical Study of Religion": Lessons from the Study of Islam', in Robert A. Orsi (ed.), *The Cambridge Companion to Religious Studies*. Cambridge: Cambridge University Press.

Sullivan, Winnifred F. 2007. *The Impossibility of Religious Freedom*. Princeton: Princeton University Press.

———. 2012. 'The World that Smith Made', *The Immanent Frame*, 7 March, http://blogs.ssrc.org/tif/2012/03/07/the-world-that-smith-made/.

Vatican Congregation for the Doctrine of the Faith. 2012. 'Doctrinal Assessment of the Leadership Conference of Women Religious', *United States Conference of Catholic Bishops*, 18 April, http://www.usccb.org/loader.cfm?csModule=security/getfile&pageid=55544.